About the Book and Author

One of the primary goals of both U.S. policy in Europe since the erection of the Berlin Wall in 1961 and the West German *Ostpolitik* was to alleviate problems in Berlin and restore normality to the city. This goal was finally achieved with the 1971 Quadripartite Agreement.

This book examines how the Quadripartite Agreement dealt with the salient problems of Berlin and what role this treaty assumed within a broader political framework. The agreement, in addition to improving daily life in and around the city, provided an important impetus for the Bonn-Moscow Treaty, the FRG treaties with Poland and Czechoslovakia, and above all, the Basic Treaty between the German states. Improvement in the Berlin situation made possible a modus vivendi between the FRG and the GDR on the basis of equality and nondiscrimination.

Although the FRG and the GDR are not parties to the Quadripartite Agreement, in reaching an accord on Berlin the Four Powers had to take into account the interests of their respective allies. This book provides an excellent study of the mechanics of international negotiations through which an enduring and workable settlement was reached in a very complex situation.

David M. Keithly is assistant to the director of the Keck Center for International Strategic Studies at Claremont McKenna College.

To my parents

Breakthrough
in the *Ostpolitik*
The 1971 Quadripartite Agreement

David M. Keithly

Westview Press / Boulder and London

Westview Special Studies in International Relations

Copyright © 1986 by Westview Press, Inc.

Published in 1986 in the United States of America by Westview Press, Inc,;
Frederick A. Praeger, Publisher; 5500 Central Avenue, Boulder, Colorado 80301

Library of Congress Catalog Card Number: 85-30410
ISBN: 0-8133-7178-3

Printed and bound in the United States of America

The paper used in this publication meets the minimum requirements
of the American National Standard for Permanence of Paper for
Printed Library Materials Z39.48-1984.

6 5 4 3 2 1

Contents

viii

Preface

This is a book about conflict and conciliation, about power and the clash of interests. Its focus is upon one of the most snarled and intricate issues of the post-war world, the issue perhaps most laden with the tangle over "legalisms." Its setting is Central Europe where two worlds collide, in a country which remains divided, with all the sorrow and suffering this circumstance has brought in its wake.

My intention in writing this book is three-fold.

First, I wish to provide an analysis of the agonizing and complex Berlin dilemmas of use to scholars, as well as to a more general audience, not completely conversant with the literature in the field, who might be interested in examining salient problems of international relations. Without doubt there is a need at present for Americans better to familiarize themselves with the political/strategic problems of Europe.

Second, I believe that more scholarship with an emphasis upon area studies is necessary. In this treatise, I have written upon the interests and concerns of the two German states, two very complex and fascinating societies which deserve our attention. That there is a uniqueness about many elements of these societies, as well as of the political/geographic situation in which they exist is beyond question; yet the two German states face problems not dissimilar from those of many other countries. A unifying element of this book is a recurrent theme: the integration of the Federal Republic of Germany and the German Democratic Republic into opposing blocs and the consequent relatively narrow operating radii, especially in the case of the latter, which have profound effects upon the policy-making process.

Lastly, I wanted to place the 1971 Quadripartite Agreement into a broader structure of European detente. The Quadripartite Agreement represented a cornerstone of a framework within which the "German problem" can be managed. I have tried to sketch out the esoteric and vexing issues of Berlin and of the post-war Central European order of which divided Berlin is a part in such a way as to make these issues understandable. It is my hope that the approach allows the reader to fathom how an international enigma has been handled.

The book is the product of years of travel, study and work in Central Europe. Sources I have employed fall into several categories. First, there are the primary sources, interviews with and memoirs of U.S. and West German officials. Most important among the memoirs are those of Henry Kissinger, which provide a wealth of information. I was able to conduct numerous interviews with U.S. and German government officials in the United States and in Europe. The oral history interviews at the Kennedy Library were useful on several issues. Second, I drew upon a number of newspapers and periodicals, the most readily-available public sources, for an overview of contemporary press coverage of events. The value of such materials in an analysis like this one should not be underestimated, since these often furnish important insights into local political dynamics. Another timely German source was Arnulf Baring's book, *Machtwechsel*, which serves as the memoirs of Walter Scheel, an instrumental figure in the SPD/FDP *Ostpolitik*. Baring's book gives the reader a new perspective on certain events. Third, I was able to examine a number of recently released, highly classified documents on the 1958-1961 Berlin crises. Fourth, as a U.S. State Department intern in 1978 in the U.S. Mission, Berlin, I gained an understanding and an interest in Berlin not obtainable through books alone. A few years later, as a young academic, I received a gracious invitation from the State Department to participate in the Scholar/Diplomat Program. In the absence of these enlightened and far-sighted programs, this project would have been inconceivable. I owe a special debt to all those government officials who have helped me over the years directly or indirectly. Few probably thought at the time that their helpfulness and kindness would contribute to a book. Most must go unnamed.

Several secondary sources have been most valuable. I should like to acknowledge my indebtedness to Honoré M. Catudal, whose numerous fine books on Berlin helped to encourage me along this path. I hope my book approaches the standards he has set, for his is a difficult act to follow. Among the old Germany hands and free men everywhere, he ranks among those most entitled to claim: "Ich bin Berliner."

Writing this book would have been considerably more difficult without the assistance and support of friends and colleagues.

My special thanks to George S. Blair, Harry V. Jaffa, and P. Edward Haley, the finest dissertation committee any young scholar could hope for. Without their guidance and support, this project, as well as a great many other things, would not have been possible. I owe them more than I can say and I hope that I shall never disappoint any of them.

Many thanks to James Swihart, FSO, who took a State Department intern under his wing and entrusted him with tasks a graduate student would not usually be assigned.

I am indebted to my friends at Claremont McKenna College, especially to Jack Merritt, mentor, friend, and co-editor of my first book, who has always provided encouragement. My gratitude to the Earhart Foundation which furnished financial support. Thanks also to the bright and hard-working student assistants at the Keck Center who saved me hours of work.

I wish to thank Coral Janssen for her invaluable services typing and formatting the manuscript.

I am most grateful to the editors of Westview Press, who are among the most competent and congenial people with whom an author could hope to work. It is their interest in this project which ultimately made it possible.

David M. Keithly

Introduction

An anomaly in international relations, Berlin remains under Four-Power control as a direct result of World War II agreements, the city's status having been initially established through accord on occupied Germany. The rights of the United States, Great Britain, France and the Soviet Union are of an "original" nature in that they constitute an integral part of quadrilateral treaties on occupied territories in Central Europe and they precede the founding of post-war German regimes. Perhaps no other single post-war European issue has been encumbered by as much political enmity and bickering over legalisms as has Berlin.

Despite the tremendous political changes that have taken place in Central and Eastern Europe since World War II, the point of departure of the Western Powers concerning Berlin's political/legal status has not changed considerably from the wartime agreements on occupied Berlin (the London Protocols of 1944) to the Quadripartite Agreement of September 1971, the only major post-war international accord on Berlin.

This is not to say that political developments, including U.S.-Soviet confrontation, the division of Germany, the emergence of two separate German states and the partition of the city have not significantly affected the Berlin situation or that the Western Powers do not recognize this fact. In addition to representing an affirmation of the validity of existing accords, in particular those guaranteeing Western presence in designated sectors of Berlin, the Quadripartite Agreement is an East-West *modus vivendi*. In treaty provisions assuring the rights of the four former allies, the parties to the 1971 Quadripartite Agreement, "without prejudice to their legal positions," upheld the status-quo in Berlin and the quadrilateral responsibility for it. Thus, as specified in the Quadripartite Agreement, Berlin retains an amount of its immediate post-war status, a manifest aspect of which is the maintenance of Four-Power prerogative.

As Daniel J. Nelson has so aptly pointed out, Berlin is above all a symbol: a symbol of Allied victory and occupation, of the East-West conflict, of Cold War tension, of Soviet as well as U.S. foreign policy goals.[1] In the 1960s Berlin became a sort of seismograph of East-West tensions, and in the early 1970s, a test-case for detente policies. In a sense, Berlin is a microcosm of the German problem: it is the divided former capital of a divided land. No other part of Europe was as directly and assiduously affected by Cold War conflicts as was Berlin. In effect a battleground of the Cold War, Berlin experienced a blockade, numerous Soviet threats to its independence, constant insecurity and, finally, physical division.

Berlin has, however, been more than a symbol of East-West conflict and a peripheral theater of the Cold War. A flash-point for dispute, the city at times ignited Soviet-U.S. altercations. Geography and the drawing of occupation zone boundaries have been in no small way responsible. The most salient peculiarity of post-war Berlin is its location 110 miles inside the former Soviet zone of occupation, now the German Democratic Republic (GDR). Because of its bizarre geographics, Berlin has been repeatedly subjected to the interdiction of its lines of supply and communication. It has thus been unavoidable that the most decisive question for the Western Allies concerned access to and from the city. By restricting access, the Soviet Union has attempted to pressure the Western Powers into relinquishing their respective sectors of the city, to eliminate the quadripartite status, and to incorporate the Western sectors into the Soviet zone, or, later into the GDR.

The three air corridors into West Berlin allowed the United States to supply the city by air during the 1948-49 blockage, foiling Soviet aggression. In fact, the Western right to use the air corridors has never been directly challenged. But throughout the 1950s and 1960s, the overland transit routes, i.e., highway and railroad, were liable to obstruction and chicanery; general international tension often prompted Soviet and East German incidents on routes to West Berlin. So long as such insecurity existed and Berlin remained a focal point of confrontation, the inhabitants of the Western sectors of the city remained hostages of international discord.

One of the primary goals of U.S. policy in Europe since the erection of the Berlin Wall in 1961, and later of the West German *Ostpolitik*, was the alleviation of Berlin problems and the subsequent creation of some semblance of normality in the city. This goal was achieved in large part with the 1971 Quadripartite Agreement which formed a cornerstone of the *Ostpolitik*.

The narrowness of German authority in Berlin remains one of the principal ironies of the situation. Although an improvement in the daily conditions in West Berlin was seen by the West German architects of *Ostpolitik* as a *sine qua non* for new policies vis-à-vis Eastern Europe, negotiations on Berlin were officially within the exclusive jurisdiction of the Four Powers: the USSR, the U.S., Great Britain and France. Despite the diplomatic and military limitations that integration into blocs has placed upon the Federal Republic of Germany (West Germany, or FRG) and the GDR, the Four Powers, on the other hand, could not ignore the interests of their respective allies in reaching an accord on Berlin. Berlin negotiations were carried on by the Four, with the two German states anxiously observing developments. The complexity of the situation in Berlin is a function of the unfolding of post-war political events as well as the impingement of Berlin issues upon the vital interests of six nations. Any Four-Power agreement on Berlin had to meet with FRG and GDR acceptance, since it was primarily the Germans who must live with Berlin accords.

The purpose of this book is to examine how the 1971 Quadripartite Agreement dealt with the salient problems of Berlin and what role this treaty assumed within a broader political framework. The analysis is cast in such a way that the following basic questions will be posed:

1. What were the Western and Eastern positions on Berlin on the eve of the *Ostpolitik*?
2. How had the emergence of two German states, integrated into respective, opposing blocs affected the Berlin situation?
3. What are the interests of the six states in Berlin and to what extent were these interests upheld in the quadripartite accord?
4. To what extent did perceived West German interests in Berlin, and more broadly in Eastern Europe, not coincide with those of the United States?

4

5. How was the Quadripartite Agreement integrated into a larger framework?
6. How has the Quadripartite Agreement dealt with the seemingly insurmountable obstacles to accord and what is the broader significance of the treaty?

NOTES

1. Daniel J. Nelson, *Wartime Origins of the Berlin Dilemma* (University, Alabama: University of Alabama Press, 1978), pp. 1-3.

1
The Dilemmas of Post-War Berlin

The current political status of Berlin is the result of an interaction of East-West conflict and cooperation. To begin an inquiry into what the Quadripartite Agreement is and what it is not, a few general observations can be made. First, the 1971 agreement serves as a legally binding Soviet affirmation of the 1944 London Protocols, establishing the right of the Western Allies to occupy the city of Berlin. Second, this agreement constitutes the recognition of chief post-war realities such as the division of the city, the integration of East Berlin into the GDR and the creation of an East German state in the former Soviet zone of occupation. Third, the agreement leaves the "German question" open--at least theoretically. Since it involves in the main a recognition of the status-quo and does not alter the European political situation in a manner that would permanently hinder eventual German reunification, the Berlin accord represents an acceptable diplomatic arrangement for the FRG.

By 1949, the year of the founding of the FRG and the GDR, the antithetical positions on Berlin which had already emerged seemed to exclude any possibility of an accord on the city. Intrinsic to the establishment of an East German state was the granting of allegedly sovereign control over territory, including the "capital" of the GDR in the Eastern sector of Berlin, and over the Berlin access routes which passed through East Germany. According to the standard Soviet argument, put forth within a few years of the creation of the GDR, previous Soviet rights and duties in its zone would be transferred to the East Germans in accordance with the exercise of complete sovereignty.

The intentions of the Soviet Union were apparent. By the transfer of sovereignty, Moscow could selectively deny the validity of wartime agreements and thus posture eventually to expel the U.S., France and Great Britain from the city, something it had failed to do with the blockade. The official Soviet position throughout the 1950s--inasmuch as one finds any consistency--was that the Western presence in Berlin, and above all, any West German affiliation with the city, were contingent upon GDR consent. Any sort of original rights of occupation were disclaimed outright.

The Western Allies continue to maintain that all of Berlin (greater Berlin) remains under quadripartite control as a result of Allied victory and the collapse of Nazi Germany. According to their argument, the 1944 London Protocol, establishing zones of occupation in Germany and delineating a separate and distinct region of occupation in the former German capital, was legally binding upon the Soviet Union in the absence of a comprehensive German peace treaty which would render such agreements *clausula rebus sic stantibus*. Soviet transfer of authority to a third party, i.e., the GDR, so the position of the Allies, constituted a unilateral abrogation of multi-party treaties. The Allies adamantly insisted upon their right of overland and air access to their designated sectors in Berlin, denying that such access could be restricted or infringed upon, and rejecting out-of-hand that this access rested upon GDR consent. Even a brief analysis of the Western standpoint and of the eventual Quadripartite Agreement shows that Western premises have not changed considerably since the European Advisory Commission made its recommendations in the final phase of the Second World War.[1] The Western Three acquired rights and sovereignty in this area through international agreement. No side is permitted to abrogate this accord or to alter the existing situation unilaterally.

Crucial to this Allied argument is that the emergence of any sort of sovereign political entity in the Soviet zone of occupation neither altered nor affected rights acquired by the Western Allies through military victory. Neither German state had any rights or responsibilities in Berlin or on its access routes except those officially sanctioned by Four-Power agreement. The Berlin blockade provided the Allies with sufficient proof that any modification of their political/legal position on Berlin would invariably jeopardize their presence in the Western sectors, and, ultimately, the freedom of West Berlin.

At the center of Berlin conflicts have been two problems: the maintenance of quadripartite rights and access to the Western sectors. Soviet attempts to eliminate the Western presence focused initially upon the restriction of access, then later, particularly in the 1958 crisis, involved a campaign of access limitation, coupled with the systematic denial of occupation rights. It was not until the 1971 Quadripartite Agreement that the Soviet Union explicitly reaffirmed quadripartite status, including Allied rights. Most of the original Four-Power administrative instruments, such as the Berlin Kommandatura, remain in place although the Soviet Union has refused to participate in this forum since 1947.

The rights of the three Western Powers in Berlin are inextricably linked with questions of access since these rights depend upon the unrestricted use of transit routes. Inherent in the right to occupy a territory is a guarantee of access to the area, a guarantee the Soviet Union reneged upon in denying overland transport to the Western Three as well as to West Germans. The primary reason for such Soviet measures has been the ability to undertake them so easily, with a minimum fear of reprisal, because of Berlin's unusual geographic position deep in East Germany.

Repeatedly exploiting gray areas, Moscow was seldom at a loss to justify deliberate hindrance of overland transit. No written agreement concerning either road or railway access to Berlin existed until the Quadripartite Agreement of 1971. The U.S. did not require formal written access accords in 1944, much to its later chagrin, and merely assumed that the Soviet Union would accept all responsibility for access into and through its zone.

The twenty-mile wide air corridors to Berlin, Berlin-Hamburg, Berlin-Bückeburg, Berlin-Frankfurt/Main, were created by written accord, the Air Corridor Agreement of November 30, 1945. These air corridors saved the Western sectors of Berlin from being incorporated into the Soviet zone as a result of the blockade. The Air Corridor Agreement of November 1945 also established the Berlin Control Zone for aircraft, encompassing greater Berlin with a radius of 32 km., and the Berlin Air Safety Center (BASC), which has continued to function as a Four-Power institution. The corridors, the Control Zone and the BASC together comprise the quadrilateral Berlin "Air-Regime," which despite the spates of political/legal squabbling, remains in place. One of the many oddities of post-war Berlin has been that although the Soviet Union has attempted to hinder overland transit and has bid defiance to Allied authority in the Western sectors of Berlin, it has never directly challenged the Allied right to use the air corridors, nor has it attempted to eliminate the "Air-

Regime."

With the lifting of the blockade in 1949, the Soviet Union explicitly agreed to end restrictions upon overland transit to Berlin's Western sectors. The Soviet communiqué of May 1949 stated, "All restrictions imposed since March 1, 1948, by the Government of the Union of Soviet Socialist Republics on Communications, transportation, and trade between Berlin and the Western zones will be removed on May 12, 1949.[2] But it is notable that the Soviet Union judiciously precluded formally guaranteeing any overland access to Berlin. Thus, the termination of access restrictions was no more than a temporary Soviet pledge to end the blockade, prior to renewed pressure to jettison the Western Powers from Berlin.

A quadripartite communiqué released on June 20, 1949, provided for discussion on three points:

1. The mitigation of the "effects of the present administrative division of Germany and of Berlin" in areas of "trade and development of the financial and economic relations between the western zones and the eastern zone and between Berlin and the zones."

2. The facilitation of the "movement of persons and goods and the exchange of information between the western zones and the eastern zone and between Berlin and the zones."

3. Consideration of "questions of common interest relating to the administration of the four sectors in Berlin with a view to normalizing as far as possible the life of the city."[3]

This communiqué allowed for merely a discussion of salient issues and did not specify any workable solutions to existing problems. It was one of only two post-war, quadrilateral accords on Berlin to be reached until 1971. In that the communiqué set a precedent for quadripartite agreement, it can be viewed as a precursor to the later Four-Power treaty. However, Berlin would suffer several serious crises in the more than two-decade interim between the two accords.

On May 23, 1949 came the pronouncement that the *Grundgesetz*, or Basic Law, which would serve as a provisional West German constitution, had been accepted by nationwide plebiscite and had been approved by Allied military authorities. Some months before, the first elections to the *Bundestag*, or Federal Parliament, had taken place. Thus, a separate West German state, the FRG, became a reality.

In the Soviet zone in March 1948, institutions already in place selected a *Volksrat*, or "People's Council," to prepare a constitution for an East German state. In May 1949 a bogus national election with single lists and candidates was held to designate representatives to the "People's Congress." In the same month this body endorsed the proposed constitution and on October 7, 1949, the German Democratic Republic was founded as a "workers' and farmers' state." Thus, by 1950 the two zones of the divided nation had become states with opposing political, economic, and social systems.

In 1952 there were major efforts physically to separate an already politically divided country. The border between East and West Germany was sealed with concrete block and barbed wire. Telephone connections between East and West Berlin as well as between the GDR and West Berlin were cut. The border between the GDR and West Berlin--although not the sector-sector boundary in the city itself--was secured, permitting virtually no passage between West Berlin and the surrounding areas. Chicanery on the access routes became commonplace and included confiscation of property, inspection of luggage and deliberate blockage of traffic for hours.

The Bolz-Zorin Agreement of September 1955 marked the origin of an offensive against Berlin, which culminated in the crisis of 1958. This agreement was an indication of how Moscow planned to alter the city's status. The Soviet Union afforded the GDR extensive authority to control all overland transit to West Berlin as well as water traffic between the FRG and West Berlin. Such authority did not extend to U.S., French or British military vehicles of any kind, for which the Soviets continued to assume responsibility. The intention was to bolster the alleged sovereignty of the GDR in the hope of eventually inducing the Allies to deal officially with East Berlin. The Soviet Union also hoped to undermine any semblance of Four-Power responsibility for the city by shunning its contractual obligations and granting control rights to the GDR. Since East German police and military would thereafter be manning border posts and controlling traffic, the FRG would be left with no choice but to start doing business with the East German state and thus provide *de facto* recognition to it.

As Dennis Bark points out, the timing of the Bolz-Zorin Agreement was significant, since a week earlier, the Soviet Union had recognized the FRG.[4] Moscow thereafter maintained that two separate, independent German states had emerged from the defeated German *Reich*, and, it would follow, at least in Soviet thinking, that the FRG should accept the *fait accompli* and accord full diplomatic recognition to the GDR with its capital, "Berlin." Moscow would further argue that, because any extraterritoriality, i.e., occupation, air corridors, or use of transit routes without explicit permission of the state in which such arteries were located, contradicted the principle of sovereignty in international law, West Berlin had become an untenable anachronism.

The 1958 Berlin crisis demonstrated beyond any doubt Soviet purposes. While encouraging GDR officials to create havoc on Berlin transit routes, the Soviet Union could disavow all responsibility and refer Western governments to those ostensibly in control of "sovereign" East German territory. Any official Western-GDR contacts would enhance the political position and prestige of the latter. Furthermore, by claiming the capital of the GDR to be "Berlin," Moscow could begin incorporating the entire city into East Germany. With no regard for existing treaties or the actual situation, "Berlin," according to the new East Bloc interpretation, had become the sovereign territory of the GDR.

According to Article 23 of the Basic Law as well as Article 1 of the West Berlin Constitution, greater Berlin is a *Land* (state) of the FRG. In order that FRG authority not impinge upon Allied occupation rights in the city, the Western Powers suspended the provisions applying to Berlin. As such suspension placed certain restrictions upon FRG jurisdiction in the city, West Berlin representatives to the *Bundestag* are not entitled to vote in parliamentary sessions, and the Western Powers maintain sole responsibility for defense and security. West German civil and criminal law do, however, apply in the Western sectors of Berlin, and in economic and financial realms, West Berlin became quickly integrated into the FRG.

East Berlin has served as the *de facto* capital of the GDR since the establishment of that state. The 1968 GDR constitution which replaced the 1949 law declared the capital of the East German state to be simply "Berlin," as if the city were a single entity or the Western sectors did not exist. "East Berlin" does not constitute a part of GDR vocabulary; reference is usually made to the Eastern sector as "Berlin: Hauptstadt der DDR" (Capital of the GDR).

The proviso of the 1968 constitution specifying East Berlin as the official capital of the GDR altered the status from *de facto* to *de jure* and represented a technical violation of all Four-Power accords on Berlin. This modification of status was little more than academic, since all major state organs of the GDR were already located in East Berlin. Moreover, the Eastern sector had been remilitarized in transgression of quadripartite status even prior to the GDR's founding. All were legal matters about which the Soviet Union and the Western Powers quarreled for years.

It should come as no surprise that few Berlin problems can be viewed in isolation. Most issues are in some way or another intertwined with others, and have resulted in acerbic discussions of all matters ranging from major violations such as the deployment of East German troops in a theoretically demilitarized area to the seemingly trivial such as inspection of identity cards and stamps on visas.

Beginning in the 1950s, the GDR itself began to deny that Four-Power status had any validity whatsoever in East Berlin. Thus a pattern emerged, whereby the Western Powers were pressured meticulously to adhere to all provisions of Allied occupation status, lest even the slightest alteration lead to an unfortunate precedent. Maintenance of freedom in the Western sectors required scrupulous, sometimes pedantic, insistence upon every aspect of original Four-Power status. Following the June 1953 uprising in East Berlin, the GDR accelerated its policies of strict isolation of its population from the West. By that year both German states were already becoming integrated into the respective blocs. In 1954 serious discussion of FRG remilitarization commenced, with the attendant bitterness and trepidation brought on by painful memories.

Throughout the 1950s, all six states involved--the four wartime allies along with the two German states-- continued to pay lip-service to the elusive goal of reunification. In accordance with provisions of the Basic Law, the government of the FRG claimed to speak on behalf of all Germans, including those whose misfortune it was to be living in the Soviet zone of occupation. At the Four-Power conference of foreign ministers in early 1954, both sides put forth reunification proposals. Differences between the two sides were enormous: the proposals were, in the main, non-starters. The conference adjourned with no progress having been made.[5]

The 1954 Soviet announcement that Moscow was establishing the same diplomatic relations with the GDR it maintained with other states under international law, while retaining occupation rights and authority, seemed to indicate a new determination on Moscow's part to preserve the GDR. In January 1955 the Supreme Soviet officially terminated the state of war with Germany.[6]

1955 represented a watershed for the two German states. As already mentioned, the Bolz-Zorin Agreement was signed in that year. Prior to the signing of this accord, the GDR entered the newly-established Warsaw Pact. After the failure of plans to establish the European Defense Community (EDC), the FRG joined NATO. Thus the German states became members of antagonistic military alliances.

The 1954 Paris Agreements, terminating the occupation status of the FRG, granted it national sovereignty, but reaffirmed the continued special status of Berlin and Allied rights there. The Western Powers accepted Bonn as the sole legitimate and free German government, thereby agreeing to the so-called "Alleinvertretungsanspruch" or exclusive right of representation. This claimed right would give rise to the "Hallstein Doctrine" internationally, whereby the FRG viewed any third-power recognition of the GDR as an unfriendly act.[7]

NOTES

1. See Daniel J. Nelson, *Wartime Origins of the Berlin Dilemma*, chapters 5 and 6, pp. 75-136.
2. U.S. Department of State, *Documents on Germany 1944-1959* (Washington, D.C.: GPO, 1959), pp. 59-60; Lucius D. Clay, *Decision in Germany* (Garden City, N.Y.: Doubleday and Co., 1950), chapters 2 and 3.
3. Dennis L. Bark, *Agreement on Berlin* (Washington, D.C.: American Enterprise Institute, 1974), p. 13; *Documents on Germany 1944-1959*, pp. 59-60.
4. Bark, op. cit., pp. 19-20.
5. See: Ernst Zivier, *Der Rechtsstatus des Landes Berlin* (Berlin: Berlin Verlag, 1977), p. 31; Walther Hubatsch, et al, eds., *The German Question* (New York: Herder Book Center, 1967), pp. 170-172. Minutes of the conference appear in: *Archiv der Gegenwart* 1954, pp. 4361A, 4372A and 4383C.
6. Wolfgang Heidelmeyer and Guenter Hindrichs, *Documents on Berlin 1943-1963* (Munich: Oldenbourg Verlag, 1963), p. 170.
7. The "Hallstein Doctrine" would later pose

tremendous difficulties for the FRG as well as its allies. The doctrine specified that the opening of diplomatic relations with the GDR would be regarded by the FRG as an unfriendly act and would have resultant consequences. As a rule the FRG refused to maintain diplomatic relations with any state recognizing the GDR. There was, however, a major exception to this pillar of West German foreign policy, namely, diplomatic relations with the Soviet Union, which the FRG established as early as 1955. Needless to say, by the late 1960s, the Hallstein Doctrine and the *Ostpolitik* became mutually exclusive. See: "Erklärung des Auswärtigen Amtes der Bundesregierung" of December 11, 1956, in: *Dokumente zur Deutschlandpolitik* III/2 (Bonn: Bundesministerium für gesamtdeutsche Fragen, 1969), pp. 984-988.

2
The Crises of 1958–1961

The 1958 offensive against West Berlin began with the verbal blast of East German Communist Party (SED) leader, Walter Ulbricht, on October 27 of that year. In his speech, Ulbricht described West Berlin as an island of the Cold War in the middle of the GDR.[1] Insisting upon expeditious "normalization," Ulbricht demanded "joint negotiations on the basis of parity."[2] Ulbricht condemned the Allied presence in Berlin as illegal. Berlin was no longer a zone of occupation, according to Ulbricht; Four-Power control must end and Berlin should become GDR territory.

Ulbricht's harangue doubtless had the full blessing of the Soviet Union and constituted part of a coordinated East Bloc scheme. Moscow's prodding of Ulbricht was intended to promote the Soviet goal of coercing the West into *de facto* recognition of the GDR by jaw-boning and through the fostering of harassment on the access routes, all calculated to offer no choice but to deal with East German officials.[3] Underscoring existing quadripartite responsibilities in Berlin, the U.S. responded with a rejection of Soviet-initiated abrogation of quadrilateral agreements on Berlin.[4]

On November 10, 1958 Soviet Premier Nikita Khrushchev publicly supported his East German ally, stating that it was time to "draw conclusions" from the alleged Allied violations of the Potsdam Agreement. His speech was followed by a Soviet note of November 27, 1958 that reiterated the thrust of the demarche of July 14, 1948 in which the Soviet Union accused the West of transgressing major provisions of the Potsdam Agreement, making the establishment of an East German state unavoidable.[5] The note declared existing quadripartite accords "null and

15

void" on the basis of *clausula rebus sic stantibus*, that is, changed circumstances rendering heretofore existing treaties no longer binding on the signatory powers. The "changed circumstances" were above all the emergence of two sovereign German states.[6] Khrushchev upheld Ulbricht's position that Allied occupation of the Western sectors of Berlin was illegal, demanding the Western Powers begin immediate evacuation of their sectors. According to the Kremlin's argument, Berlin's special status was inseparable from the Potsdam Agreement: since the Potsdam Agreement was no longer binding, Berlin enjoyed no special status.

> Berlin's quadripartite status did not originate and exist independently of all the other Allied agreements on Germany, it was wholly intended to fulfill the basic purpose of Germany's occupation in the initial postwar period, . . . purposes laid down in the Potsdam agreements. Having embarked upon the road of rearming West Germany, and drawing it into their military alignments, the United States, Great Britain and France crassly violated the Potsdam agreement and therefore forfeited all legal rights for the perpetuation of Berlin's present state.[7]

Moreover, there was the standard fare of accusations about the FRG "fanning passions" and heating up the situation around Berlin "to the point of incandescence in order to insure the preservation of the occupational regime in West Berlin."[8] Moscow alleged the Allies to have yoked West Germany "onto the road of militarism and revanchism."[9] But Khrushchev was only warming up. West German "revanchism" and "illegal" Allied occupation regimes were weighty matters, necessitating concerted action. The Soviet Union delivered an ultimatum to the effect that, in the event the three Allies had not terminated their "illegal" occupation within six months, Moscow would initiate discussions with the GDR with an aim toward a separate peace treaty, "proceeding from the principle of respect for the sovereignty of the German Democratic Republic."[10] The Western Powers would thereafter have no choice but to negotiate access with the East German leaders.

Moreover, the note advanced the notion that only a West Berlin problem existed. A separate peace treaty with the GDR would, in the Soviet view, transform West Berlin into an "independent political entity" or a free city, devoid of the vestiges of the occupation regime or West

German militarism.[11]   Allied rejection of the Soviet
proposal, the Soviets stated, would eliminate all
possibilities for further negotiation on Berlin.

The treaty would invalidate all Allied rights and
duties in East Germany and in Berlin, Khrushchev insisted,
while entitling GDR authorities forcibly to expel any
"uninvited" foreign troops on their soil.   Khrushchev also
carefully called attention to the military arrangements
inherent in Warsaw Pact integration, meaning, presumably,
the Soviet Union would assist its ally in the invitation of
foreign troops to leave.   Although Khrushchev did not
explicitly state the Soviet intention to incorporate West
Berlin into the GDR, but rather to transform it into a
"free" city, given the Soviet track record in Eastern
Europe, few in the West had any delusions about the meaning
of Khrushchev's term.

Reviewing the Berlin situation, the North Atlantic
Council officially repeated on December 16, 1958 the
Western position that no state is justified in withdrawing
from or abrogating a unilateral accord and thus the Soviet
Union would continue to be held responsible for respecting
Allied rights.[12]   Separately the U.S. government informed
Moscow that Berlin agreements would remain operative.[13]

An upshot of the breakdown in U.S.-Soviet cooperation
after World War II, the partition of Germany, and the
ultimate emergence of opposing blocs in Europe was that a
unified German state envisaged in wartime accords never
evolved.   There is no German state to sign a peace treaty
with the victorious powers.   In the absence of such a peace
treaty, Four-Power accords on occupied territory in Central
Europe, such as those on Berlin, retain their validity.   As
West Germany came into existence as the child of the Cold
War, so West Berlin had become a sort of pawn of great
power rivalry.   The Berlin situation involved the
credibility, and hence the national interests of the
superpowers.   The very presence of a separate Berlin zone,
occupied by Western military forces, impinged upon the
sovereignty of the Soviet client state, the GDR, and
represented an affront to Soviet predominance in Eastern
Europe.[14]   Validity of existing wartime accords with the
ensuing rights of the Allies in Berlin became inextricably
linked with U.S. strategic credibility, particularly the
willingness to defend Western Europe.[15]   Equally interested
in upholding the Four-Power status of Berlin was the FRG,
since an occupied Berlin not only guaranteed the freedom of
some two million West Berliners, but ensured the
transitoriness of the post-war order, leaving open the

German question and allowing for the possibility of a
reunified Germany, to which the West German government is
constitutionally committed.[16] Recognizing the threat that
the Khrushchev ultimatum posed to the security of West
Berlin, the Western Allies protested the Soviet maneuver in
the strongest terms, and insisted that they would continue
to hold the Soviet Union responsible for its treaty
obligations in Berlin.

The Berlin situation was the subject of U.S.-Soviet
discussions on three separate occasions following the
Khrushchev ultimatum: in Geneva in 1958, at the Paris
summit in 1960 and at the Kennedy-Khrushchev meeting in
Vienna in 1961. At none of these encounters was any
progress made on the Berlin problem, but the six-month
period, specified in the 1958 ultimatum, expired without
the Soviet Union making good on any of its threats. The
ultimatum had, nonetheless, unleased a crisis which lasted
intermittently until after the erection of the Berlin Wall
in August 1961.

The Soviet legal position on Berlin at that time is
decisive to understanding the Soviet viewpoint at the
opening of negotiations for the 1971 Quadripartite
Agreement. Moscow based its argument upon three reference
points: treaty expiration, Allied treaty violation and
significantly-changed circumstances rendering adherence no
longer possible. International law recognizes all three as
adequate reason for treaty termination.[17] Yet it is
dubious whether any of the aforementioned justifications
actually applied to the Berlin situation.

For example, the Soviet Union maintained the Allies
had violated the Potsdam Agreement of 1945 and were
therefore no longer entitled to occupy the city. As the
Allies pointed out, however, the Soviet argument was a *non
sequitur* because Allied rights in the separate Berlin zone
of occupation were of an original nature, outlined in the
London Protocols on occupation, and had nothing to do with
the Potsdam Agreement. Even if the Three had violated the
Potsdam Agreement, such a violation could in no way
jeopardize their position in Berlin.[18]

The Allies insisted in their rejoinder that the London
Protocols had no specified expiration date and therefore
any retroactive imposition of a time limit on the treaty
would amount to outright abrogation. Most important to the
Allies--and to the West Germans--was that the circumstances
in Germany had not changed to the extent that the Allied
position in Berlin had become politically untenable. The
West Germans and their allies would continue to uphold the

goal of eventual German reunification. The German question should remain open and East Germany should not be allowed to swallow up Berlin. Such an action would not only be detrimental to Western security but would lend credence to the East Bloc assertion about the permanency of the post-war political order in Central Europe.[19]

Unilateral exit from binding treaty commitments is possible under international law only when the conditions specified by the treaty become an unacceptable imputation for a treaty partner.[20] But the Soviet claim that the continuing Four-Power status of Berlin imposed an undue demand upon the sovereignty of the East German state was unsustainable, and, indeed, flew in the face of logic. The Soviet Union was arguing not that wartime accords had in some way become an unacceptable imputation on it, but upon the GDR, which was not a partner to the treaty and did not even exist at the time of ratification.

What serious observer would conclude that the Soviet Union in 1958, in 1970, or at present, for that matter, would have renounced its acquired rights either in East Germany or in Berlin? Soviet purposes prior to August 1961 focused primarily upon eliminating all vestiges of Four-Power control in East Germany, and terminating Western rights there. But the Soviet Union did not have the slightest intention of diminishing *its* clout in East Germany. The 1955 Bolz-Zorin Agreement is evidence of such Soviet purpose. Although this agreement ostensibly grants the GDR sovereign rights, a careful reading reveals how the Soviet Union actually confirmed its own rights in East Berlin as well as on the overland transit routes on the "sovereign territory" of the GDR.

In Khrushchev's 1958 ultimatum, the Kremlin leader suggested with little subtlety that West Berlin should become a "free" city. What about all of Berlin? On this matter Khrushchev had precious little to say, since it was never his purpose to withdraw Soviet garrisons from the Eastern sector which had become the capital of the GDR. A particularly shrewd understanding of Soviet policies vis-à-vis East Germany is hardly required to detect Moscow's intentions. Soviet notes were quite explicit:

As for Germany's occupation in general, the Soviet Union has always observed and observes its international commitments, including those on Germany. Moreover, no one can reproach the Soviet Union that it did not serve warning when the western powers scrapped one Allied agreement after another, yoking West

Germany onto the road of militarism and revanchism.[21]

Khrushchev's proposal was thus completely in accordance with a not unusual Kremlin adage: what is mine, stays mine; about yours we can negotiate.

Another example of the same stratagem can be found in June 1964, when Khrushchev once again labeled the occupation regime an anachronism and declared it permanently terminated as a result of the GDR-Soviet Friendship Treaty of the same year. The Soviet Union scrupulously avoided having any accord impact upon its original rights in East Germany, explicitly stating it would maintain this prerogative.[22]

Hartmut Schiedermair calls attention to another important fact about Soviet control in East Germany.[23] In addition to maintaining original occupation rights in East Berlin as well as the responsibility for Allied military vehicles and aircraft, the Soviet Union can invoke the principle of socialist internationalism in order to protect those areas in which socialist achievements are endangered. Such a rationale was offered in Hungary in 1956 and in Czechoslovakia in 1968 and would undoubtedly be used once again in East Germany in the event of political instability.

By 1958 four salient points of contention regarding Berlin's status had emerged between Moscow and the Western Powers. Analysis of these points shows how post-war political developments affected the positions of the two sides.

The first political/legal dispute centered on the quadripartite status of the city and the Soviet notes of 1958 and 1959 are based upon the assumption that Western, though not Soviet, rights in Berlin are anchored in the Potsdam Agreement. Western rights, according to the Soviet position, were the result of a *quid pro quo* and depended upon Soviet consent. It would follow that Allied occupation rights were subject to certain conditions specified by the Soviet Union. Western treaty violation or a unilateral Soviet decision could result in a termination of Western presence in Berlin. As already mentioned, the Western rebuttal had as its point of departure that occupation rights are of an original nature and have nothing to do with the Potsdam Agreement, let alone some sort of *quid pro quo*, such as Western evacuation of Thuringia. The Potsdam Agreement itself did not specify areas of occupation in Germany but merely created specific instruments and institutions for the execution of existing occupation accords.

The second dispute concerned access to the Western sectors. The Allied position noted that the right of overland access was intrinsic to the legal authority to occupy. In their view, access rights were accorded by international agreement, as were original occupation rights; neither was in any way dependent upon Soviet consent. Moreover, because of treaty obligations, the Soviet Union was bound by international law to guarantee overland and air transit to Berlin. Free access, as defined by the Allies, meant unhindered transport of personnel and supplies in company with Soviet pledges of safety. Included in this right of access were the air corridors, established as sovereign Allied air space. In this realm, the GDR had no authority whatsoever and any Soviet attempt to delegate to the GDR control of the air corridors was tantamount to treaty abrogation. The Allies asserted that the emergence of an East German state could not affect established rights and prerogatives in Eastern Germany. Neither GDR claims of sovereignty nor separate GDR-Soviet agreements would terminate Allied rights or render existing treaties invalid.[24]

Intertwined with the access question was the contention over the geographic extension of Allied sovereignty. In the November 1958 note, the Soviet Union argued that greater Berlin, i.e., all four sectors of Berlin, as specified in original quadripartite agreements, had been a part of the Soviet zone of occupation. The Soviet Union had then granted the Western Allies certain rights within this area. It would follow, so the argument goes, that the Soviet Union could withdraw such permission to occupy and the Allies would be obligated to evacuate their sectors. In this view, greater Berlin was sovereign territory only of the Soviet Union, which had the authority to alter the situation unilaterally, for example, by assigning certain control powers to the GDR.

In response to this argument, the Western Powers alluded to the provisions of the wartime accords that specified a Four-Power occupation regime in Germany and established greater Berlin as a separate zone under sovereign quadripartite control: the Soviet Union would thus have no authorization to require Allied evacuation or to grant powers to a country not a party to the agreements, i.e., the GDR. In accordance with the London Protocol, each of the four signatory powers exercised sovereign authority in its respective sector and the Three enjoyed full legal rights in the air corridors.[25]

Finally, there was the fourth point of conflict--the Soviet insistence that the former quadripartite administration and institutions affiliated with it had neither authority nor jurisdiction in Berlin.[26] The Soviet Union argued that, as a result of new developments and changed circumstances, Four-Power jurisdiction in Berlin lapsed, and, "as a logical result of the existing situation," all accords ceased having any validity.[27] To substantiate all arguments, the Soviet Union cited the customary grounds: expiration, Western violations of the Potsdam Agreement, and *clausula rebus sic stantibus*.

The Western Powers asserted all Soviet positions and claims were themselves violations of international law: since there was never any connection between Allied occupation rights and the Potsdam Agreement, the Soviet Union was misconstruing the latter and shirking responsibilities vis-à-vis treaty partners. The wartime accords, the established administrative organs in Berlin as well as the air corridors had no specific expiration date, and, as originally envisaged, these would end only following the ratification of a comprehensive German peace treaty: no treaty, no expiration. Expiration arguments amounted to abrogation.

Furthermore, a separate peace agreement with the GDR, the Allies argued, could not be a comprehensive peace agreement. Such an agreement would not allow the Soviet Union to disregard its treaty obligations and would, in itself, violate prior existing international accords. The Allies emphasized that any separate GDR-Soviet peace agreement would be "without effect."[28]

Two important points should be made about the Soviet legal positions, "legal" being somewhat of a misnomer but continually employed by both sides in presenting their respective arguments about the Berlin situation. As is often the case in international relations, political positions are expressed in legal terms in the interest of augmenting the validity of the arguments.

First, the Soviet position was instructive about Kremlin designs. While it undertook a campaign to expel the Western Powers from Berlin, the Soviet Union was careful about asserting its own rights in East Germany. As was the case in the Bolz-Zorin Agreement, the Soviet Union maintained its occupation authority, even going so far in 1958 as to argue that its were the only "original" rights in East Germany.

Second, although Khrushchev did not make good on his threats--never, for example, signing a separate peace treaty with the GDR--the Soviet legal positions on Berlin in 1958 were analogous to those which would be the starting points for the 1970 quadripartite negotiations. The differences of Eastern and Western positions in 1958 provide a good indication of the extent of the Berlin dilemma.

If the crisis of 1958 is viewed as continuing at least until the construction of the Berlin Wall in August 1961, this crisis reached its climax in the summer of 1961. In a June 15, 1961 speech, Ulbricht specified Eastern demands for the future status of Berlin. According to Ulbricht, the following conditions would constitute prerequisites for the "free city" of West Berlin:

1. Termination of granting political asylum.
2. The elimination of all spy and "human-trade" organizations.
3. Closing of the refugee facilities in West Berlin.
4. Western guarantees of GDR sovereignty vis-à-vis overland transit routes and in the air corridors as well as the renunciation of all Western rights in eastern Germany.[29]

Ulbricht's fourth demand was the Soviet position on sovereignty that had precipitated the crisis in late 1958. The emphasis Ulbricht placed upon the other three points indicated what had become the predominant East Bloc concern by 1961: the hemorrhaging of the GDR.

The steady stream of refugees crossing the still-open sector-sector boundary between East and West Berlin had reached flood levels by 1961. Those leaving East Germany were primarily young professionals and skilled workers, human resources a country can least afford to lose, and the GDR was confronted with the very real prospect of economic collapse. The Soviet Union could ill permit its most loyal Eastern European ally to become economically languid.

Thus, the mass exit of East Germans catalyzed the crisis. After the establishment of the GDR in 1949, over 2,600,000 East Germans fled to the West.[30] In the first half of 1961, about 150,000 people left East Germany. In July of that year, the numbers of refugees hit record highs--30,000.[31]

Khrushchev's speech via radio and television on the same day as Ulbricht's press conference portended the opening round of a new East Bloc offensive against Berlin. Hoping to convey an image of sobriety, the Kremlin leader repeated the challenges made in 1958. First there was the "changed political circumstances" and the "need for a treaty" argument:

> It has always been recognized that after a war a peace treaty should be concluded among the states. This has already been a custom and, if you will, a rule of international law. Examples of it can be found in international practice after the second world war too. Peace treaties were signed more than 14 years ago with Italy and other states that fought on the side of Hitlerite Germany. The United States, Britain and other countries concluded a peace treaty with Japan in 1951. Yet the governments of these same countries will not hear of concluding a peace with Germany.[32]

Second, there was the "complete GDR sovereignty" argument and the threat to defend alleged GDR interests with force:

> If any country violates the peace and crosses another's borders—land, air or water—it will bear the full responsibility for the consequences of aggression and will be duly repulsed . . . we ask everyone to understand us correctly: The conclusion of a peace treaty with Germany cannot be put off any longer; a peace settlement in Europe must be achieved this year.[33]

Finally, Khrushchev stated that the Soviet Union was negotiating from a position of strength, resulting from new strategic circumstances favoring the Soviet Union. The West would have no choice but to accede to the Kremlin's demands on Berlin. There could be little doubt what the "peaceful settlement of issues" referred to by Khrushchev would mean for Berlin.[34]

Some observers have perceived maximum and minimum East Bloc objectives regarding Berlin in the series of 1958-61 crises.[35] The evidence would indicate that a disparity between Soviet and GDR goals existed even in the summer of 1961. The maximum objective in Berlin would have been the incorporation of the entire city into the GDR, resulting in a solution to many East German problems and making Ulbricht's political life a good deal easier. GDR absorption of greater Berlin would have eliminated with one stroke refugee outflow so endangering to East German stability, elevated the international prestige of the GDR, and disposed of the affront to the East German state that

c, to be employed against the West at propitious moments, an
area to be "heated-up" when the Soviet Union was off on
adventures elsewhere. Increasingly, the Kremlin tired of
Ulbricht's petty concerns with his unwillingness to hold
the tenets of "socialist internationalism" in highest
esteem. One of the most visible threads of continuity in
the 1960s and into the Berlin quadripartite negotiations in
the early 1970s was the growing divergence between East
German and Soviet objectives in Berlin. There is
considerable evidence that the Kremlin triumvirate which
deposed Khrushchev as a "hare-brained schemer" became ever
more disinclined to use Berlin as a pressure point against
the West, preferring order and quiet in the East German
state. In August 1961 Ulbricht got his wall, but it was
not a sector-sector wall in Berlin that the East German
leader favored. He likely wanted a successful blockade of
the Western sectors, the expulsion of the Allies from West
Berlin, with the consequent opportunity for the GDR
formally to annex Berlin. Ulbricht's statements at his
June 15 press conference were quite informative upon
careful reading. He publicly renounced the "minimum
objective":

> . . . there are people in West Germany who would like
> us to mobilize the building workers of the GDR capital
> to put up a wall. I am not aware of any such
> intention, since the building workers in our capital
> are chiefly engaged in the housing program, and their
> time is fully occupied. Nobody intends to put up a
> wall. As I said before, we are in favor of a
> contractual settlement of relations between West
> Berlin and the GDR Government. This is the simplest
> and most normal way to solve these questions.[37]

There is every reason to believe Ulbricht meant what

he said: erection of a wall was not the best option for
him. He wished to terminate the occupation regime with the
maximum application of Eastern pressure. He seemed to calm
reservations that some might have had about pursuing the
"maximum objective" in case the United States resisted with
military force. One need barely read between the lines:

> What nonsense all this is. We simply do not want to
> believe and cannot believe that it is the desire, the
> ambition of the United States to appear before the
> whole world as an aggressor. I don't think I need to
> say any more about this. We would be pleased if
> certain people were to refrain in the future from
> answering our many peace offers time after time with
> foolish saber-rattling of other weapons. We would
> like to tell them amicably; stop that noise with your
> weapons, stop the rattling, and wait until we have
> reasonable negotiations on equal terms.[38]

Most revealing of all--and most foreboding for
Berliners--was Ulbricht's stated intention to shut down
West Berlin's Tempelhof Airport "in the interest of air
safety," once West Berlin became a "free" city. There
could be no doubt about Ulbricht's desire to eliminate this
escape route once and for all or about the East German
leader's broader scheme to batten down the hatches in his
soon-to-be "capital."

> . . . if such arrangements are made for air traffic,
> the inhabitants of the central boroughs of Berlin will
> benefit greatly. There will not be so much noise in
> the central boroughs, and there will no longer be the
> danger that planes will hit them on the head.
> Everything will be settled in an orderly manner.[39]

The next parlay came with Khrushchev's speech of June
21 marking the 20th anniversary of Hitler's attack on the
Soviet Union. Speaking initially in global terms,
Khrushchev came to the point after a while about Berlin:

> We propose giving West Berlin the status of a free
> city. We do not at all intend to change West Berlin's
> social and political system. This is the internal
> affair of its population. Neither the Soviet Union
> nor the German Democratic Republic intends to restrict
> West Berlin's ties with all countries of the world.
> But in accordance with international law, the

sovereign rights of the German Democratic Republic, through whose territory the communications linking West Berlin with the outside world pass, must be respected.[40]

Then came the threat to sign a peace treaty with the GDR that would terminate all Soviet dealings with the Allies on Berlin matters. Presenting the West with yet another of his deadlines, Khrushchev insisted the treaty would be signed at the end of the year.

For all Khrushchev's blustering, his challenge to Berlin's status was tangential to the much longer address on defense issues and Soviet strategic concerns, laced with a bit of rocket-rattling and underscoring the Kremlin's view that Berlin was merely one of an array of Soviet power instruments, not an end in itself. Khrushchev even linked the Berlin issue with other matters, hinting at least that he would be satisfied with the "minimum objective."[41] Although the 1961 Soviet-East German verbal blasts showed obvious coordination, a divergence of positions even in the summer of 1961 is not beyond the realm of possibility. That Moscow would have consented to Ulbricht's schemes under any circumstances, at least so long as the U.S. threatened to go to war with the Soviet Union to defend the Western sectors of Berlin is improbable.[42] Slusser argues that Khrushchev's "economic rivalry" speeches, stressing peaceful economic competition with the United States, given in Alma Ata, Kazakh SSR on June 24 and 25, lend considerable credence to the thesis of "minimum objectives" in Berlin.[43] The content of these speeches seem inconsistent with the June 21 speech and completely incompatible with the showdown with imperialism, necessary for accomplishing Ulbricht's maximum Berlin objectives.

Arthur Schlesinger advances the hypothesis that Berlin in the summer of 1961 for Khrushchev was not "a problem but a pretext."[44] The Kremlin leader's demarche had little or nothing to do with Berlin or Germany.[45] This clearly goes too far. The refugee figures from East Germany were doubtless cause of great concern in the Kremlin. Khrushchev was not about to allow Moscow's proteges to lose control in the most important Soviet strategic asset in Central Europe. Khrushchev and Ulbricht were in complete agreement that immediate action had to be taken to quell the refugee tide. Schlesinger is right only insofar as Khrushchev was testing general U.S. will worldwide on the issue of Berlin. Khrushchev apparently hoped he could induce the U.S. to back down on a long-standing commitment to Berlin, while Moscow held the trump of a sector-sector wall in Berlin in its hand. Khrushchev probed, but there is no evidence that he viewed maximum East Bloc objectives as the *only* solution to East German difficulties.

Outlining the U.S. administration's response to the mounting tension in Berlin, President Kennedy in a June 28 press conference labeled the new crisis "Soviet-manufactured" and rejected Soviet demands that the Allies do business with the GDR. Kennedy specified three Soviet objectives in the latest Berlin flare-up: first, "to make permanent the partition of Germany"; second, to "bring an end to Allied rights in West Berlin and to free access for that city"; finally, to produce a situation "in which the rights of the citizens of West Berlin are gradually but relentlessly extinguished."[46] He asserted:

> This is not just a question of technical legal rights . . . It involves the peace and security of the peoples of West Berlin. It involves the direct responsibilities and commitments of the United States, the United Kingdom, and France. It involves the peace and security of the Western world.[47]

On the same day, Khrushchev upped the ante. Determined to save his East German ally, Khrushchev apparently became convinced that the closing of the Berlin sector border was the *sine qua non* for East German viability. Khrushchev described what he wanted in the new situation:

> West Berlin will be able to maintain free relations with all states at its own discretion. But since the communications to West Berlin run through the territory of the German Democratic Republic, according to established international traditions and laws an agreement with the government of that state is required for making use of them. No one is permitted to violate the ground, air or water frontiers of a sovereign state. Any attempt to disregard generally accepted standards of international intercourse has always met with, and it will meet with, a fitting rebuff.[48]

Two GDR announcements following the Khrushchev speech indicated that the East German party leadership was up to no good. A decree appearing in the official GDR gazette stated that the GDR would initiate restrictions on foreign air traffic to and from Berlin on August 1. Claiming the air corridors to be its sovereign air space--a notable violation of existing accords with the Soviet Union in the absence of a peace treaty--the GDR announced that foreign air traffic would be obliged to register with an East German controlled safety center.[49]

In July the official mouthpiece of the GDR Ministry of Justice, *Neue Justiz*, delineated plans for administration in Berlin, once a Soviet-GDR peace treaty was signed. Basing its concept upon the premise that all of Berlin would become GDR territory, *Neue Justiz* proclaimed the peace treaty would be operational "for the entire territory of the GDR, on which West Berlin is situated."[50]

What role the Kremlin had in either of these East German announcements is not possible to determine, although neither received explicit Soviet endorsement as is often the case. In his June 28 speech, Khrushchev insisted there would be no more Berlin blockades. The dubiousness of Kremlin pledges notwithstanding, unilateral East German usurpation of air traffic control in the corridors was a probe of Western will never before attempted. Even in the 1948 blockade, the Kremlin was loathe to provoke such a direct military confrontation. It is unlikely therefore that the Soviet Union was prepared to run such risks for a rather minor East German objective, for loyalty like patience, as time would later show, has its limits. It is not entirely unthinkable that Ulbricht was acting on his own with the air safety center scheme.

Then came stiff Western responses to the East Bloc challenge. In the middle of July, the U.S., Great Britain and France sent notes to the Soviet Union, rejecting the most recent threats to Berlin's status and affirming preparedness to resist any attempt to infringe upon their rights. In a July 25 television address, Kennedy sketched the administration's military, diplomatic and financial measures to counter Khrushchev's new offensive.[51] The U.S. beefed up conventional forces and the President vowed to stand firm in Berlin. "We cannot and will not permit the Communists to drive us out of Berlin, either gradually or by force," Kennedy declared.[52]

Western resolve drove home to Khrushchev the alternatives confronting him. Slusser describes this choice as one between raising the bid and pushing for the maximum objectives on Berlin--signing a peace treaty with the GDR with the consequent termination of all Allied rights--or opting for the "minimum" of sealing the border in the interest of sustaining the East German regime.[53]

Achievement of the "maximum" would doubtless have entailed an almost immediate conclusion of a peace agreement, since the domestic situation in the GDR was urgent and Ulbricht was becoming hot under the collar. It was entirely possible that Khrushchev had already chosen the "minimum" prior to the Allied replies of July. Moreover, the Kremlin wanted to keep Ulbricht on a relatively short leash and Khrushchev was reluctant to give the East German party boss the kind of free hand in Berlin the latter had in mind. East German delay in closing the sector border in Berlin to dam the refugee stream was likely a play for time by Ulbricht, who hoped the Kremlin would push to the limit in Berlin and berid him of the Western Powers permanently. Somewhat remarkable, though, were the Western comments at the time about GDR hesitancy permanently to lock up its population.[54] Perhaps few in the West saw the situation in "maximum" and "minimum" terms, nor did many realize the differences between the GDR and Moscow even at that time.

The Soviet Union issued rejoinders separately to all three Allied notes, making noises about Western warmongering and about the insidiousness of imperialism. Contained in all three notes were complaints about FRG activities in Berlin, marking a new direction in East Bloc assaults against West Berlin following the construction of the Wall. Thereafter Moscow would fix its sights more on FRG rather than Allied presence in the city. According to the Soviet notes: "The population of West Germany lives amid the rampaging of revanchist passions. The Government of the Federal Republic of Germany continually brings forward demands to alter the existing frontiers."[55]

Conspicuously absent from the Soviet notes, even after Kennedy had matched Khrushchev's tough talk, was any reference to the issue of most consequence in bringing on the crisis in the first place, the pledge to conclude a Soviet-GDR peace treaty and the ensuing threat of an across-the-board elimination of Western rights. Khrushchev had other matters of concern for his energies. Ulbricht would have to be content with his Wall. Frustrated, the East German leader was dead-set upon dividing Berlin by the first week of August.

In a speech on July 6, 1961, Ulbricht took aim at the "border crossers" (Grenzgänger), some 60,000 living in East Berlin but working in West Berlin. On July 22, East German police began efforts to prevent exit from the GDR. Those caught leaving faced prison sentences, but so long as the sector border remained open, control remained difficult.

This aspect of the crisis alone was cause for great

concern in Washington. The Soviet Union might have no choice but to take drastic action to bolster the East German regime, thereby occasioning superpower confrontation in Berlin. The question was: what options were available to the Soviet Union? A recently declassified secret cable alluded to problems ensuing from the Berlin crisis:

-After reviewing information available, Department has impression either of two contingencies could arise. First, and more likely, if refugee flood continues, East German regime might take measures to control it. They could do this either by tightening controls over travel from Soviet Zone to East Berlin or by severely restricting travel from East to West Berlin. Second, situation in zone could deteriorate sufficiently to lead to serious disorders.

-We believe Soviets watching situation even more closely than we, since they are sitting on top (of a) volcano. For the moment at least, Soviet policy is to tolerate loss of refugees, while pressing toward decision on Berlin. Continued refugee flood, could, however, tip balance toward restrictive measures. If Khrushchev became seriously concerned (about) situation (in) East Germany, he could either call for showdown on Berlin or slacken pressure in order (to) give regime time (to) get economic house in order.

-Like Soviets, U.S. is faced with dilemma on East Germany. While we would like (to) see unrest there cause Soviets to slacken pressure on Berlin, we would not like (to) see revolt at this time. Nor would U.S. like (to) see drastic measures taken (to) halt refugee flow, particularly since this might fan flames in East Germany.[56]

Given the situation in summer 1961, the Soviet Union had three alternatives for sustaining East Germany. First, as mentioned in the State Department cable, the GDR could impose restrictions on travel between the GDR proper and East Berlin. Such an action would not only have posed considerable practical difficulties, but would have made a mockery of GDR claims to sovereignty in its capital. Second, the GDR could erect a barrier on the sector boundary through the center of Berlin, interdicting any crossing from East to West Berlin. Third, the Soviet Union could attempt to impose its maximum demands upon the Allies as specified in the June 15 Ulbricht speech. The realization of these demands would have necessitated the expulsion of the Western Powers from Berlin and undoubtedly would have precipitated a U.S.-Soviet showdown with the inherent risk of nuclear war.

Ulbricht flew to Moscow on August 3 to argue his case before the Kremlin leadership. Short of having the Soviets seize West Berlin, Ulbricht wished to seal the border as tightly and as quickly as possible.[57] The Soviet Union accepted the proposal, but in a way that would not be viewed by the West as direct confrontation. East Germans were forbidden to leave, but Ulbricht would have to live with Allied military patrols crossing the sector boundary and entering East Berlin. Allied military vehicles in the "sovereign capital" of the GDR were an insult to Ulbricht and an indignity for his regime, but the Soviet Union realized the denial of such Allied access would blatantly violate Four-Power accords and risk a U.S.-Soviet showdown. Notwithstanding Khrushchev's threats in 1958 and Ulbricht's noise in 1961, the Soviet Union was not ready to go to war over Berlin. Khrushchev was interested only in shoring up his East German ally. He did not pursue his earlier challenges to Allied rights in East Germany, although the official Soviet position on Berlin had not changed. Khrushchev said to the East Germans: "this much and no more."

With the building of the Wall and the subsequent stabilization of the East German regime, new possibilities were open to Soviet foreign policy toward the West. The sealing of the border on August 13, 1961 allowed Moscow to negotiate on Berlin separately without much risk to East German stability. By the end of the decade, the Soviet Union was in a position to cut a deal on Berlin. The closure of the sector-sector boundary anchored Berlin's eastern sector in the territory of the GDR and enabled the GDR to consolidate its power. The last exit for East Germans had been slammed shut and Berliners on both sides of the Wall were denied access to the other half of their city.

Added to Berlin's ironies is the dubiousness of whether the erection of the Berlin Wall represented an explicit violation of the city's quadripartite status. Unilateral Soviet termination of Four-Power administration notwithstanding, the Wall did not directly affect the quadripartite accords on Berlin, as would have, for example, the implementation of any of Khrushchev's threats in 1958. Technically, the Soviet Union enjoyed sovereign jurisdiction in its own sector and was obligated only to ensure complete Allied access to West Berlin and free movement within greater Berlin. No agreements prohibited the Soviet Union from erecting a wall in its own occupation sector to restrict the passage of Germans. In light of repeated Soviet assurances that the newly-erected "border fortifications" would not impinge upon Western rights of access, the Western Allies had little choice but to accept the Eastern action as a *fait accompli*.[58] Many Western officials realized that the erection of a wall was the least provocative and distasteful enterprise the Soviet Union could have undertaken. Bark suggests that, had the United States attempted to dismantle the Wall, the East Germans simply would have proceeded to erect another wall 100 meters farther into the Soviet zone.[59] The Allies certainly would not have challenged Soviet authority so deep in its own zone.

The closing of the sector boundary, in the Eastern view the protection of the GDR from espionage and "human-trade," and the subsequent consolidation of the East German regime actually paved the way for change. Moscow had less reason to fear that a modicum of East-West accommodation would endanger GDR stability. Following the construction of the Wall, the Soviet Union modified its tune on Berlin considerably. It made no overt attempts to expel the Western Allies from Berlin as it had done in 1948-49 and again in 1958. Instead, it concentrated its efforts on a campaign against any West German presence in Berlin, thereby testing Western resolve in another way.

As underscored in the GDR-Soviet Friendship Treaty of 1964, the East Bloc officially adopted the view that West Berlin was an "independent political entity" under Allied control with no ties to the FRG.[60] This position was legally correct only in the sense that the Allies had suspended Articles 23 and 144 (2) of the West German Basic Law specifying West Berlin as the twelfth state of the FRG. The Soviet Union was determined, however, to eliminate all social, economic, administrative and cultural ties between the FRG and West Berlin allowed by the Western Powers. The long-term purpose of the Soviet tactics was all too apparent: without West German ties with and financial support of West Berlin, the city would cease to be viable. If sufficient pressure could be applied, political divisions between the FRG and its Western allies were probable.

After 1961, Allied military vehicles and convoys maintained regular access to the Western sectors and free movement throughout the city. But the GDR was quick to assert its "sovereignty" over West German traffic on

overland transit routes. It would deliberately harass
traffic, resulting in snarls lasting hours, every time an
FRG official traveled to West Berlin. "Demonstrative
federal presence," such as visits by the FRG chancellor or
parliamentary meetings in West Berlin, resulted in shrill
East German condemnation and swift reactions. The GDR
labeled any West German presence in Berlin "provocatory
activity" and openly accused the FRG of attempting to annex
West Berlin. Standing shoulder to shoulder with its German
ally, the Soviet Union protested West German presence in
West Berlin in the strongest terms, emphasizing that the
FRG had no business in Berlin and asserting that all FRG
activities in Berlin endangered peace.

Yet there was another important result of the Berlin
Wall. Its erection made clear to most Germans that
reunification was all but impossible in the foreseeable
future. A viable East German regime had been established
and the capital of the former German *Reich*--the presumed
capital of a unified Germany--had been dissected. The FRG
had succeeded in a remarkably short time in becoming a full
member of the Western community, but at the price of
shutting itself off from the East almost completely. FRG
policies, instead of moving Germany in the direction of
reunification, were actually perpetuating division. The
risk of Konrad Adenauer's policy was that all vestiges of
German "nationhood" might eventually disappear. Hence,
many Germans became convinced that a thorough reevaluation
of this policy was necessary.

NOTES

1. *Dokumente zur Deutschlandpolitik* III/4 (Bonn:
Bundesministerium für gesamtdeutsche Fragen, 1969), pp.
1831-1850; *Dokumente Deutschland-Frage* I (Bonn:
Bundesministerium für gesamtdeutsche Fragen, 1961), p. 885.
2. Ibid.
3. Secret Telegram from U.S. State Department,
Washington, to U.S. Embassy, Bonn, Nov. 24, 1958; "A Status
Report on Berlin in the Light of the Khrushchev Statement
of November 10," undated State Department Report, 1958.
4. Secret Telegram, Polto 1829, U.S. Embassy Paris to
State Department, Dec. 30, 1958; *Dokumente Deutschland-
Frage* II, p. 54.
5. "Note from the Government of the Union of Soviet
Socialist Republics to the Government of the United States

of America on the Situation in Berlin, November 27, 1958,"
Documents on Berlin 1943-1963, pp. 180-196.

6. Dieter Mahncke, *Berlin im geteilten Deutschland* (Munich: R. Oldenbourg, 1973), pp. 84-85; Alois Riklin, *Das Berlin-Problem* (Cologne: Verlag Wissenschaft und Politik, 1964), pp. 276-278.

7. "Soviet Note to the U.S. Government on Berlin," Joint Chiefs of Staff Official Use Only Report, Jan. 10, 1959, pp. 7-9.

8. Ibid.

9. Ibid.

10. *Documents on Berlin 1943-1963*, pp. 191-192.

11. "Soviet Aide-Memoire," Joint Chiefs of Staff Official Use Only Report, Jan. 5, 1959, pp. 1-2.

12. *The German Question*, op. cit., pp. 273-74; for the classified version see for example: State Department Confidential Telegram to U.S. Embassy Bonn, Nov. 24, 1958.

13. *Documents on Berlin 1943-1963*, pp. 220-224.

14. Secret Telegram, Polto 1829, U.S. Embassy Paris to State Department, Washington, Dec. 30, 1958.

15. Henry Kissinger, *White House Years* (Boston: Little, Brown and Company, 1979), pp. 403-5; for a contemporary discussion of such connections see: Top Secret Minutes of memorandum of Conference with the President, March 17, 1959, pp. 1-2.

16. The preamble of the Basic Law (*Grundgesetz*), the FRG's *de facto* constitution obligates Germans to work for reunification.

17. Dieter Mahncke, "Das Viermächte-Abkommen über Berlin," *Europa-Archiv*, Vol. 26, No. 19 (1971), pp. 703-4; Mahncke, *Berlin im geteilten Deutschland*, pp. 84-85.

18. *Documents on Berlin 1943-1963*, pp. 211-224.

19. Memorandum of Conference with the President, March 17, 1959, pp. 1-3; Secret Telegram from U.S. Embassy Paris to Department of State, Dec. 30, 1958.

20. Mahncke, *Berlin im geteilten Deutschland*, pp. 84-85.

21. Soviet Note to the U. S. Government on Berlin, January 10, 1959, p. 7.

22. *Dokumente zur Deutschlandpolitik* III/4, pp. 352-55; *Dokumente Deutschland-Frage* III, p. 400; David Childs, *The GDR: Moscow's German Ally* (London: Allen and Unwin, 1983), pp. 67-70.

23. Hartmut Schiedermair, *Das völkerrechtliche Status Berlins nach dem Viermächte-Abkommen von 3. September 1971* (Berlin: Springer Verlag, 1975) p. 17.

24. U.S. Department of State, *U.S. Reply to Soviet*

Note on Berlin (Washington, D.C.: U.S. Government Printing Office, Department of State Publication 6757, 1959) p. 32; Bark, op. cit., pp. 22-23.

25. "Protocol Between the United States, the United Kingdom, the Union of Soviet Union Regarding the Zones of Occupation in Germany and the Administration of Greater Berlin," September 12, 1944; Robert M. Slusser, *The Berlin Crisis of 1961* (Baltimore: The Johns Hopkins University Press, 1973), pp. 4-6.

26. Mahncke, *Berlin im geteilten Deutschland*, p. 109; Riklin, *Das Berlin-Problem*, p. 229; Nelson, op. cit., pp. 169-170.

27. *Documents on Berlin 1943-1963*, pp. 190-193.

28. *U.S. Reply to Soviet Note on Berlin*, pp. 33-34; Bark, pp. 36-38.

29. Ulbricht's Press Conference of June 15, 1961: U.S. Senate, Committee on Foreign Relations, *Documents on Germany 1944-1961* (Washington, D.C., GPO, 1961), pp. 652-663.

30. Honoré Catudal, *The Diplomacy of the Quadripartite Agreement on Berlin* (Berlin: Berlin Verlag, 1977), pp. 34-35; "Intelligence material reported to the President," Secret CIA Report, January 1961.

31. Catudal, *The Diplomacy of the Quadripartite Agreement on Berlin*, pp. 34-35.

32. *Current Digest of the Soviet Press*, XIII/24, p. 4.

33. Ibid., p. 6.

34. Slusser, op. cit., pp. 9-10, 16-19.

35. The "maximum-minimum" thesis is presented cogently by Robert Slusser, see chapter 5 of *The Berlin Crisis of 1961*, pp. 88-107; also, Honoré M. Catudal, *Kennedy and the Berlin Wall Crisis* (Berlin: Berlin Verlag, 1980) pp. 208-211; NSC top secret meeting, "Memorandum of Conference with the President," March 6, 1959.

36. Slusser, op. cit., p. 9.

37. Ulbricht's Press Conference of June 15, 1961: *Documents on Germany 1944-1961*, p. 652.

38. Ibid.

39. *Documents on Germany 1944-1961*, p. 658; *Der Spiegel*, June 28, 1961.

40. *CDSP*, XIII/25, p. 7.

41. Slusser, op. cit., pp. 16-17.

42. Slusser, op. cit., p. 9; preparedness to defend Berlin by whatever means necessary was a known tenet of U.S. policy, see for example: Secret Telegram, Polto 1829, from U.S. Embassy Paris to State Department, Washington, Dec. 30, 1958; Top Secret Minutes of Memorandum of

Conference with the President, March 6, 1959, pp. 1-2.

43. In lieu of specifying a deadline of 6 months, Khrushchev said only that the peace treaty abrogating Western rights in Berlin would be signed in "the near future"; Slusser, op. cit., pp. 18-20; *CDSP*, XIII/25, p. 19.

44. Arthur M. Schlesinger, Jr., *A Thousand Days: John F. Kennedy in the White House* (Boston: Houghton Mifflin, 1965), p. 381.

45. Ibid.

46. Slusser, op. cit., 29-30; Office of the Registrar, *John F. Kennedy. Containing the Public Messages, Speeches, and Statements of the President* (Washington, D.C.: Government Printing Office, 1962), pp. 476-77.

47. Ibid.

48. *CDSP*, XIII/26, p. 12.

49. Slusser, op. cit., p. 43; *New York Times*, June 30, 1961.

50. *New York Times*, July 17, 1961.

51. *U.S. Department of State Bulletin*, 45 (1961), pp. 267-73.

52. Ibid.

53. Slusser, op. cit., pp. 88, 93-95.

54. Examples are not difficult to find: *New York Times*, July 23, 1961, sect. 4, p. 1.; Chairman of the Senate Foreign Relations Committee, J. William Fulbright remarked: "I don't understand why the East Germans don't close their border because I think they have a right to close it."

55. JCS Official Use Only Report, Soviet Note to the U.S. Government on Berlin, Jan. 10, 1959, pp. 3-4; Moscow stated the view that would become a salient theme through the 1960s: "the FRG did not and does not have rights of any kind in West Berlin," Slusser, op. cit., p. 100. *Selected Documents on Germany and the Question of Berlin 1944-1961* (London: H.M.S.O., 1961, Command 1552), p. 457. In light of statements like the following, one cannot help wondering how the Soviet Union could justify some of its policies without the West German bogeyman:

> It would be dangerous to lose sight of the fact that the Federal Republic of Germany even now has more than enough armed forces and arms at its disposal to bring about a general military conflict. After all it is not necessary to be the commandant of a powder-magazine in order to blow it up. It is enough that there should be a madman among those in attendance on the commandant to strike a match.

56. See: Honoré M. Catudal, *Kennedy and the Berlin Wall Crisis*; Secret Cable on U.S. Policy Regarding Unrest in GDR and Refugee Flow, Secretary of State Dean Rusk to U.S. Mission (Berlin), July 22, 1961.

57. *Der Spiegel*, Aug. 2 and Aug. 9, 1961.

58. Catudal, *Kennedy and the Berlin Wall Crisis*, pp. 239-42, 251-53; Slusser, op. cit., pp. 133-38.

59. Ibid.

60. Bark, op. cit., p. 22; Catudal, *Kennedy and the Berlin Wall Crisis*, p. 227-28; Slusser, op. cit., pp. 111-114.

3
The Berlin Question as an International Legal Problem

There are considerable grounds for skepticism about international law and the application of international legal dictums.[1] International law can only be analyzed within the framework of power relationships. Admonishing the Soviet Union for unilateral abrogations of solemn treaties hardly prevented the Berlin blockade or deterred the Soviets from precipitating the 1958 Berlin crisis. A close consideration of legal problems is crucial to a serious examination of the Berlin political situation for two reasons:

1. Since the Second World War, the actions, positions and protests of both sides have been studiously couched in intricate legal arguments. Without understanding such arguments, one cannot fathom the Berlin problem, much less grasp its significance in a broader framework.
2. The Allied position in Berlin continues to depend substantially upon basic respect for the tenets of wartime occupation. Ignoring even the most minor status-related issue could have the "slippery-slope" effect, whereby the GDR could succeed in undermining the Western position. Soviet concessions in the 1971 Quadripartite Agreement represented above all an acceptance of an existing status-quo as well as a reaffirmation of wartime accords.

Allied rights of occupation are inexorably linked with all legal problems affiliated with Berlin. Thus, the stationing of Allied garrisons in the Western sectors, access to the city, as well as FRG authority in West Berlin are all contingent upon the maintenance of occupation prerogatives. The FRG and the Western Powers insist that

the Allies gained their rights of occupation through the
unconditional surrender of the Third *Reich* and not by any
sort of Soviet consent.[2]   The Allies claim the right to
uphold the validity of the London Protocols until a
provisional government of a reunified Germany signs a peace
treaty, rendering wartime accords invalid.[3]   What the West
most adamantly rejects is the alleged ability of the GDR or
the Soviet Union to bring about such circumstances
unilaterally.[4]

Despite the vacillations of the Soviet and East German
positions regarding Berlin, one thread of continuity seems
to have remained: that Berlin was never a separate zone,
but constituted a part of Soviet-occupied areas.[5]   In the
case of East Berlin, the Eastern side presented the West
with a *fait accompli*, the ramifications of which lie at the
very core of the German problem. The establishment of the
Eastern sector as the capital of the GDR, the building of
the Wall and the long denial of access to the East for West
Germans are not merely problems of Berlin, rather they are
aspects of broader questions of Germany's post-war
division.

As was best exemplified in the 1958 crisis, a salient
point of conflict between the two sides was the question
whether or not political developments or treaty expiration
in themselves could be cause for the termination of
Berlin's Four-Power status. The recurrent argument of the
East Bloc in 1958 was that the very existence of the GDR as
a sovereign state, i.e., greatly modified political
circumstances, eliminated all vestiges of Four-Power
status.[6]   In later communiqués, the Soviet Union would
assert that the political situation would change once the
Kremlin signed a separate peace treaty with the GDR.[7]
Combining this position on the GDR with the long-held
premise that Berlin was a part of the Soviet zone, the
Kremlin apparently believed itself to have an air-tight
case. All Eastern legal arguments, however, were
tangential to the overriding political concern of
preserving the GDR.

The Soviet Union had yet additional arguments, not
least of which was Western violation of the Potsdam
Agreement.[8]   Repeatedly the Soviets accused the Western
Powers of treaty infractions whose consequences could only
be the terminus of Four-Power responsibility in German
occupation zones. The currency reform in the Western zones
in 1948, in the Soviet view, represented the first major
violation of wartime accords. Additional violations
included other steps leading to the establishment of a West

German state, and later the integration of the FRG into NATO. Furthermore, all major state organs of the GDR have been located in East Berlin for decades. Maintenance of Four-Power status, so the argument goes, constitutes an infringement upon the sovereign authority of an independent state.[9]

In the strictest technical sense, these East Bloc positions are seriously flawed. International jurists do not recognize the violation of a treaty by one or more parties to it as grounds for its termination, especially its unilateral termination.[10] Neither can the existence or location of the institutions of a state not party to an agreement possibly justify any sort of unilateral alteration or abrogation of an international accord.[11]

These are nonetheless matters over which Eastern and Western legal advisers squabbled for years. The basic Western position on Berlin has remained the same: prior to the ratification of peace agreements with a unified Germany, the Soviet Union will continue to retain responsibilities in Berlin. What is far more important than the rightness or wrongness of a particular position, the strength or weakness of a particular argument under recognized international law, is that the United States has no choice in the matter. Its security interests in Europe are closely bound to the meticulous preservation of Four-Power status in Berlin. Thus, the examination merely of the legal cogency of certain positions is insufficient in any analysis of international law. Political/security considerations underpinning official positions are equally if not more important.

Soviet actions in Berlin often ran parallel to Moscow's policies vis-à-vis Germany. After 1953, with the Soviet Union committed to the continued existence of a separate, communist state in the former Eastern zone of occupation, the Kremlin rather consistently followed a plan to augment the political authority of the GDR. In 1955 the Soviet high commissioner was replaced with an ambassador in East Berlin.[12] Shortly thereafter East German border troops and police replaced Soviet soldiers on the German zonal borders as well as on the sector boundaries in Berlin. By 1958 the Soviet Union increasingly maintained that matters of Berlin's status, including access and border control, were exclusively within the jurisdiction of the GDR, not the Soviet Union. The Kremlin hoped to be in a position whereby its proxy could carry out its policies, without the Soviets having any accountability.[13]

A decisive step in the incorporation of East Berlin

came in January 1957 with the GDR law on the application of *Volkskammer* (GDR parliament) statutes throughout East Berlin.[14] With this law, East Berlin became fully integrated into the legal system of the GDR. Such integration amounted to *de facto* annexation of the Eastern sector of Berlin, although the *Volkskammer* has scrupulously respected Soviet appurtenances.[15]

Yet another step was taken in December 1960, when the *Volkskammer* eliminated the office of president of the GDR, replacing it with a collective organ, the *Staatsrat*, or Council of State. The GDR president was primarily a ceremonial figure, exercising no political authority. In comparison, the *Staatsrat* was established as a second executive power with its seat in East Berlin and jurisdiction far exceeding that of the nominal parliament.[16] In fact, this executive organ often functions as a parliamentary institution in that it replaces the *Volkskammer* when the latter is not in session. The erection of the Wall thus represented one of a series of actions against Berlin's Four-Power status, but a maneuver with one practical purpose: to thwart the flow of refugees from the GDR.

Gradually, East Berlin came to be incorporated into the legal, administrative and economic system of the GDR. By 1953 East Berliners were issued GDR passports. The GDR carried out all foreign and international trade relations. Few differing administrative organs existed for East Berlin. Most apparent of all was the remilitarization of East Berlin, whereas West Berlin maintains no military forces apart from those of the Western Powers and no FRG military personnel are permitted to be stationed in West Berlin.

A few notable peculiarities in East Berlin's status continue to exist in the East Bloc interpretation. Though dismissed by many as a minor point, neither the first or the second GDR constitution explicitly stated that East Berlin itself comprises GDR territory, regardless of the reference to "Berlin" as the GDR capital.[17] The matter is not insignificant, and a modicum of deliberation will bring one to the reason for this ambiguity. The Soviet Union undoubtedly wished to leave open the possibility that greater Berlin would eventually become part of the East German state, hence the avoidance of reference only to part of Berlin. The ambiguity later opened the way for various Soviet legal positions. It is ironic, though, that this odd aspect of the 1968 GDR constitution later made possible a far-reaching accord between the powers--the 1971

Quadripartite Agreement--without the Soviet Union formally violating the GDR's highest law.

How then, given the ostensibly unbridgeable positions of the two sides concerning the issue of East Berlin, could any sort of accord on Berlin's status ever be reached? The answer is two-fold: first, political developments in the 1960s led to environs in Central Europe facilitating agreement on Berlin; second, the Quadripartite Agreement in structure and wording is a workable accord.

Reference is made in the General Provisions of the Quadripartite Agreement not to "Berlin" specifically, but rather to the "relevant area." This term allows a great deal of flexibility without jeopardizing the Western interpretation or political/legal position. Thus, the agreement does not state explicitly whether or not East Berlin is to be included in the "relevant area" or not.[18] The ambiguity, nurtured in the agreement, permits the Soviet Union and its East German ally to save face and maintain certain tenets of former legal positions, as will be discussed in detail in chapter 11, while disallowing them from endangering either West Berlin's freedom or Allied rights. The 1971 agreement has successfully separated practical political matters, such as access, Allied occupation rights, and West German authority in the Western sectors, from the presently-irresolvable abstract international legal issues like the legitimacy of the GDR, the legality of the *de facto* annexation of East Berlin or the actual status of greater Berlin in international law.

Such is not to argue, however, that differing interpretations do not result in controversy or that the Quadripartite Agreement is the panacea for Berlin problems. One example of the practical difficulties of the accord involves GDR border guards shooting escapees on the Berlin Wall.[19] The Soviet Union asserts that this brutal action is a completely justifiable measure for the protection of state borders, a long-recognized right of sovereign nations and therefore strictly a domestic political matter of the GDR.[20] The Allies protest the "Schusswaffengebrauch" (use of weapons) against refugees in the strongest terms, asserting such acts to be in violation of the renunciation-of-force provisions of the Quadripartite Agreement.[21] The Allies continue to refuse to accept the Berlin sector/sector boundary as a *de jure* international border. Closed borders and refugee persecution are hardly out of the ordinary in the Eastern Bloc and to expect an accord on Berlin's status in some manner to modify these unfortunate occurrences is not realistic.

On the employment of force issue, the Soviet Union and the Allies also have very disparate views. Since, according to the Soviet positior, East Berlin is the capital of the GDR and thus lies outside of the Quadripartite Agreement's jurisdiction, the renunciation-of-force proviso does not apply to East Berlin. Since Paragraph 2 of the General Provisions offers no solution to the dilemma, one might hasten to characterize the agreement as seriously flawed and to accuse its negotiators of sophistry.

No. 4 of the Quadripartite Protocol, providing for quadripartite negotiations on difficulties in the administration of the accord, suggests a partial solution.[22] Decades of East-West altercation about the legality of GDR actions have demonstrated the futility of abstract discussions of East Berlin's status. But the requirement for consultation of administrative difficulties has made possible the serious consideration of the "Schusswaffengebrauch" issue in various forums. In fact, the West has succeeded in discouraging the GDR from arbitrarily shooting suspected escapees by linking the issue to political matters of importance to the GDR. It has not been theoretical legal discussion, but instead political horse-trading within the framework of the Quadripartite Agreement, that has resulted in the GDR's refraining from extensive brutality.

Equivocalness in international agreements is certainly no recent discovery of statesmen. The breadth of the Quadripartite Agreement's framework and its laxness on legal interpretation were necessary in order to provide the possibility of ancillary treaties with the GDR and the FRG, neither of which is a party to the Quadripartite Agreement. The general accord structure allowed, for example, the two German states to reach traffic and transport arrangements between themselves. Also, the accord did not run athwart of premises or basic designs of FRG *Ostpolitik*.

NOTES

1. Much ink in the area of international law has been spilled on the subject of Berlin. A skeptic could cite the case of post-war Berlin as an example of the ascendancy of the political over the legal in international relations;

legalisms aside, the Soviet Union carried out the Berlin Blockade and repeatedly attempted to expel the Western powers from the city. German literature--Alois Riklin, Hartmut Schiedermair, Doeking Ress, for example--tends to be legalistic in approach, whereas English-language analyses as a rule deal with Berlin in the broader context of East-West conflict.   For a brief discussion of differences in approaches to the Berlin problem, see: Ernst R. Zivier, "Vorwort zur dritten Auflage," *Der Rechtsstatus des Landes Berlin* (Berlin: Berlin Verlag, 1977), pp. 10-12.

2. The Allied position has remained unchanged and has been repeated during the various crises on Berlin; see: U.S. Department of State, *The Soviet Note on Berlin: An Analysis* (Washington, D.C.: Government Printing Office, 1958); Daniel J. Nelson, op. cit., pp. 1-9.

3. U.S. Department of State, *Berlin-1961* (Washington, D.C.: Government Printing Office, 1961); United States Foreign Policy: A Report of the Secretary of State (Washington, D.C.: GPO, 1972).

4. Joint Chiefs of Staff Official Use Only Report, "Soviet Note to the U S Government on Berlin," and, "Soviet Aid-Memoire," Jan. 10, 1959; "Top Secret Memorandum of Conference with the President," March 6, 1959, pp. 1-2; Secret NSC Report, "A Status Report on Berlin in the Light of the Khrushchev Statement of November 10," undated.

5. See: Ernst Zivier, op. cit., pp. 60-64; JCS Official Use Only Report, "Soviet Aid-Memoire," Jan. 10, 1959, pp. 7-9.

6. *U.S. Department of State Bulletin*, Nov. 7, 1955, pp. 734-35.

7. See: JCS Report, "Soviet Note to the U S Government on Berlin," Jan. 10, 1959, pp. 4-6; Zivier, p. 60; Khrushchev speech, *CDSP* XIII/25, p. 7.

8. See: Notes from the Government of the U.S.S.R. to the German Democratic Republic and the Federal Republic of Germany, *Documents on Berlin 1943-1963*, pp. 196-209.

9. JCS Report, "Soviet Note to the U S Government on Berlin," Jan. 10, 1959, pp. 6-10.

10. See: Georg Dahm, *Völkerrecht*, Vol. 3 (Stuttgart: Deutsche Verlags-Anstalt, 1961), pp. 143-46; Mahncke, *Berlin im geteilten Deutschland*, pp. 84-85.

11. Zivier, op. cit., pp. 51-54.

12. See Zivier's discussion, pp. 30-33.

13. John F. Kennedy Library, "Oral History Program," Interview with Dean Acheson, pp. 20-22; Top Secret NSC Document No. 174, 1954, pp. 9-10; Secret NSC Report, "A Status Report on Berlin in the Light of the Khrushchev

46

Statement of November 10," undated.

14. Zivier, op. cit., pp. 81-82.

15. Ibid.

16. Siegfried Mampel, *Der Sowjetsektor von Berlin* (Frankfurt: A. Metzner Verlag, 1963), pp. 355-58.

17. Mampel, op. cit., pp. 94, 336-38; Zivier, op. cit., pp. 83-84.

18. See: Zivier, pp. 86-88; Hartmut Schiedermair, *Der völkerrechtliche Status Berlins nach dem Viermächte-Abkommen vom 3. September 1971* (Berlin: Springer Verlag, 1975), pp. 14-18.

19. Schiedermair, op. cit., pp. 42-43; Zivier, op. cit., pp. 87-89.

20. Schiedermair, op. cit., pp. 46-48; Soviet attempts to refer the Allies to the GDR authorities on important Berlin matters is no new problem: see for example, Secret NSC Report, "A Status Report on Berlin in the Light of the Khrushchev Statement of November 10, 1958," undated.

21. *Süddeutsche Zeitung*, July 28, 1972; *Le Monde*, Feb. 8, 1973; *Frankfurter Allgemeine Zeitung*, Feb. 8, 1973.

22. Schiedermair and Zivier both point out that the provision for consultations facilitates the management of various problems and isolated issues, see: Schiedermair, op. cit., pp. 42-44; Zivier, op. cit., pp. 207-209.

4
Occupation Rights and German Authority

The Paris Agreements granting sovereignty to the FRG contain certain provisions for maintenance of Allied rights and authority in Berlin.[1] Thus, according to Article VI of the "Germany Treaty," the Western Powers are obligated to consult with the FRG on matters concerning the exercise of existing prerogative in Berlin. For its part, the FRG agreed to cooperate closely with the Allies in the administration of their rights and to facilitate the exercise of those rights.[2] The FRG explicitly assented to assist Berlin economically and financially, in effect, integrating the Western sectors into its economic system. Moreover, the Agreements provided for the inclusion of West Berlin in international treaties made by the FRG, contingent upon Allied approval on security concerns. As a rule, FRG civil law applies in the Western sectors.

As West German officials were quick to observe in the 1950s and some Americans seemed less able to grasp, the viability and the freedoms of West Berlin depended upon the "organic links" with the FRG politically and economically.[3] The question of ties between the Western sectors and the FRG was as crucial to West Berlin's future as were Allied security guarantees.

Correctly perceiving this axiom, former West Berlin governing mayor, Willy Brandt, repeatedly expressed doubts about mere defense of the Berlin status-quo.[4] Although one may fault some of Brandt's conclusions, he recognized the need not only to preserve aspects of a status-quo in Berlin but to assure an expansion of West German influence and jurisdiction in the Western sectors. An accord on Berlin sanctioning such necessary connections with the FRG, as the Quadripartite Agreement of 1971 does, was of particular value to the West, preventing what Brandt called an eventual "status-quo minus."

So long as the provisions of the Basic Law dealing with Berlin and paragraphs 2 and 3 of the First Article of the Berlin Constitution remain suspended, FRG statute laws do not automatically apply to the Western sectors of Berlin, but instead must be individually voted upon by the Berlin House of Representatives.[5] The Kommandatura originally determined the procedure for approval of West Berlin civil law and has simplified the process considerably. For example BK/L (52) 19 provides for parliamentary approval of several FRG laws through a so-called Berlin "Mantelgesetz."[6] BK/O (51) 56 established the general use of "blanket laws" in West Berlin, paralleling FRG codification.

The Allies retain the right to examine all laws in West Berlin and to annul any--including "blanket laws" as well as FRG laws--deemed not in accordance with West Berlin's Four-Power status.[7] It is, however, unusual for Allied authorities to intervene directly in West Berlin law-making processes. Potentially objectionable clauses in FRG laws are either scrutinized prior to passage in the *Bundestag* (FRG Parliament) for any Berlin-related difficulties or else contain provisions for the non-application of such laws in the Western sectors. Often FRG laws are drafted with special attention to West Berlin and to the security concerns of the Allies there.[8]

The only major difference between the FRG legal system and that of West Berlin, with the exception of military law, is in regard to the role of the West German Constitutional Court, the *Bundesverfassungsgericht*. The Constitutional Court is not authorized to pass judgment upon Allied decisions in Berlin, nor to rule on Berlin issues.[9] Because the Constitutional Court is generally regarded as a major governmental institution of the FRG, consignment of court authority in the Western sectors would impinge upon Allied prerogative and represent a violation of valid Four-Power accords.

Even though the foreign relations of the Western sectors lie within the exclusive jurisdiction of the Allies, the latter have delegated much authority outside the defense and security realm to the FRG. An Allied communiqué from May 21, 1952 designates certain FRG foreign-political responsibilities for West Berlin and specifies how West Berlin is to be included in FRG international agreements.[10] As a general rule, an agreement applying to Berlin will include a specific Berlin clause.[11] Trade and financial agreements usually employ the term "DM-currency area" of which Berlin is a part. The Allies maintain the right either to exclude the Western sectors from an accord or to place limitations upon the accord's validity in West Berlin.

A note now part of the 1955 Paris Agreements allows the FRG to represent the interests of West Berliners abroad.[12] Such authority permitted the FRG to provide consular services as well as to represent West Berlin in international organizations. Neutral and Western-oriented nations accepted this international FRG role.

The East Bloc, however, did not. The question of FRG international jurisdiction in the Western sectors was a point of East-West contention for years. Accusing the Western powers of violating existing accords on Berlin's status, the Soviet Union made a great deal of noise about the inclusion of West Berlin in any FRG agreements, while maintaining the GDR did have such authority vis-à-vis East Berlin.[13] Tacit Soviet assent to the inclusion of the Western sectors in the Soviet-German Trade Agreement of April 25, 1958 notwithstanding, a concession appearing to set a precedent, the East Bloc continued adamantly to oppose any FRG representation of West Berlin interests abroad. This disapprobation amounted to discrimination against West Berliners, whose identity cards and passports were not recognized in Eastern Europe or the Soviet Union. Only in the 1971 Quadripartite Agreement did Moscow finally accept the principle of FRG responsibility for West Berliners. Poland, Hungary and Bulgaria did consent to limited West German authority for West Berlin in the 1963-64 commercial agreements establishing FRG trade missions in those countries. Nonetheless, the Soviet Union and the GDR repeatedly attempted to prevent FRG representation of West Berlin in multilateral treaties and international organizations; the FRG-jurisdiction issue continued to strain relations with Eastern European states.[14]

FRG ties with West Berlin have customarily been referred to as the "Bundesprasenz" or federal presence in West Berlin. As FRG authority in the Western sectors increased, it became necessary for one to differentiate between "demonstrative federal presence" and FRG economic, legal, cultural connections with the city. The former term alludes to the activities of major FRG political institutions in West Berlin, such as *Bundestag* sessions or the convention electing the FRG's president. The convention met four times in West Berlin (1954, 1959, 1964 and 1969). This "demonstrative federal presence" has precipitated several serious confrontations with the Soviet

Union and the GDR.[15] Without infringing upon vital FRG
ties, the Quadripartite Agreement significantly reduced
"demonstrative federal presence."

The question of the legality of the "demonstrative
federal presence" which the FRG pursued for years is still
controversial among FRG legal analysts. Some, like Riklin,
argue that the "demonstrative federal presence" was not in
conformance with the Four-Power status of the city.[16]
Other observers justify such action in retaliation to
repeated East Bloc violations of Berlin's status.[17] In all
likelihood the motive behind "demonstrative federal
presence" was a combination of the desire to assert FRG
authority, reprisals against the GDR, and the wish to
maintain some semblance of nationhood in a divided land--
all major political concerns of the FRG.

Another salient question of the post-war era has been
that of nationality. Should, for example, the division of
Berlin and the continuing validity of Allied treaties in
West Berlin, result in a separate citizenship for West
Berliners? Because the Basic Law was formulated to apply
to all Germans, and since the FRG refuses to recognize the
GDR as a separate nation, the former does not view East
Germans as foreigners in the sense they are citizens of a
different country.[18] Hence, customary precepts of
international law do not apply.[19] For its part, the GDR
claimed the existence of a single German nationality until
1957, at which time the GDR in a notable *volte-face* adopted
the position that two separate German states developed
after the Second World War with distinctly different
nationalities. Shortly thereafter the GDR began to speak
officially of "citizens of the GDR," as opposed to Germans.

The Berlin situation complicated matters even more.
On account of Berlin's special status--not a constituent
part of the FRG, or, theoretically of the GDR--the issue of
the nationality of its inhabitants is singularly vexing.
Until 1971 the East Bloc was adamant about refusing to
recognize West Berliners as West German citizens and was
loath to have FRG officials speak on Berliners' behalf in
any way. Subjected to blatant discrimination, West
Berliners were in a sort of juridical limbo. In a May 1952
Allied communiqué, the Western Powers explicitly accepted
FRG legal procedure on nationality issues in Berlin. Such
was little help to West Berliners throughout the East Bloc
or even in East Berlin.[20]

The problem became more acute in the 1960s and not
until 1971 was it settled. In a letter of the three
ambassadors to the Federal (FRG) Chancellor concerning

interpretation of Annex II of the Quadripartite Agreement, the Western Powers explained that the term "ties" in the agreement permitted West Berliners in practice to have the benefits of FRG citizenship.[21] The agreement thereby affirmed the validity of the May 1952 Allied communique and the Soviet Union has accepted the Western interpretation.

NOTES

1. Article 2 of the "Germany Treaty" of May 26, 1952 and in the protocol of October 23, 1954. Zivier, op. cit., pp. 90-91. *Documents on Berlin 1943-1963*, pp. 132-134 and pp. 141-143.

2. *Documents on Berlin 1943-1963*, p. 145.

3. Willy Brandt, *People and Politics The Years 1960-1975* (Boston: Little, Brown and Co., 1976), pp. 20-21. Brandt was governing mayor of Berlin from 1957-1966.

4. Brandt, *People and Politics The Years 1960-1975*, pp. 14-19, 20-21. Brandt was convinced that the West should recognize in the erection of the Berlin Wall: first, the failure of Adenauer's "Deutschlandpolitik"; second, the mere adherence to a status-quo was short-sighted and would exacerbate the German problem. He later advocated positive, sometimes bold steps toward the acceptance of Central European realities and a relaxation of tensions insofar as this was possible.

5. Zivier, op. cit., p. 95.

6. BK/O (51), *Documents on Berlin 1943-1963*, pp. 128-129; BK/L (52), *Documents on Berlin 1943-1963*, pp. 129-130.

7. Richard Lush, "The Relationship between Berlin and the Federal Republic of Germany," *The International Comparative Law Quarterly* 3 (1965), p. 762. Zivier, op. cit., pp. 97-98.

8. Lush, op. cit., p. 767. An example is legislation concerning civilian air traffic to Berlin. The Allies have exclusive jurisdiction in the three air corridors to the Western sectors. The *Bundestag* and the Berlin House of Representatives avoid parliamentary action that could in any way impinge upon Allied prerogative.

9. BK/O (52) 35 and BK/L (51) 29 forbid the Federal Constitutional Court from exercising any jurisdiction in Berlin, *Documents on Berlin 1943-1963*, pp. 121-131.

10. BKC/L (52) 6, May 21, 1952, *Documents on Berlin*

1943-1963, pp. 130-132.

11. Zivier, op. cit., pp. 116-17.

12. Zivier, op. cit., p. 117; *Documents on Berlin 1943-1963*, pp. 303-306. Until the Quadripartite Agreement, the Soviet position was that the FRG could not legally represent West Berlin interests. The Soviets even took the matter to the United Nations in 1958: see Zivier, p. 118; Schiedermair, op. cit., pp. 90-91.

13. *Documents on Berlin 1943-1963*, pp. 176-180.

14. Zivier, op. cit., pp. 118-119; *Die Berlin-Regelung. Das Viermachte-Abkommen über Berlin und die erganzenden Vereinbarungen* (Bonn: Presse-und Informationsamt der Bundesregierung, 1972), p. 275.

15. Zivier, op. cit., p. 126. The most thorough treatment of the problem of "demonstrative federal presence" is: Ottfried Hennig, *Die Bundesprasenz in West Berlin* (Cologne: Verlag Wissenschaft und Politik, 1976).

16. Alois Riklin, "Berlin als völkerrechtliches Problem," *Schweizer Monatshefte* 4 (1966), pp. 707-716. The review of esoteric German international law treatises is beyond the scope of this essay. In the view of this author, some legal analyses indeed border on the irrelevant since determination of legality or illegality hardly alters GDR actions in East Berlin, for example, that are largely political issues. See also: Hennig, op. cit., pp. 147-49.

17. Riklin, "Berlin als völkerrechtliches Problem," pp. 708-710.

18. *Grundgesetz*, Art. 116 (1). For analysis: Arnold J. Heidenheimer and Donald P. Kommers, *The Governments of Germany*, 4th ed. (New York: Harper and Row, 1975), pp. 73-77.

19. Zivier, op. cit., pp. 132-33; H. Kreutzer, "Berlin im Bund," *Zeitschrift fur Politik*, No. 1 (1960), p. 139; Lush, op. cit., p. 742.

20. Zivier, op. cit., pp. 159-60.

21. Zivier, op. cit., pp. 161; Schiedermair, op. cit., pp. 94-96; Karl Meesen, "Das Problem der Staatsangehorigkeit nach dem Grundvertrag," *Europa-Archiv*, Vol. 28, No. 15 (1973), pp. 515-24.

5
Political Developments After 1961

Reflecting a developing new mood in the FRG regarding the East, Foreign Minister Gerhard Schröder described his government's approach in 1965 in the following terms:

> No German government, constitutionally sworn as it is to act on behalf of all Germans and to restore German unity, could abandon the policy of reunification . . . our policy must be not to arouse false hopes, but to establish relations between East and West based on mutual trust and thus enable us to remove, first of all, the minor sources of tension, but subsequently the major ones as well.[1]

The stabilization of the East German regime brought about primarily by the sealing off of East Berlin made plain to most Germans that the policy of "maintained tensions" with the GDR was failing positively to affect the German situation and risked the ossification of FRG policies. New concepts were needed by virtue of the fact that Ulbricht had demonstrated his willingness to take any measures to secure the East German state and to isolate it from the West. By the mid-1960s the yawning gap between West German policy aims toward the East and the realities of divided Europe had become apparent. Confrontation tactics devoid of fresh concepts were yielding the FRG nothing.

There were yet other considerations West Germans had to make. The euphoria over European integration was warming. A Gaullist France was pursuing an increasingly nationalist foreign policy that had a two-fold effect for Bonn: first, French policies diminished FRG hopes to enhance its position toward the East through a politically integrated Europe; second, and more importantly, France was developing its own ideas about relations with Eastern Europe, with the resultant likelihood of independent, albeit limited, French reconciliation with individual East Bloc countries. The U.S. also began exploring new avenues of rapprochement in Eastern Europe, raising the specter in Bonn of the FRG either being at odds with the Allies or of the latter making accords over the FRG's head.

With the formation of the so-called Grand Coalition of CDU and SPD in Bonn in December 1966 came the first augury of policy shifts. The SPD had entered the governing coalition upon the stipulation that the FRG initiate new Eastern policies, widely known as the *Ostpolitik*. Many in the SPD as well as in the CDU realized that Bonn should begin dealing with individual members of the East Bloc, a notion requiring overhauling the Hallstein Doctrine. Wiser heads in Bonn perceived that this policy dictum had outlived its usefulness, threatening the FRG with eventual diplomatic isolation.[2]

In the first months of the CDU-SPD coalition, West German Chancellor Kurt Georg Kiesinger offered to meet with GDR Premier Willi Stoph to discuss inter-German problems. Both the CDU and the SPD dispatched notes to the SED, encouraging the opening of negotiations on an array of problems. Thus, Bonn for the first time was fostering high-level government contacts with the East Germans in a complete reversal of former policies of proscription. Ostensible validity of the Hallstein Doctrine notwithstanding, high-level contacts with the GDR were in themselves tantamount to *de facto* recognition of the East German regime, an action almost unthinkable under Adenauer's chancellorship.

It was not only with the GDR that Bonn was nurturing significant political change. In January 1967 the FRG established full diplomatic relations with Romania and one year later with Yugoslavia. The FRG entered into talks with Hungary, Bulgaria and Czechoslovakia on matters of mutual concern, i.e., mutual recognition. For an alleged political dwarf, threatened in the early 1960s to be sodden by the tide of change, the FRG in 1968 was not faring badly.

In the same period the FRG-East European trade curve moved steadily upwards. Beginning in 1965 the FRG extended five- and eight-year credits to Eastern European countries. The Grand Coalition proceeded to further encourage economic relations with the East and to liberalize lending. Lacking sources of foreign exchange, it was only through the extension of liberalized credits that Eastern European countries could acquire Western industrial products. The catalyst for the surge in trade with the East Bloc in the 1960s was political motivation; economic and political goals were inextricably linked. Likewise, trade difficulties were--and continue to be--political as well as financial. In the former case, the dominant Soviet role in COMECON and GDR reservations about increased East-West contacts in many instances place a damper upon trade relations. In the latter, the Eastern lack of hard currency often excludes extensive commercial relations, unless provisions can be made for availability of credit.

Despite Bonn's not insignificant successes in Eastern Europe from 1966-68, such as with Romania and Yugoslavia, seemingly insurmountable political obstacles to the improvement of relations with other states remained. First, there was the burning question of Germany's eastern boundaries--the Oder-Neisse line. Few could deny in the late 1960s the existence of the Oder-Neisse as a *de facto* international border or would presage any revision of this boundary in the foreseeable future. Yet the policy of "maintained tensions" in the FRG died hard. Acceptance of a status-quo in Eastern Europe had foreign as well as domestic ramifications for any government in Bonn. Poland's position on the matter was unyielding: the opening of negotiations with the FRG on any issues was predicated upon prior acceptance of its western borders.

Next, the theoretically-valid Hallstein Doctrine was a continuing problem for Bonn in that it amounted to a codification of the policy of "maintained tensions." Flexibility in foreign policy and a successful *Ostpolitik* depended upon its eventual revision; Bonn's goals after 1967 were actually at cross-purposes with this former pillar of West German policy. Yet the coalition was not quite able to handle the political dilemmas created by the doctrine.

Finally, East German intransigence posed the greatest difficulty of all for Bonn. Ulbricht, a dyed-in-the-wool Stalinist so long as he drew breath, had his own ideas about maintained tension policies. Not enchanted with Bonn's initiatives in Eastern Europe and highly suspicious of anything smacking of liberalization, Ulbricht was determined to sabotage all efforts at detente. Complacently satisfied behind the fortress of his walled-in nation, Ulbricht dreaded change that might have had adverse effects upon the GDR's security. To make the point, the East German party boss developed a policy maxim bearing his name. The so-called "Ulbricht Doctrine" stipulated that Bonn must grant *de jure* recognition to the GDR with the establishment of full diplomatic relations previous to any discussion of inter-German issues. Hence Ulbricht's standard reply to all FRG initiatives before 1970 was a vociferous demand for unconditional acceptance of the GDR.

Ulbricht was hardly renowned for his discretion, as evidenced by the 1966 "Workers' Parties of two Germanies Letter," sent to the West German SPD. Riddled with distortions and half-truths, the letter from Ulbricht appealed in an insulting manner to the "solidarity" of the German "workers' parties."[3] Typifying GDR diplomatic approaches, the letter would set the tone for future East German notes to the FRG for upcoming years.

As if each of the aforementioned problems was not in itself profound, all difficulties regarding Eastern Europe that confronted Bonn were interrelated. Even though the CDU-SPD coalition recognized that its *Ostpolitik* had to form part of a more general Western detente, West German foreign policy in the years 1966-68 was in need of a conceptual breakthrough; that is, it had to determine its priorities carefully in order to concentrate on individual phases of a step-by-step approach. Only by taking small steps in Eastern Europe could the FRG possibly succeed in sorting out foreign political dilemmas. The following excerpts from the new West German government's state of the nation address in December 1966 illustrates the dilemmas facing the FRG: " . . . we have not forgotten . . . (Poland's) sorrowful history . . . and we can appreciate . . . more than ever before Poland's desire to live within a state of secured boundaries."[4] Agreeing to guarantees of Polish security seemed feasible enough, but such was hardly the case. Kiesinger went on: "However, the boundaries of a reunited Germany can only be determined by an agreement, freely arrived at, with an all-German government; an agreement that would establish the preconditions for a good and lasting relationship acceptable to both."[5] Here was the rub. A reunited Germany was little more than a dream. Ulbricht was willing to play ball with Bonn on few issues. The FRG would have tacitly to accept Germany's division before major foreign policy successes were to be achieved. Paying lip-service to eventual German reunification was one thing, but shackling one's foreign policy to its actual realization was quite another. So long as the FRG remained inflexible on the matter, Ulbricht enjoyed a right of veto over most of Bonn's actions.

There were signs as early as 1967 that the East German

leadership was becoming very edgy about increasing West German influence in Eastern Europe and penetration of markets there. The SED cranked up its propaganda machinery, launching blistering attacks against Bonn's policies, as Ulbricht dug in his heels.[6] To Ulbricht's discomfiture, Hungary, Czechoslovakia and Romania rejected East German proposals for a "united front" against Bonn in early 1967.[7] All were interested in new trade deals, none in Ulbricht's crusty outlook. To boot, the GDR party boss announced a new corollary to the so-called Ulbricht Doctrine. Full West German recognition of the GDR in accordance with international law should be a precondition for further normalization of relations between the FRG and East European states. Ulbricht hoped thereby to pull off a maneuver augmenting the GDR's international standing and securing a veto for him on crucial issues in Eastern Europe. It was to prove a dreadful miscalculation.

In a New Year's message to the entire German people, Ulbricht spurned all possibilities of reunification "under the prevailing circumstances."[8] This rejection was complemented with an East German ten-point program, tempered with icy Cold War blasts and designed to set back the clock in Eastern Europe.[9] Intended for immediate rejection in the West, the program outlined by Ulbricht was a non-starter. So long as he remained in power, Ulbricht would hardly budge, concerned as he was about domestic tranquility in the GDR. On some occasions, Moscow supported Ulbricht in his unconditional demands for full West German recognition of the GDR and even encouraged him as he seethed with indignation about imperialist machinations.

Few in the West could have had illusions about the possibility of accords with Ulbricht. In examining the East German leader's address to the German people, one West German newspaper commented remorsefully that "the lord and master of the other part of Germany made his aspirations more apparent than ever: division of Germany once and for all into two German states."[10] Doubtless Ulbricht was intractable. The genius of later West German approaches to *Ostpolitik* and Henry Kissinger's concept of Central European detente lay in the ability to circumnavigate Ulbricht by doing business directly with Moscow. The redoubtable party boss proved an impediment to acquiring the concessions dangled before the Kremlin leaders' noses, whereafter an open rift emerged between Ulbricht and his mentors. Outflanked, Ulbricht would eventually lose his clout in Eastern Europe and find himself almost completely isolated when the Kremlin decided to reach major accords with the West.

Ulbricht's insistence in 1967 of a series of high-level East Bloc meetings to reestablish what he perceived as eroding bloc solidarity was further evidence of his increasingly defensive position. Ulbricht set the tone for the first of these meetings--the Warsaw Foreign Minister's Conference of February 8 and 10--with the East German party organ, *Neues Deutschland*, printing a scathing attack on Romania for that country's dealings with the FRG.[11] In conformity with the corollary to the Ulbricht Doctrine, the GDR arrogated to itself in the article the right to be fully consulted on all Eastern European efforts at rapprochement with the FRG. Romania's public rebuke of Ulbricht's moves as "unjustified interference in domestic affairs," was an ominous sign for the GDR.[12]

The conference, hardly a paragon of accord, was concluded with a communiqué stating merely that the "consultations were conducted in an . . . atmosphere of . . . mutual understanding."[13] The salient point of contention was Ulbricht's demand for complete consultation prior to any member of the Warsaw Pact embarking upon any negotiations with Bonn. Such prior audience with GDR leaders, as Laszlo Gorgey points out, amounted to a veto right and was hardly something self-respecting satellites, not to mention the Soviet Union, were willing to concede to Ulbricht.[14] Moscow had maintained full diplomatic relations with the FRG since 1955, had concluded a number of significant agreements with the latter since that time, and was not about to have East German party functionaries obstructing its transactions with the West. As in 1961, the Kremlin was again wearying of Ulbricht's maneuvers. Far from being undertaken at Soviet behest, East German public criticism of Warsaw Pact members and the demand for a veto within the East Bloc must have infuriated the Kremlin.

Ulbricht was inadvertently playing with fire in Eastern Europe. His faultfinding was drawing additional attention to the growing polycentrism and discord in the Warsaw Pact. These differences could be probed and exploited by astute officials, both West and East. Perhaps carried away by anxiety about East German security or overwhelmed by his fervent belief in Marxist-Leninist ideology, Ulbricht was engaging in an affront to the national pride of Eastern European states, whereby he might well have demonstrated to certain Pact leaders that the national interests of their respective countries do not always coincide with the canons of East Bloc unity.

Ulbricht's objectives transcended merely the perpetuation of German division and ideological confrontation with Bonn. His strategy is often characterized as the "all or nothing" policy, entailing full diplomatic recognition of the GDR, official Western acceptance of all borders, with sundry, fluctuating demands about Berlin. But it is doubtful that the realization of all these goals would have made Ulbricht completely content. As leader of a state lacking cultural or national identity, the gruff old cold-warrior fathomed that a Europe devoid of international tensions would not be a desirable place for the GDR.[15] Only with the continuation of discord and imagined external threats could Ulbricht's regime maintain even a superficial semblance of legitimacy. As a child of the Cold War, the East German state saw in expanding East-West contacts a direct challenge to its vital interests.

In March and April 1967 the FRG began backing off from its heretofore resolute claim to the "right of sole representation" of the German people, as the only legitimate, elected government in Germany. Such a "right of sole representation" was tantamount to a permanent denial of the GDR's legitimacy. Rendering mandatory formalisms to the principle of eventual reunification, Kiesinger and Foreign Minister Brandt stated their continuing adherence to the concept of a single German nation. According to the new interpretation, however, Bonn's exclusive representation claim was above all an obligation to the German people, assuring adequate West German input into a future settlement.[16] Shortly thereafter the SPD began to describe Bonn's claim as primarily a moral obligation.[17]

Ulbricht would hear nothing of all this. In an April 1967 speech at the SED Party Congress, he raved about imperialist aggression, the heightening of international tensions and the danger of war.[18] He called for the "abandonment of Bonn's claims to represent all Germans," characterizing such claims as a potential "declaration of war on the GDR."[19] This remark was a particularly interesting response to Bonn's recent pronouncements on the issue. Ulbricht concluded with the assertion that, "Nobody can seriously expect the German Democratic Republic to open its borders to revanchism and exploitation."[20]

With the new GDR Constitution and the Penal Code, both promulgated in 1968, the East German leadership struck hard at those striving to devise new concepts for dealing with the German question. Both documents strengthened Ulbricht's "Abschirmungspolitik" (screening-off) and widened the official rift between the two Germanies. The 1949 GDR Constitution contained at least some vestiges of liberal democratic ideas and made no specific reference to separate German states, in principle leaving the unification question open. In contradistinction the 1968 Constitution is laced with Marxist-Leninist rhetoric and is best characterized as studiously unambiguous on issues of German division.[21] The Preamble to the Constitution specifies that Germany's future lies in "peace and socialism," which have been excluded from the West by "the forces of imperialism and capitalism."[22] The East German regime thereby relegated to itself the role of future sole legitimate representative of the German people. According to the Constitution, relations with Bonn must be of the normal interstate type, based upon mutual recognition and national sovereignty. With the document, Ulbricht codified the policy he had been following for over a decade, in anticipation of fortifying his position.

The new Penal Code farther distanced the two German states. Gone were all traces of the old 1871 Penal Code. Grounded on 1967 legislation on East German citizenship, the 1968 Penal Code stipulated that "treasonable disloyalty" to the GDR by anyone deemed as being one of its citizens was an act punishable by death. The code could without doubt be applied to refugees who had left the GDR. Also, "discriminatory criticism" of the GDR, according to the Code, could be prosecuted as "agitation hostile to the state," a high crime in the GDR. Some observers stated that such a provision could be used to prosecute West German journalists and government officials, and even non-Germans; indeed the Code has since been so employed.[23] "Economic subversion" drew a penalty of two to fifteen years in prison, with "extremely aggravated cases" punishable by death.[24]

Such was Ulbricht's answer to Bonn's initiatives and he considered himself vindicated when the "Prague Spring" later in 1968 posed a bodeful challenge to Moscow's hegemony in Eastern Europe. Ulbricht played no small role in the crushing of the Czechoslovak government intent upon liberalization and in the return of the dissident satellite to the Warsaw Pact fold. The occupation resulted in only a temporary set-back for efforts at normalization of the situation in Central Europe. New governments in the U.S. and the FRG ushered in new approaches and new initiatives. The Warsaw Pact action in Czechoslovakia was evidence enough that the way toward diplomatic progress on the German question was through Moscow; preliminary bilateral negotiations held the greatest chance for success.

Through the 1960s no breakthroughs had been made on the Berlin situation with the exception of the temporary "pass agreements" between the two German states lasting from 1964 to 1966, allowing West Berliners to transit the Wall to visit relatives in the Eastern sector. The GDR refused to renew these transit arrangements after 1966, and so once again West Berliners were denied entry into the East.[25]

The FRG frequently pursued "demonstrative federal presence" in West Berlin with visits of high government officials or meetings of parliamentary committees. These FRG actions usually triggered Eastern reprisals in the form of autobahn harassment and chicanery, making life in Berlin miserable. Scathing Eastern protests were habitual, and at times Soviet aircraft flew over the Western sectors, shattering windows with sonic booms.

In 1968 a major provocation took place as the GDR ventured to set new precedents for its authority through the application of transit fees and the requirement of visas for road and rail users. These new regulations would apply only to West Germans and West Berliners, not to Allied forces. Though an affront to Bonn, the East German maneuver did not affect Berlin's status or directly jeopardize the security of the Western sectors. Following consultation with the Allies, the FRG grudgingly increased the already sizable subsidies it paid to West Berlin in order partially to offset the new expenses to travelers. But the GDR was once again engaging in the "salami-tactics" game with a degree of success. In the absence of an accord, the GDR would have little incentive to refrain from such practices. Bark suggests that the episode illustrated the dilemma of Western policies in Berlin, since the Western powers depend upon West German commitment to West Berlin.[26] It is, however, highly unlikely that a government of the FRG would back off from its responsibilities in the city; the ties are too close, the stakes too high.

NOTES

1. Gerhard Schröder, "Germany Looks at Eastern Europe," *Foreign Affairs*, Vol. 44, No. 1 (Oct. 1965), pp. 16-17.

2. Whetten, op. cit., pp. 32-33, 43-45; Roger Morgan, "The Ostpolitik and West Germany's External Relations," in Roger Tilford, ed., *The Ostpolitik and Political Change in Germany* (Lexington, Mass.: Lexington Books, 1975), pp. 104-6.

3. "Offener Brief an die Delegierten des Dortmunder Parteitages," *Neues Deutschland*, Feb. 11, 1966; *Offensive Auseinandersetzung* (Bonn: Vorwaerts Druck, 1966) pp. 151-62.

4. "Regierungserklärung von Bundeskanzler Dr. Kurt Georg Kiesinger vor dem Deutschen Bundestag am 13. Dezember 1966," *Bulletin des Presse-und Informationsamtes der Bundesregierung*, no. 157, Dec. 14, 1966.

5. "Regierungserklärung von Bundeskanzler," quoted in: Laszlo Görgey, *Bonn's Eastern Policy 1964-1971* (Hamden, Conn.: Archon Books, 1972), p. 79.

6. See: *Der Spiegel*, Jan. 9, 1967; Görgey, *Bonn's Eastern Policy 1964-1971*, pp. 95-98; Childs, "The Ostpolitik and Domestic Politics in East Germany," pp. 64-66.

7. Whetten, op. cit., pp. 42-44; *Neues Deutschland*, Dec. 16, 1966; Heinrich Bechtholdt, "Ulbrichts Niederlage in Osteuropa," *Aussenpolitik*, Vol. 18, No. 3, March 1967, pp. 129-32.

8. "Neujahrsbotschaft des Staatsratsvorsitzenden der DDR," *Europa-Archiv*, Vol. 22, No. 1 (1967), pp. 6-9; *New York Times*, Jan. 1, 1967.

9. Ibid.

10. *Christ und Welt*, Jan. 6, 1967; for an East German statement, see: "Die Europäische Sicherheit und die sogenannte neue Ostpolitik der westdeutschen Regierung," *Deutschlandpolitik* V/I (1966-67), pp. 127-134.

11. *Der Spiegel*, Feb. 6 and Feb. 13, 1967.

12. "Ulbricht's Hard Line Vexes," *Christian Science Monitor*, December 14, 1967.

13. "Kommuniqué über die Konferenz der Aussenminister der Mitgliedstaaten des Warschauer Paktes," *Europa-Archiv*, Vol. 22, No. 6 (1967), pp. 123-24.

14. *Scinteia*, Feb. 4, 1967, quoted in: *Deutschlandpolitik* V/I (1966-67), pp. 475-479; "Das Dreieck Ostberlin-Warschau-Prag," *Neue Zürcher Zeitung*, March 30, 1967.

15. *Der Spiegel*, April 3, 1967; Childs, *The GDR: Moscow's German Ally*, pp. 77-83; Croan, *East Germany: The Soviet Connection*, pp. 16-18.

16. See: Görgey, op. cit., pp. 109-110.

17. "Deutschlandpolitik im Zeichen der Entspannung," *Neue Zürcher Zeitung*, April 2, 1967; also, "Interview des Bundesministers Wehner," April 16, 1967, *Deutschlandpolitik* V/I (1966-67), pp. 939-948.

18. *Der Spiegel*, April 24, 1967.

19. *New York Times*, April 21, 1967; *Christian Science Monitor*, April 20, 1967; *Deutschlandpolitik* V/I (1966-67), pp. 949-968.

20. *New York Times*, April 21, 1967.

21. Childs, *The GDR: Moscow's German Ally*, pp. 118-139; Heidenheimer and Kommers, op. cit., pp. 297-304.

22. *Der Spiegel*, Feb. 5, 1968; *New York Times*, April 9, 1968.

23. See Görgey's discussion, pp. 118-120; Childs, *The GDR: Moscow's German Ally*, pp. 120-22.

24. *Der Spiegel*, Feb. 5, 1968; *New York Times*, Feb. 1, 1968.

25. "Protokoll der Passierscheinvereinbarung," *Duetschlandpolitik* IV/12 (1966), pp. 291-294; "Mitteilung des Presse-und Informationsamtes des Landes Berlin zur Passierscheinfrage," *Deutschlandpolitik* V/I (1966-67), pp. 93-94.

26. Bark, op. cit., p. 23.

6
The Beginning of Detente

Following the Czechoslovakia crisis, Moscow made a conscious effort to refurbish its image and to improve its relations with the West, especially with the FRG. In September 1969 on the eve of West German elections, the Soviet Union proposed reconvening the bilateral talks suspended in the wake of the occupation of Czechoslovakia. Moscow's greater confidence as a player in world affairs was doubtless an important factor in Soviet overtures to the West in certain areas. Strategically, the Soviet Union attained parity with the United States and the former longed for bilateral arms agreements attesting to the fact. After significant challenges to Soviet predominance in Eastern Europe, a modicum of order had been restored, albeit quite brutally. Soviet naval power was on the upsurge worldwide, and Warsaw Pact force projection in Central Europe had been augmented.

More important to the Kremlin than arms agreements was the long-desired aim of a European security conference confirming the post-war status in Europe and the sanctity within some international legal context of the new borders. Such a conference with its attendant agreements was one of the priority items on Moscow's foreign policy agenda. There was in 1969 no lack of evidence for Soviet avidness to deal. German issues were far and away the most perplexing of all European security problems and it was generally accepted that any modification of the Cold War standoff would have to begin with a discussion of such problems. GDR reservations about East-West contact and basic intransigence would constitute obstacles even for Soviet bilateral negotiations with the FRG; Moscow at times cajoled, at times bullied its devout ally. At the December 1969 Moscow conference, the GDR was given the final word on the "Ulbricht Doctrine." The protocol of the Moscow conference specified only that "all states establish equitable relations with the German Democratic Republic on the basis of international law."[1] "Equitable relations" meant a good deal less than the full legal recognition Ulbricht had in mind, and, moreover, the former condition had long since been accepted by the FRG and its NATO allies.

Short years after the construction of the Wall, there was a growing realization in the West that it would be in the interest of the Western Powers as well as of the FRG to achieve a *modus vivendi* on the Berlin situation to ease tension and facilitate East-West contact. Farther down the road, such a political arrangement could serve as a stepping stone for improvement in the relations between the two German states. Five weeks after taking office, U.S. President Richard Nixon visited Berlin and underscored U.S. resolve to protect the city, while at the same time sending a signal to Moscow by asserting that Berlin crises were of benefit to neither side. The new president arrived in Berlin in the middle of a typical mini-showdown on the access routes. The GDR had been harassing traffic between the FRG and West Berlin in retaliation for the proposed convening of the *Bundesversammlung* (federal election committee) in the Western sectors to choose a new FRG president on March 5. The GDR and the Soviet Union claimed the planned election was a violation of Berlin's status and was evidence of FRG "aggressive intentions" in West Berlin. Access route obstruction discharged by GDR officials assured the new administration—as if additional proof were needed—of the precariousness of the Berlin situation and the desirability of a workable accord.

Nixon announced that his trip to Europe was aimed at setting the stage for East-West discussion of security issues.[2] The new administration was cognizant of the fact that all was not rosy for the Soviet Union, internationally and domestically, notwithstanding recent increases in the Soviet arsenal. In several areas an easing of confrontation could be of mutual benefit. Nixon reopened the suspended arms control talks with the Soviet Union and hinted at his willingness to convene the European security conference long advocated by the Soviet Union.

He also outlined the basic tenets of the U.S. position on Berlin by publicly stating his commitment to President Kennedy's "three essentials," laid down during the highpoint of crisis in 1961: (1) securing free access to and from Berlin; (2) stationing Western garrisons in

Berlin; and (3) preserving the city's cultural, political and economic vitality, i.e., its affiliation with the FRG.[3]

These continued to comprise the "minimum position" of the West on Berlin. If the Soviet Union were prepared to negotiate, it would have somehow to accept the "essentials" as non-negotiable Western conditions.

In 1969 many forces were at work that would catalyze movement toward an accord on Berlin. Nixon's apparent willingness to talk became quite tempting to the Soviet Union as Chinese-Soviet relations took a turn for the worst. In March 1969 reports of heavy fighting between Soviet and Chinese units on the Ussuri River surfaced. If they had not been aware of the dire situation prior to the clashes, the Kremlin leaders must have realized at the time of the confrontation the extent of the Soviet geostrategic problem in Asia. It is likely that the exacerbation of the Sino-Soviet conflict convinced many Kremlin leaders to strike a bargain with the West on Berlin. Some undoubtedly feared two concurrent "hot spots" threatening Soviet security. Examining the contingency of a pre-emptive surgical strike against Chinese nuclear facilities in the event of further deterioration of the situation, Moscow was in no mood to play strategic poker with the West. Besides, the Nixon Administration offered a sweetener: it was willing to disattach disarmament negotiations from the overall discussion of East-West relations. This U.S. move opened wide the door to strategic arms reduction talks.

Some observers have speculated that the Soviet Union undertook an "agonizing reappraisal" of its foreign policy in 1969.[4] In the early part of that year, the Kremlin pushed for beginning a European security conference, intimating a preparedness to make concessions, changed some aspects of policy toward the FRG, and consented to discussion on Berlin.[5] The stage had been set for the start of accommodation in Central Europe.

Nixon's National Security Advisor, Henry Kissinger, argues that there was widespread impatience in Europe at the beginning of the Nixon administration finally to reduce the severity of the Cold War.[6] Kissinger was convinced that the new administration should emphasize its adherence to the principle of detente in the interest of Atlantic solidarity. Thus the administration's public "gospel" would be serious discussion and the emergence of an "era of negotiations."

Kissinger alleges that several Western European governments had been pushed by the left into toeing the detente line.[7] European leaders were beginning to believe--De Gaulle had been playing the game since the mid 1960s--that they should serve as a sort of bridge between East and West in the event of continuing U.S. "hard-line" rhetoric and intransigence on issues. Kissinger feared that the U.S. risked estrangement from its European allies in the absence of some movement toward reconciliation with the East.

On July 10, 1969 Soviet Foreign Minister Andrei Gromyko invited the Powers to "exchange views as to how complications concerning West Berlin can be avoided now and in the future."[8] Gromyko's comment vividly reflected what the Soviet Union had in mind, namely, negotiations on *West* Berlin. To the Soviets, East Berlin had long ceased being a problem and was non-negotiable anyway.

Foreign Minister Willy Brandt encouraged the United States to approach the Soviet Union on the Berlin issue in order to gauge the possibilities of an accord. The upcoming FRG elections, held in September 1969, were crucial to Brandt's sense of urgency for beginning negotiations. As leader of the SPD, Brandt had a shot at becoming the FRG chancellor. Visible progress in East-West talks would significantly enhance SPD chances at the polls, since in 1969 the SPD seemed to offer an alternative to what many West Germans considered the spent policies of the major coalition partner, the CDU.

Brandt had no qualms about expressing his belief that a new *Ostpolitik* in coalition with the CDU was not possible.[9] The party was too polycentric, the desire to pursue Adenauer's "maintained tension" policies still strong, and opposition to accords with the GDR too widespread. The smallest of the FRG parties, the FDP, had for a number of years shown fresh thinking on the East much more in line with that of Brandt. It was in collusion with the FDP in 1963 that the SPD-led government of Berlin negotiated the 1964-66 "pass agreements" with the GDR, one of the very few breakthroughs achieved in inter-German matters prior to 1970. In the 1960s FDP politicians and academics were examining various new channels for East-West contact and accord.[10] In 1966 the FDP succeeded in arranging a meeting with GDR officials to discuss specific German issues. Even prior to 1966, when the FDP was in a coalition with the CDU, certain FDP politicians advocated certain compacts with the East Germans that were later to become tenets of Bonn's policies vis-à-vis the GDR, namely, the reuniting of families and the "Haftlingsfreikauf" (buying the release of political prisoners).[11]

A common misreading of the political constellation in

the FRG is that each party has its own separate and distinct foreign-political conception, e.g., the CDU/CSU places primary foreign policy emphasis upon the Western alliance, while the SPD directs its attentions to the *Ostpolitik.* The situation is hardly so simple. By the late 1960s there were at least three discernible groupings in West German politics.[12] These did not always coincide with party divisions, but rather ran somewhat across the grain, athwart party lines. The first group is best characterized as strongly Atlanticist, those placing primary, sometimes exclusive, emphasis in foreign policy upon close ties with the United States and the Atlantic Alliance. In the 1960s most members of this group still considered relations with NATO of paramount importance, although many favored greater FRG input into the Alliance. Even this group was somewhat suspicious of an organizational arrangement dominated by the United States if Alliance loyalty excluded dialogue with the East Germans.

The second basic group was comprised of those like Brandt, Herbert Wehner and Walter Scheel who, though loyal to the Atlantic Alliance, believed Adenauer's policies to have become empty rhetoric of confrontation with the East and damaging to the FRG in the long-term. Rather than representing a demonstration of Atlantic solidarity, FRG rigidity was the principal cause for increasing West German diplomatic isolation--witness the Hallstein Doctrine--and risked the conclusion of bilateral and even multilateral agreements behind Bonn's back and not in FRG interests, so the view of this group. Certainly the two groups had much in common, the second, however, advocated greater dialogue with the East Bloc with an aim toward the modification of the Central European situation insofar as this was possible, despite the multiplicity of hazards. A new course would be a gamble; few had any illusions about it, but in the long-run, the FRG might have had no alternative. In the 1960s Bonn's European partners were engaging in limited rapprochement with the East Bloc, usually without Bonn's consent, sometimes in disregard of perceived West German interests. The United States was also exploring new avenues. The most troubling question was: would Bonn be forced to look on helplessly?

The third group might be categorized as the West German Gaullists: the proponents of French-German bilateralism in Europe. What was lacking in concept, was partly made up for in the enthusiasm of the promoters of a new European bloc, with a French-German nucleus and considerable independence from the United States. The powerful role the FRG would have in such an organization would enable Bonn to exercise sufficient clout to bring about changes in Eastern Europe and eventually to achieve reunification.

As early as late 1961 there were those in Washington tilting toward the second group. This tilt was far less the result of admiration for people like Brandt and Wehner than it was of Washington's desire to begin pursuing detente policies with the East. Adenauer and many in the CDU/CSU posed a potential obstacle to change. Perspicacious observers in the U.S. also began to realize that FRG policies were sometimes extremely rigid. Commenting on a new outlook, a top CDU politician ruefully mentioned in September 1961: "There are circles in Washington that want Brandt to be chancellor. These people do not want the old man (Adenauer) around any longer; he is too tough for them. The U.S. is looking for an understanding with Moscow and the FRG is in the way."[13]

Those advocating more West German flexibility toward the GDR were by no means a variety of appeasers. The former high commissioner of Germany, John J. McCloy, remarked in 1962 that it was about time the FRG began coming to grips with some Central and Eastern European realities, citing the Oder-Neisse line, the existence of the GDR and the situation in Berlin as examples.[14] Few observers in the West even suggested that the FRG forget about the German question, but the GDR was not to be wished away and the Berlin Wall was not going to disappear.

In 1969 there had emerged an almost startling modicum of consensus in the FRG among the three groups and in the parties on several points, the first being that the FRG should reconsider its long-practiced "demonstrative federal presence" in Berlin in light of the intensity of GDR reactions during the 1969 presidential election. FRG posturing in Berlin, though not overtly illegal, was causing friction with the Allies and resulted above all in aggravation for West Berliners. At no time had the "demonstrative federal presence" facilitated West German contacts with the East or pressured the GDR to cease shooting refugees on its border.

Second, FRG officials, so the emerging mood, should at least consider concluding a renunciation-of-force agreement with Moscow to serve as an *ersatz* peace treaty. In the absence of such an agreement, the Soviet Union had the theoretical right under the "enemy state clause" of the UN Charter (Articles 53 and 107) to intervene with military

force in the FRG. Soviet leaders had at various times
mentioned the possibility of armed intervention in Central
Europe under particular circumstances.[15] Moreover, the FRG
had a good deal to gain from a mutual renunciation-of-force
agreement with the Soviet Union, since the approach would
bypass the GDR and undercut Ulbricht's demand for full
diplomatic recognition of his state as a precondition for
any such compact. Soviet willingness to sign would in
itself be a rebuff to Ulbricht. And in end effect, the
agreement would amount to little more than a reaffirmation
of adherence to the U.N. Charter.

Third, the FRG's trade with Eastern Europe was already
booming in certain areas by 1969 and no one in the FRG had
any intention of reducing it. Most welcomed this expansion
as a positive development. The Soviet Union held out to
Bonn the prospect of more lucrative business deals. In the
late 1960s Soviet economic growth was slowing down and the
Kremlin had become keen on acquiring Western technology to
boost productivity. Soviet leaders were actually going out
of their way to make their wishes for closer economic
cooperation with West Germany known. During a visit to
Moscow in July 1969, several leading SPD officials received
an extensive briefing on Soviet economic problems by
Premier Alexei Kosygin. Thereafter, economic issues became
a common discussion topic in meetings between West German
and Soviet leaders.[16]

The FRG Foreign Office stood in the forefront of those
in Bonn who surmised that a deal with Moscow on practical
Berlin matters was in the cards if the FRG were willing to
make some concessions on "demonstrative federal presence"
practices. Interested in beginning talks with the Kremlin
on Berlin, the Western Allies were nudging the West Germans
to ease off from demonstrations and to probe for Soviet
willingness to compromise. Some in the Foreign Office were
aware of the possibilities of driving in the narrow wedge
between Ulbricht and the Kremlin. The following classified
FRG Foreign Office background paper of August 5, 1969 is
most instructive about Western strategy on Berlin:

1. It appears to us that the present situation is
   favorable for the initiative planned at the Nato
   Ministers' Meeting in Washington by the four foreign
   ministers on April 9, 1969. Gromyko's speech of July
   10, 1969 clearly showed Soviet interest in an initial
   exchange of views with the Western powers concerning
   the avoidance of complications in Berlin. We agree
   fully with our Allies that Soviet interests in an

improvement in the Berlin situation should be explored. To this point the GDR has reacted negatively to all FRG attempts to begin inter-German discussions. We, however, do not exclude the possibility of Moscow's seeing the advantage for it of bringing East Berlin to the negotiating table. We might be able to exploit Moscow's possible interests in a stabilization of the Berlin situation to prepare the way for inter-German discussions.

2. We consider it most important that Four-Power Berlin discussions under no circumstances lead to an alteration of greater Berlin's status. Above all the upcoming discussions should strive for a solution to Berlin's practical problems, especially for securing the access routes. Insofar as it is possible, basic political questions, about which no accord is conceivable at present, should be avoided. Whether such improvements without concessions on the question of status are actually achievable at present is uncertain to us. We believe, however, that the Berlin problem cannot be left out of Western efforts to improve East-West relations.[17]

Thus Berlin was to serve as the first step toward broader East-West accord. The Western Powers had informed the Foreign Office of their preparedness to conclude an agreement with the Soviets to decrease animosity in the former German capital. The GDR would remain a problem and Ulbricht would commence with discussions only if ordered to do so by Moscow. But if the Soviet Union would so induce the East Germans to back off from their unacceptable demands, the West would have gained a significant diplomatic victory.[18]

Eagerness in the FRG to talk seriously with Moscow about a renunciation-of-force agreement and about Berlin also transcended party demarkation lines. West German politicians of all coloring seemed willing to be flexible.[19] In a note of September 13, the Soviet Union declared its preparedness to deal with any political constellation, be the SPD or the CDU in the foreground, on Berlin issues.[20]

The September 1969 elections in the FRG resulted in the formation of a Social Democrat-Free Democrat (SPD-FDP) coalition committed to an improvement of relations between the Germanies and to greater dialogue with Moscow; the new leaders assumed the former to be largely dependent upon the latter. A State Department paper asserted that "under an

SPD-FDP coalition an active all-German and Eastern policy will have the first priority."[21] Kissinger explained in a memorandum:

> It should be stressed that men like Brandt, Wehner and Defense Minister (Helmut) Schmidt undoubtedly see themselves as conducting a responsible policy of reconciliation and normalization with the East and intend not to have this policy come into conflict with Germany's Western association. There can be no doubt about their basic Western orientation. But their problem is to control a process which, if it results in failure, could jeopardize their political lives and if it succeeds could create a momentum that may shake Germany's domestic stability and unhinge its international position.[22]

Kissinger correctly perceived the FRG's need to develop fresh concepts on the situation in the East and somehow to come to grips with the existence of the GDR. The new FRG government was not only firm about achieving these goals, it wished to accomplish them quickly and it would devote tremendous energies to the effort. FRG leaders needed U.S. cooperation, but insisted upon their right to pursue certain policies. For over two decades it had been America's most devoted and faithful ally; now it was time for the U.S. to help the FRG with the German problem. Over and above the Nixon Administration's desire for negotiation was pressure from Bonn to seek change in the European political order.

Walter Scheel, leader of the FDP and Foreign Minister of the new coalition, argues that both superpowers grudgingly agreed to begin sorting out German problems largely as a result of the compulsion of events.[23] Surely this is somewhat of a simplification, although the significance of certain events, i.e., the open Sino-Soviet rift with the somber possibility of war, must not be underestimated. It was in the interest of the West to modify many aspects of policies in Central Europe. John J. McCloy's suggestion in 1962 that all sides should begin accepting basic realities had gained wide currency by the late 1960s and leaders on both sides of the Atlantic increasingly shared this opinion. Adenauer's accomplishments notwithstanding, the West had good cause to question those of his policies so lacking in long-term conception or inventiveness. Astute West German as well as non-German officials realized that a breakdown in the foreign policy consensus so carefully forged by Adenauer in the FRG might be forthcoming in the absence of considerable innovation.

For its part, the Soviet Union's patience with Ulbricht was wearing thin. Doubtless there were Soviet officials who legitimately feared Ulbricht's input into Moscow's foreign policy becoming too extensive. By the end of 1969 the Soviet Union was ready to reach accord with the West on issues it was hardly willing to discuss in the early 1960s. Moscow could not help but fathom that an official sanctioning of the basic Western position on Berlin, using the "three essentials" as a foundation would have as a consequence the permanent embedding of a thorn in the flesh of its East German ally.[24] According to Scheel, many in Washington saw the advantages of such a development; other policy-makers tended to balk, a notion confirmed by Kissinger.[25] The SPD-FDP government made its intentions clear to the U.S. and urged the latter to make Berlin a test case for detente.

Even Kissinger saw the logic in the SPD-FDP position. If an accord could be achieved on an issue as prickly as Berlin, this would be tangible evidence of the possibility of further East-West agreements. Whether or not it was recognized at the time--Brandt and Scheel were probably shrewd enough to be mindful of the situation in the GDR-- SED leader Ulbricht stood in the way of any deal on Berlin. Moscow would have to rein in Ulbricht prior to reaching accords with the West on issues directly affecting East Germany. One of the greatest fears of any East German leader has been the prospect of the Soviet Union making agreements with Western countries over the GDR's head, or worse yet, agreements smacking of "throwing the GDR to the wolves."

A time-honored aphorism in diplomacy is to trade the inevitable for a concession. As Kissinger observes, "the inevitable" for the FRG in 1969 included a *modus vivendi* with the GDR falling short of complete diplomatic recognition. Such an arrangement necessitated the elimination of the Hallstein Doctrine in favor of some policy allowing the FRG more leeway. Bonn to its chagrin had waited too long to modify some of the hollow dogmas of its foreign policy; gaining meaningful concessions for a renunciation of the Hallstein Doctrine in 1969 was unrealistic. The FDP specified as one of its conditions for entering a coalition with the SPD the final abjuration of this doctrine. This action would at a minimum bring Bonn's official pronouncements more in line with policy.

Speaking for the government, a principal FDP official outlined the new direction of Bonn's policies:

> The new FRG government wishes to state unequivocally that it strives for treaties with the GDR, which aim toward human amelioration in divided Germany. The treaty negotiations between Bonn and East Berlin shall be carried out on the basis of equality, without discrimination and devoid of preconditions.[26]

This statement was a signal to Moscow as well as to East Berlin. Bonn was willing to deal with the East Germans on an equal footing, but it would not accept unreasonable Eastern prerequisites nor make conciliatory gestures to Ulbricht. Were East Berlin not willing to play ball, the Kremlin knew what it had to do.

Brandt made an even more startling pronouncement shortly thereafter, asserting that the new government was proceeding from the acceptance of two German states. It was the first time an FRG official had been so explicit. Brandt's policy proclamation established the new point of departure for relations with the GDR: namely, that two German states exist in one German nation. The two German states would, however, in the FRG view, never be considered foreign countries (Ausland) to each other.[27]

The FRG announcements sent the East German functionaries scurrying for cover. Ulbricht could not have been more suspicious and mistrustful of Bonn's actions, since the door was then ajar for a relaxation of tensions between the Soviet Union and the FRG—likely at East German expense. No East German leader could be oblivious to the fact that these tensions were a major *raison d'être* of the GDR and a diminution could be ominous to its future. A fortnight's delay in any East German response to the new initiatives was a sure indication of the extent of Ulbricht's quandary. Commenting on the FRG's position, the party organ *Neues Deutschland* spoke blandly of "some new accents, ubiquitously noticed, naturally in the GDR also."[28]

The utterance barely concealed East German concerns. A position warranting universal notice might produce certain reappraisals in the Kremlin. Moreover, Bonn's prior consultation with its allies was a foregone conclusion, paving the way for quadrilateral negotiations on a number of issues.[29] In October the Soviet ambassador to the GDR, Pyotr Abrasimov, a CPSU functionary and one of the most powerful figures in the Foreign Ministry, hinted to the governing mayor of West Berlin what the Soviet Union had in mind for openers.[30] Conceding his "understanding" for FRG goals of maintaining and expanding economic relations with the Western sectors, Abrasimov alluded to Soviet willingness to accept such coupling in a Four-Power contractual arrangement. In addition, the ambassador spoke of the feasibility of guaranteed access to West Berlin and of Soviet-authorized respect for the status-quo in Berlin. He required only one Western *quid pro quo*: the termination of "demonstrative federal presence" in Berlin, described by Abrasimov as "provocations." There was no mention of full recognition of the GDR, no challenge to Allied rights in the city, nor any demands for explicit Western approbation of East Berlin as the capital of the GDR.[31] Abrasimov's probe had to have been cleared at the highest Kremlin levels. The importance of the Soviet ambassador's suggestions could not have gone undetected in Western ministries, for Moscow was ostensibly offering terms it never before had. Ulbricht was surely aware of what Moscow was proposing, in all likelihood, however, Abrasimov had not consulted with him, but merely told him.

Brandt stood at the forefront in the dramatic surge forward and the coalition wasted little time in getting *Ostpolitik* in high gear. Concrete proposals were made to the Kremlin in November 1969 and serious negotiations began in early 1970.[32] Bonn made its intentions known that it would be prepared to sign a renunciation-of-force agreement, tacitly acknowledging the existence of post-World War II German borders and the reality of Germany's partition. This treaty would make a similar accord with Poland possible. Brandt's and Scheel's calculations were quite correct on the principal point: the key to progress and change in relations with Eastern Europe lay in Moscow and there all initiatives had to begin. But a vexing question haggled Western observers: could the SPD-FDP coalition sustain a dynamic *Ostpolitik* and *Westpolitik* at the same time, in spite of the apparent constricting demands?

For more than 20 years there had been no contact for all practical purposes between Poland and the FRG. Affinities were perhaps the most frigid of any in the Cold War and the establishment of Bonn-Warsaw relations patterned on other examples in Eastern Europe was not possible because of the disputed Western borders of Poland, the Oder-Neisse line. Bolstered by its known willingness to sign a renunciation-of-force agreement with the Soviet Union accepting the European status-quo, the FRG formally approached Warsaw in late 1969 for an exchange of views leading to a normalization of relations. What Moscow considered sufficient was satisfactory for Warsaw and a treaty with Bonn offered not inconsiderable advantages to Poland previously unavailable: the prospect of secure borders, enhanced international prestige, as well as the possibility of trade and credit. The Soviet Union could be only too happy to see the conclusion of a Bonn-Warsaw accord following in the wake of a Bonn-Moscow agreement. Once a proposal for an accord was cleared with Moscow, the chances for its completion were high. Gromyko remarked cynically to West German officials in March 1970, that the latter need not lose sleep over the position of third states, e.g., Poland and the GDR, on *Ostpolitik*. The Soviet Union would "speak" to them about the situation.[33]

That Moscow began to lean heavily on East Berlin was evident. In the first week of December 1969, the Warsaw Pact Political Consultative Committee officially discarded the "Ulbricht Doctrine." Two weeks thereafter Ulbricht, acting as chief of state, not party secretary, wrote a letter to the FRG president expressing East German volition to convene inter-German discussions the following month.[34] He failed to address himself to main West German concerns— guaranteed access to West Berlin or "human amelioration"— and he did include the usual buzzwords about exchange of ambassadors, recognition of borders and equality of discussion partners.[35] But reticence about preconditions and a noticeable absence of sweeping demands indicated Ulbricht's amenability to some sort of negotiations and underscored the pressure coming from Moscow.

In attempting to mediate between Bonn and East Berlin, Moscow was eager to be heard in both capitals and to present itself in the best possible light. It had been crucial in getting the two German states to make tolerant gestures to one another. Each would begin trying to outmaneuver its adversary.[36]

For its part Moscow seemed convinced that the policy approach it had developed in the late 1960s could somehow be made suitable for dealing with the *Ostpolitik* in the 1970s. Soviet policy employed the following tactics: (1) approach Western Europe with an olive branch while portraying the U.S. as a enemy of detente; (2) promote the obliquity of Bonn's positions from those of other NATO allies; and (3) encourage a European security settlement, the purpose of which would be to dissolve the "artificial barriers" between Eastern and Western Europe and to guarantee the European status-quo.

If East and West could agree on anything at the beginning of 1970 it was on the prominence of Berlin. At stake for the U.S., Britain and France was first of all the maintenance of the occupation rights so essential to Western Europe's security. Keenly interested in the well-being and rights of two million West Berliners, the FRG viewed Berlin as the initial awkward step forward toward the betterment of decades of German misery. Berlin had long been a useful tool for the Soviet Union in the game of great power politics. As has been seen, Moscow had a readily-available trump in Berlin when dealing with the U.S. and its allies. In addition Berlin served the Kremlin well as a Central European political lever to be employed against both German states.

Soviet and East German national interests with regard to Berlin diverged after the construction of the Wall. The differences became manifest even in the rather esoteric legal views justifying states' positions and bordering on irrelevancy in power politics. In the late 1960s the Soviet Union described West Berlin as an autonomous political entity *within* GDR territory, whereas the GDR continued to view West Berlin as an entity *on* its territory.[37] The distinction is not to be missed; in exchange for order and the status-quo in Europe, Moscow consented to soft-pedal the East Bloc campaign to annex Berlin. An aspect of fresh Soviet attention to the German question in 1969 was a partial modification in the Kremlin's attitude toward the GDR.

Bonn's response to Ulbricht's December letter came with Brandt's January 14, 1970 address to the FRG *Bundestag*. Reflecting a consensus of Western views on Germany following extensive consultation, the Chancellor stated the guiding elements of negotiations with East Berlin. As a basis for discussion, both sides would be obliged to:

1. Maintain the German nation's indivisibility.
2. Apply generally recognized principles of international law.
3. Respect one another's social structure.
4. Engage in neighborly cooperation.
5. Preserve quadripartite rights and responsibilities for Berlin as well as for Germany.
6. Work with the Four Powers in realizing improvements in the Berlin situation.[38]

Banter aside, the speech evidenced Western

concentration upon Berlin. Brandt's Minister for Inner-German Affairs fleshed out the pronouncements in a follow-up in which he defined "cooperation" and "good-neighborliness" as referring to reunification of families, greater contact between East and West Germans, encouragement of cultural exchanges as well as the furtherance of trade.[39]

Ulbricht's reaction surprised nearly everyone, except perhaps the Kremlin leaders. In his first press conference since June 1961--when Ulbricht infamously denied "anyone's" intention to build a wall--he affirmed his commitment to immediate "negotiations on fundamental problems." He even went to the trouble to say: "We have no preconditions."[40]

NOTES

1. *Der Spiegel*, Dec. 1, 1969; Georg Ferdinand Duckwitz, "Die Wende im Osten," *Aussenpolitik*, Vol. 21, No. 4 (1970), pp. 649-55.

2. Kissinger, *White House Years*, pp. 403-6; *Die Welt*, Feb. 24-25, 1969.

3. Stated in address by President Kennedy, July 26, 1961, *New York Times*, Feb. 28, 1969; *Die Welt*, Feb. 27, 1969.

4. Childs, op. cit., pp. 82-83; Bark, op. cit., pp. 23-26; Kissinger, *White House Years* pp. 96-100, 114-25.

5. Bark, op. cit., p. 33.

6. Arnulf Baring, *Machtwechsel* (Stuttgart: Deutsche Verlags-Anstalt, 1982), pp. 229-243. Baring's *Machtwechsel* is actually the memoirs of FDP parliamentarian, Walter Scheel. Scheel, who was FDP party chairman from 1963-1974 and FRG foreign minister from 1969-1974, was an instrumental figure in the *Ostpolitik*. Later, as FRG president, Scheel provided Baring with large amounts of oral and written information about the period 1969-1974 and hired him to write a book that would serve as Scheel's memoirs. On the matter of reducing the severity of the Cold War, see: Kissinger, *White House Years*, pp. 405-12; Scheel is in basic agreement with Kissinger on this point.

7. Kissinger, *White House Years*, p. 403-4; Bark, op. cit., p. 28.

8. Baring, op. cit., pp. 240-41.

9. *Der Spiegel*, Dec. 22, 1969.

10. "Entschliessung zur Deutschlandpolitik des 21. Ordenlichen Landesparteitages der FDP Berlin," *Deutschlandpolitik* IV/12 (1966), pp. 733-35; "Referat des Sentdirektors Hartkopf im Arbeitskreis fur Deutschlandpolitik auf dem 18. Ordentlichen Bundesparteitag der FDP," *Deutschlandpolitik* V/I (1966-67), pp. 857-864.

11. "Entschliessung des 17. Ordentlichen Bundesparteitages der FDP in Nürnberg," *Deutschlandpolitik* IV/12 (1966), pp. 860-861; "Warum die DDR nicht anerkannt werden darf," *Die Welt*, Sept. 3, 1966.

12. These groups are so described by Baring, op. cit., pp. 205-11.

13. So CDU/CSU whip, Heinrich Krone, is said to have written in his diary in Sept. 1961, Baring, op. cit., p. 207.

14. Baring, op. cit., p. 207.

15. *Pravda*, Sept. 18, 1969; Lawrence L. Whetten, *Germany's Ostpolitik* (London: Oxford University Press, 1971), pp. 22-23.

16. Baring, op. cit., pp. 240-41; Whetten, op. cit., pp. 116-18.

17. Quoted in Baring, op. cit., pp. 241-42, (author's translation); the report concluded by underscoring the standpoint that Berlin could not be dealt with in isolation, but was an aspect of the German problem. That West Berlin constituted an "independent political entity" was an unacceptable notion for Bonn. It would be necessary to "clarify" the relationship between the two German states in the near future, according to the report.

18. That Ulbricht had numerous disagreements with Moscow concerning detente policies is not a matter of serious contention. There are several explanations for Ulbricht's eventual consent to enter negotiations devoid of preconditions with the FRG. The first is direct pressure from Moscow. A second would be the opportunity to enhance the international standing of the GDR. A third might be the wish to avoid being isolated in the midst of a scurry of diplomatic activity. Finally, Ulbricht may well have planned to do all he could to scuttle detente, to show the Soviets the perils of the course they were following and to dissuade them from going farther. See: Melvin Croan, *East Germany: The Soviet Connection* (Beverly Hills and London: Sage Publications, The Washington Papers, 1976), vol. IV, no. 36, pp. 8-13; Catudal, *The Diplomacy of the Quadripartite Agreement on Berlin*, pp. 76-78; David Childs, "The Ostpolitik and Domestic Politics in East Germany," in

The Ostpolitik and Political Change in Germany, Robert Tiford, ed., (Lexington, Mass: Lexington Books, 1975) pp. 70-72.

19. Baring, op. cit., pp. 243-46.

20. There were some Soviet leaders who wished to see the emergence of an SPD-FDP coalition in the fall of 1969. Soviet Ambassador Pyotr Abrasimov is reported to have stated he welcomed such a political development. The reasoning was that an SPD-FDP government would be "untainted" by "Cold War" rhetoric and conflict. Moscow could save face dealing with the FRG by claiming such a government would not be "revanchist." See: Baring, pp. 243-45. Given the manner in which Moscow pigeonholed Ulbricht, this account might be fairly accurate.

21. Kissinger, *White House Years*, p. 408.

22. Ibid.

23. Baring, op. cit., p. 283.

24. Brandt and Scheel were fully aware of this. See: Baring, op. cit., pp. 283-84; Kissinger, *White House Years*, pp. 409-10.

25. The two versions are surprisingly similar: Baring, op. cit., pp. 282-84; Kissinger, *White House Years*, pp. 409-10.

26. Baring, op. cit., p. 245 (author's translation).

27. Baring, op. cit., p. 246; Roger Morgan, *West Germany's Foreign Policy Agenda* (Beverly Hills and London: Sage Publications, The Washington Papers 1978), vol. VI, no. 54, pp. 19-20.

28. *Der Spiegel*, Nov. 17, 1969.

29. Childs, "The Ostpolitik and Domestic Politics in East Germany," pp. 59-61.

30. Abrasimov was interested specifically in the new coalition's position on: The Nuclear Nonproliferation Agreement, a renunciation-of-force accord and the GDR. The official apparently considered these the most salient issues and he was anxious to hear Bonn's opinions. See: Baring, op. cit., pp. 249-50.

31. Baring, op. cit., p. 250-51.

32. That Bonn was in a hurry is hardly a matter of dispute: Baring, op. cit., pp. 244-50, 253-59; *Der Spiegel*, Nov. 17, 1969.

33. Croan, op. cit., pp. 12-13; Baring, op. cit., pp. 255-56.

34. The complete text is in: Bundesministerium für innerdeutsche Beziehungen, *Die Entwicklung der Beziehungen zwischen der Bundesrepublik Deutschland und der Deutschen Demokratischen Republik* (Melsungen: Verlagsbuchdruckerei

Bernecker, 1973), pp. 49-51.

35. Baring, op. cit., p. 257.

36. Catudal, *The Diplomacy of the Quadripartite Agreement on Berlin*, pp. 75-76; Baring, op. cit., pp. 256-57.

37. Whetten, op. cit., p. 105.

38. English text is contained in a supplement to *The Bulletin* (New York: German Information Service), Jan. 20, 1970.

39. Catudal, *The Diplomacy of the Quadripartite Agreement*, pp. 74-75; K. W. Beer, "Acht Verhandlungspunkte," *Deutsche Korrespondenz*, Vol. 20, No. 4 (Jan. 1970), pp. 2-5.

40. *New York Times*, Jan. 20, 1970.

7
Western Requirements

For the West it was realistic, indeed necessary, closely to examine the implications of European developments emerging from the dynamics of continental politics. Then, as now, the U.S. and its allies had somehow to come to grips with ponderous dilemmas, since, without astute concepts of what must be safeguarded and what should be changed, the West will be confronted with insolvable quandaries.

Enormous differences in the positions of the negotiating partners on Berlin were apparent before the convening of discussions. Some assumed such clefts to be unbridgeable in less than a decade or two.[1] Yet there were grounds for some optimism in the U.S. administration on account of the chief high trump card the West held: a Berlin agreement would pave the way for the security conference so close to Moscow's heart.[2]

On this artful, and ostensibly successful, employment of linkage there is some historical controversy. The chief U.S. negotiator at the quadripartite discussions and confidant of President Nixon, Kenneth Rush, discounts the significance of the "link" between a Berlin accord and progress on a security conference, though conceding that the Soviet Union realized the connection between Berlin and increased West German–East European ties.[3] Kissinger seems to have put the matter to rest now. The quadrilateral Berlin talks were to be one of the initial probes for a broader "linkage" policy on arms negotiations, European security issues, the Middle East, etc. According to Kissinger's account, had the Soviets been intransigent on Berlin, the U.S. would have put the European security conference on hold. It is in fact not improbable that

Kissinger would have done all within his power to apply the brakes to Bonn's *Ostpolitik* in the event the Soviets stonewalled on Berlin. The existence of such a scheme would go far in explaining the not insignificant U.S.-West German differences of approach in at least the initial phase of the Brandt-Scheel *Ostpolitik*. A West German renunciation-of-force in accordance with the U.N. Charter was one thing; Western sanctioning of Soviet land grabs in the Second World War was quite another.

Kissinger had a veritable network of linkages in mind. Berlin would be linked to a more extensive FRG *Ostpolitik* and both would be precursors of the eventual convening of a European security conference. If the Kremlin stalled, Washington could play the same game. There can be little doubt about U.S. willingness to support Bonn's endeavors to normalize relations with Eastern Europe, so long as such new directions did not hazard the Atlantic Alliance, as well as encouragement to put the West German diplomatic house in order, shedding such burdensome relicts as the Hallstein Doctrine. But as Scheel recalls, Kissinger made few efforts to conceal his reservations about the urgency of and the approach to the *Ostpolitik*.[4] Had the West Germans considered the long-term implications of their *Ostpolitik*? Was Bonn not overestimating its diplomatic clout? Kissinger saw no need for haste. In advocating accords on Central Europe, he was convinced the Alliance would get a better deal by holding its hand close to the vest and waiting. Scheel says Kissinger hinted--at a minimum--that Bonn's maneuvers in 1970 bordered on the reckless and might prove damaging to U.S. interests.[5] Scheel is doubtless correct in pointing out one of Kissinger's main objections vis-à-vis the SPD-FDP coalition: he (Kissinger) wanted to hold the reins of detente in his own hands and he was suspicious of side-show performances.

What Rush was not fully aware of during the discussions on Berlin (and later might not have wanted to admit) was Kissinger's extensive use of the "back-channel" with Soviet Ambassador Anatoly Dobrynin on major political issues. Kissinger claims the "back-channel" to have become fully operational by the end of 1970.[6] Rush, as was also the case with Gerard Smith at the SALT meetings, was being "back-channeled" as Kissinger brought up matters with Moscow and dangled sugarplums in front of Soviet noses without high-level U.S. officials being privy to the goings-on. One can presume that by 1971 there were at least two tracks of Berlin negotiations, one, the quadrilateral discussions taking place behind closed doors in the city itself, the other through the White House back-channel direct to the Kremlin, with a minimum of consultation with third parties. Such an operational back-channel had its advantages and disadvantages, allowing the manipulation and probing that are difficult in multilateral negotiations and impossible in public forums, but risking discord and the mistrust of allies, indignant about lack of coordination on crucial issues. Had the channel to the Kremlin functioned as Kissinger describes--there is every indication it did--can there be much doubt that Kissinger sketched out his designs there to Soviet officials? In the ante-up on future European accords, Moscow had to come through on Berlin: no recognition of Berlin's quadripartite status, no multilateral security treaty.

Certainly the *Ostpolitik* posed looming dilemmas for the U.S. as well as for the FRG. What was to be the proper and efficacious blend of undisguised support for Bonn's initiatives in the East, and U.S. regulation of these policies? Would a point eventually be reached at which U.S. and West German interests would diverge and the two allies be at loggerheads? Moscow could not have precluded such an eventuality and indeed looked forward to such a breathtaking possibility. The outcome was a disappointment for the Kremlin; the West has nonetheless had to accept divaricating interests on some issues. In the realm of *Ostpolitik* the years have brought out differences as well as accord. As is typical of international relations there have been no easy answers, only stilted complexities, no right or wrong strategies, but unpalatable predicaments.

Catudal summarizes the Western goals at the beginning of the Berlin negotiations as the following:

1. To acquire Soviet confirmation of the continuing quadripartite status of Berlin.
2. To secure Soviet guarantees of Western access to Berlin, including civilian and military traffic.
3. "Zutritt"--the right of West Berliners to travel to East Berlin and the GDR.
4. To improve communications between West and East Berlin as well as the GDR.
5. To secure Soviet pledges to terminate the discrimination against West Berliners in East Bloc countries, allowing passage and travel.
6. "Zuordnung"--Soviet and GDR acceptance of social, cultural, economic and political ties between West Berlin and the FRG.[7]

These Western goals were an expanded version of Kennedy's "three essentials", as they came to be expressed in German: *Zugang, Zuordnung, Zutritt.* That there was little room for Western flexibility and "horse-trading," must have been discernible to all interested parties from the very beginning.

East Bloc goals are quite a good deal more difficult to determine; indeed, even a "minimum" East Bloc position is not to be found. The chief difficulty with trying to make such a determination was the disagreement that emerged between the GDR and the Soviet Union. In the course of the negotiations such disagreements nearly developed into a rift, having rather dire consequences for SED leader Ulbricht.

Ulbricht's astounding demonstration of flexibility in early 1970 notwithstanding, the SED chief surely considered all Western goals unacceptable, in particular, those directly infringing upon the sovereignty of the GDR as Ulbricht understood it. Allied overland and air transit uncontrolled by the GDR meant denial of sovereignty in areas the East Germans maintained were theirs. The presence of Western military forces in the city the East Germans claimed as their capital was an indignity of the first degree.

The "maximum" Eastern position probably coalesced around the following points:

1. The elimination of the quadripartite status of the city.
2. Western sanctioning of the removal of the FRG presence from West Berlin, and a complete separation of West Berlin from the FRG.
3. The full diplomatic recognition of the GDR by the FRG and the United States.
4. Final Western acceptance of West Berlin as an "independent political entity" under Four-Power control.
5. The eventual integration of Berlin into the GDR.[8]

In addition to the very great political/legal differences on the two sides, it is noteworthy that the room for compromise was far from equal, making bargaining difficult in the extreme. Western goals were in fact requirements, and compromise on any of them might have had most unfortunate consequences for West Berlin. Concessions on Allied rights of occupation or access were out of the question; Soviet suggestions regarding these matters were non-starters. The only point on which the West could compromise concerned FRG presence in West Berlin. A reduction of ties would certainly anger the FRG, but the Western Three had no alternative to pressing their German ally on the matter.

Moreover, if the assessment of the East Bloc position is a correct one, it is all too clear how Soviet strategy in Berlin was evolving. There was the likelihood of strained FRG-U.S. relations, had the talks broken down. Bonn had not begun its *Ostpolitik* to find itself excluded from areas in the East, especially one with which West Germans had a strong emotional as well as political attachment. Kissinger's worst suspicions might have been confirmed, with Bonn "taking its business elsewhere" and in the future setting off on a nationalistic course.[9]

In keeping with their efforts to maintain their rights in East Germany, as recodified in the Bolz-Zorin Agreement and the GDR-Soviet Friendship Treaty, the Soviets apparently hoped to establish quadripartite control over West Berlin exclusively, thereby getting a foot in the door to do untold mischief. An agreement on West Berlin--as opposed to the entire city--could augment the already-established, statutory authority of the Soviet Union in Germany.

One can cogently argue that the actual outcome of the negotiations exonerated the Bonn leaders on several points. First, there was no real advantage to stalling too long on Berlin. The city was a festering sore of the Cold War as late as 1970 and a workable solution was in the Western interest; the West was eventually offered a deal too enticing to pass up. Second, although the Soviet Union would exploit the situation in any way it could--ideally by creating unmendable splits in the Atlantic Alliance--Moscow maintained an interest in preventing the "test-case" of *Ostpolitik* from failing. Intrigue and perfidiousness are not unknown in Soviet foreign policy, but in this case Moscow was not about to acquiesce to Ulbricht's shenanigans and sabotage attempts. Events of 1971 evidenced this, and the outcome of the negotiations demonstrated Soviet eagerness to reach an accord on Berlin.

It is worthy of note that the U.S. did not officially recognize the GDR until 1974, three years after the signing of the Quadripartite Agreement, and, furthermore, that the FRG still retains its "special relationship" with the GDR, whereby the German states do not accord diplomatic recognition to one another. Hence, the most important GDR requirement of a Berlin accord went unrespected. This, in addition to Ulbricht's unyieldingness in the later stages of the quadripartite negotiations, indicates that the Soviet Union, in its readiness to conclude an agreement, disregarded some of the perceived interests of its East German ally.

On those issues where compromise was hardly possible and neither side could make concessions, the Four Powers fostered ambiguity to cover over differences, making an accord acceptable to both parties. The outstanding, but certainly not the only, example of such imprecision is in regard to GDR claims that the Eastern sector of the city is its capital. The Western Allies have always rejected these claims, upholding the quadripartite status of the city. For its side, the GDR has wished to acquire international recognition of its alleged capital. No one could deny by 1970, however, that East Berlin had become the *de facto* capital of the GDR. The political development in East Berlin represented a conscious East Bloc effort to undermine Berlin's quadripartite status.

Reference in the 1971 Quadripartite Agreement is made to the "relevant area" without specifying to what the term applies exactly. It could correspond to either West Berlin or to greater Berlin. Actually both interpretations have some validity and neither was considered unacceptable to the Western Three: on the one hand, application to greater Berlin underscores the continuing quadripartite status of the city; on the other, application to West Berlin only indicates that the chief purpose of the agreement is preservation of West Berlin's viability. Left out of the picture was the GDR with its hopes of explicit recognition of its sovereign rights in its *de facto* capital.

The yawning gap between the two sides regarding the actual status of Berlin became glaring in the first rounds of negotiations. The two sides could not reach any sort of consensus on exactly what it was they were discussing. Initially, the Soviet Union argued that it was a "well-known fact" that East Berlin had become the capital of the GDR and could neither be a negotiable item nor even a subject of discussion. The U.S., France and Great Britain insisted on the validity of existing accords on greater Berlin, concluding that the matter of discussion was the entire city which retained its quadripartite status.

In accordance with the wartime agreements, the Western Allies argued, greater Berlin constituted a separate zone of quadripartite occupation which was not in or a part of any of the other zones in Germany. There was no basis for the Soviet argument that Berlin once constituted a part of the Soviet zone; Moscow was thus not empowered to transfer any authority in this area to the GDR.[10]

The East Bloc position on this issue had never been completely clear and the Soviet standpoint on the "separate zone" imbroglio has been an example of what Kissinger terms "the inability to stick to one strand of policy."[11] In Khrushchev's offensive in 1958, the Soviets maintained that Berlin in its entirety had been a part of the Soviet zone of occupation, alleging the Allies had "illegally" divided the "capital" of the GDR. Later the Soviet position designated West Berlin an independent political entity under Western occupation, tolerated by the Soviet Union. Clearly the purpose of Eastern protests of West German presence in West Berlin was to strengthen GDR claims of sovereignty, and by the 1960s East Berlin had been established as the functional--if not *de jure*--capital of the GDR. Though the inconsistency of the East Bloc position was not conducive to fruitful discussion of issues--evidence the beginning of the quadripartite negotiations--the inability to maintain a policy strand resulted in Soviet diplomatic ineffectiveness which helped greatly to preserve the freedom of West Berlin.

NOTES

1. See for example: Rudolf Augstein, *Der Spiegel*, June 29, 1970, p. 18.

2. Baring, op. cit., p. 283; Kissinger, *White House Years*, pp. 412-16.

3. Catudal cites Rush as having said: "hope of promoting the convening of a European Security Conference, in my opinion, was at most a very minor item in influencing the decision of the Soviets . . . A desire to advance the Ost-Politik (sic) of Chancellor Brandt looking for improvement of relations between Germany and Russia and Germany and the other Warsaw Pact countries, was one of the two major considerations. I think that a further major one was the hope of pushing forward to an easing of tensions with the U.S. Of course, in fact the achievement of these objectives might lead in time to a European Security Conference." Catudal, *The Diplomacy of the Quadripartite Agreement on Berlin*, p. 123.

4. Baring, op. cit., pp. 260-63.

5. Ibid., p. 261.

6. Kissinger describes the functioning of the "back-channel" in some detail, see: *White House Years*, pp. 805-810.

7. Catudal, *The Diplomacy of the Quadripartite Agreement on Berlin*, pp. 69-70.

8. *Der Spiegel*, March 16, 1970.

9. Kissinger, *White House Years*, pp. 409-10.

10. Schiedermair, op. cit., p. 9.

11. Kissinger, *White House Years*, p. 405.

Breaking the stalemate —

8
Initiatives of the
FRG *Ostpolitik*

On February 11, 1970 GDR Premier Willi Stoph invited Brandt to East Berlin for the opening round of inter-German talks. Stoph wrote: "I believe it is necessary in the interest of peaceful coexistence and the regulation of our relationship by treaty and on the basis of generally recognized norms of sovereignty that we meet for direct negotiations."[1] Such a meeting would have been unprecedented and no one in the West could even be sure of East German intentions, let alone make predictions about the outcome of the encounter.

A meeting between the government chiefs of the two German states presented major logistical difficulties. The presence of the West German chancellor in East Berlin would have greatly increased GDR prestige by seeming to bolster claims to East Berlin as a "capital." Brandt was willing to go to East Berlin, but he could hardly have been expected not to visit the Western sectors where he was governing mayor during major crises. On this matter the East Germans balked, for the Chancellor's visit to West Berlin could be interpreted as being an affirmation of Bonn's authority there. Failure of the Chancellor to appear in West Berlin would have, in the words of the opposition in the *Bundestag*, been "a death blow against the affiliation of West Berlin with the Federal Republic."[2] Bonn rejected any plan excluding an official visit to the Western sectors. Years of bitter animosity could not be easily brushed aside. After the

The GDR finally did agree to an alternative site for the historic meeting, thereby separating summit tactics from the perplexities of the Berlin issue. Chosen was the dreary railroad junction of Erfurt in the GDR, a location as unpretentious as the meeting itself, for the GDR had

graciously conceded to avoid the brass bands and pomposity
associated with official visits. Because of the very real
possibility of domestic fall-out, Brandt was keenly
interested in a low-key encounter.

Despite GDR eagerness to emphasize national standing,
the East Germans were true to form in showing paranoia.
Erfurt was barricaded and rail traffic stopped, lest an
influx of well-wishers and spectators be on hand for the
first visit of a West German chancellor to the GDR.
Nonetheless, thousands of East Germans welcomed Brandt as
he stepped off the train and walked to the Hotel Erfurter
Hof. "Willy, Willy," shouted the crowd until it dawned on
people that there were two Willies attending the meeting.
In the unlikely event one of the insipid East German
leaders--not renowned for their ability to stir public
passion--begin to acquire illusions about his popularity,
the crowd changed its cry to "Willy, Willy Brandt!"[3]

The incident led to some unavoidable speculation about
its origins. The spontaneous outpouring of public emotion
in the GDR on the occasion of an FRG chancellor's visit
represented a major embarrassment to East German leaders,
especially in the wake of their not negligible efforts to
put a damper upon publicity. Most plausible is that this
was another example of the insults GDR officials have had
to take in stride, but there is another more cynical
interpretation. Some West German observers suggested at
the time that the Erfurt demonstration might have been
staged by the East German leadership as a warning to Moscow
of the dangers inherent in the course it was following.[4]
GDR party bosses had legitimate fears about domestic
turmoil resulting from increased contact with the West. In
the view of some, Erfurt would be Ulbricht's concession to
Soviet pressure; thereafter he favored discarding such
risky business.

The meeting began with summations of the positions of
the two sides. Stoph initiated the proceedings with a
lengthy tirade about Western evils and the division of
Germany.[5] He demanded Bonn recognize the GDR and insisted
that the former accept the permanency of German division
and the consequent elimination of the German question. As
if to add insult to injury, He maintained Bonn should pay
one hundred billion marks in reparations for the "economic
damages" inflicted on the GDR before 1961, i.e., the tide
of refugees exiting East Germany prior to the sealing of
the border.

For his part, Brandt reminded his East Germans
interlocutors of his constitutional obligation to strive

for German unity. He rejected demands for full diplomatic recognition out of hand, but spoke of the possibility of mutual acceptance or "semi-recognition," allowing the conclusion of inter-German accords and unlimited relations of the two Germanies with third states. Brandt placed particular emphasis on Berlin, stating that any German compacts must not impinge upon the continued quadripartite status of the city. Underscoring FRG commitment to eventual reunification as well as to Berlin's security, Brandt remarked: "We do not want to change the status of Berlin, as long as the German question has not been resolved."[6] In an exchange concerning FRG ties with West Berlin, Brandt said that "neither the three Western powers, nor the FRG nor the directly affected Berliners would agree to any change in Berlin's status, as laid down by the Four Powers, that would lead to a change in these links." Stoph's riposte was a repudiation of "Four-Power responsibility for the German Democratic Republic and its capital Berlin."[7]

Both sides did, however, agree to sign a renunciation-of-force agreement and to begin the process for entry of the two German states into the United Nations. Brandt consented unilaterally to terminate West German claims to sole legal representation of the German population and to assist the GDR in obtaining membership in international organizations. Stoph's return visit took the form of a meeting to be held in the West German city of Kassel in May. 21st 1970 *handwritten* really 96.7

Despite the very great differences as well as the lingering East German rancor (one should consult Brandt's memoirs to get an appreciation for it) the West German chancellor was determined to come to terms with his country's division and to reach an accord with the GDR.[8] In his view the approach of his government was founded upon two premises not previously considered decisive.[9] First, Germany's partition, largely a function of superpower policies, was a consequence of the division of Europe into power blocs. Thus, according to Brandt, the "national problem" cannot be solved in isolation.[10] Second, an improvement in East-West relations and a West German opening to Eastern Europe could not be made contingent upon the reunification of Germany. The latter was not immediately in the cards and Adenauer's policies are often seen as having made German division in some ways even more wretched. Circumstances as they were in the 1960s left Bonn with little choice but to acknowledge the existence of the GDR. "Patriotism," in Brandt's words, "called for a

94

recognition of what existed and repeated attempts to discover what was possible. It called for courage to face facts."[11]

Brandt's *Ostpolitik* rested upon the pillars of Western integration, Alliance solidarity and detente with the Soviet Union. These are abstractions, and reality does not often spare leaders the necessity of handling contradictions and of making weighty decisions. Brandt's policies were often lacking in concept, devoid of grand design. Successful foreign policy involves the management of crosscurrents. In a variety of ways the elements forming the bases of the *Ostpolitik* were potentially contradictory and latently unstable. Though Brandt had for years been dissatisfied with what he viewed as the spent policies of Adenauer and the CDU, the *Ostpolitik* of the SPD-FDP coalition consisted primarily of a series of probes without definite long-term goals.

In fairness to the coalition, alternatives to its approach are difficult to conceive of. It is impossible to judge even years later how the German enigmas are to be solved or what longer-term possibilities there are for the *Ostpolitik*. In a sense, the *Ostpolitik* was from its inception the pursuit of policies without grand design, but rather a strategy of small steps. According to Brandt's own account, the primary objective of his government's policy toward the East was to arouse confidence and to eliminate distrust. Such a course would, in the view of its architects, eventually alleviate the problems affiliated with the division of Europe. Brandt provides few specifics about an overall strategy in his writings and he avoids discussing long-term concepts; nevertheless, one can discern at least in part what the leaders of the coalition had in view.

As an initial step, Brandt and Scheel intended to diminish the abiding trepidation of Germany in Eastern Europe. The attenuation of fear would augment West German influence in Europe, and, in the longer term, was likely to enhance the FRG's bargaining position vis-à-vis the Soviet Union. The FRG would be able to increase the role it would be playing in East-West relations, averting the possibility of Bonn's diplomatic isolation. The reduction of the perceived German threat with the ensuing gradual reemergence of West German prestige and ascendancy in Eastern Europe would contribute to a semblance of normalcy in the European power balance.

Alternatively, Bonn's influence might upset the apple cart, causing regime-threatening reverberations in the GDR, as Ulbricht feared. Intrinsic to the *Ostpolitik* was the readiness on the part of the FRG to manage its own affairs, to achieve greater independence and to come to grips with a regrettable past. It is therefore not by coincidence that Brandt emphasized in election campaigns that Germans could once again be proud of their country. Bonn's new approach required greater coordination of *Ostpolitik* and *Deutschlandpolitik*, whereby tensions in Eastern Europe would be relaxed and a German dialogue would commence.

Within the realm of the German problem, Bonn's course comprised a willingness to deal with the GDR as an equal partner, though inter-state relations would not amount to mutual recognition. Realism allowed an acceptance of the GDR's existence as a satellite state that had consolidated its internal control and was becoming firmer and more permanent. The coalition's idea was to increase contacts with East Germany in an effort to thwart the perpetuation of division. Through contact, not confrontation, through dialogue, not acrid rhetoric, Bonn attempted to alter the German situation. In light of the parameters within which the politics of the two Germanies must operate, and given a European status-quo that will not soon change, neither showdown nor reconciliation was feasible; Bonn sought above all to handle the circumstances of Germany's fate.

In the late 1960s the FRG stood at a crossroads. The SPD-FDP coalition had come to power with promises of movement in Eastern Europe and a betterment in inter-German relations. Brandt and Scheel had to follow the fine line between alliance cohesion and the pursuit of interests that were, in part, primarily West German ones. It was their government that bore the onus of consensus-building and of the rallying of domestic support for the acceptance of the European status-quo necessary for the significant alteration of the unfortunate, at times heart-wrenching, conditions in Central Europe. The trick was to manage the process, to reach some sort of *modus vivendi* with the GDR, to demonstrate to the West German electorate positive accomplishments of the coalition's program, to reassure allies that no "mad race" to Moscow was taking place, and not to lean against the wind. If concrete results of the *Ostpolitik* were to become apparent to West Germans, then, Brandt and Scheel assumed, public support for some once-unthinkable concessions would be forthcoming. The dilemma facing the coalition was, on the one hand, to foster sufficient change in FRG policies to make human amelioration possible, while preventing the occurrence of excessive mistrust on the other. Notwithstanding the ambiguities of Brandt's *Ostpolitik*, the salient theme of the approach was evident: Bonn wished to normalize relations with the East Bloc insofar as possible and to increase inter-German contacts, but in a way that would leave the German question and a nexus of European options open.

Brandt's primary concern was to ease the human misery attendant to partition but within the framework of existing power structures. <u>Brandt's vision lay in the acknowledgement of his country's inability to alter the basic political framework.</u> His focus was thus upon conditions affiliated with it. Indeed, some of Bonn's post-1969 policies brought considerable results in solving practical matters and in alleviating daily problems. Brandt's claims to innovative approaches and new premises are, however, somewhat overstated. Many Western policy-makers before Brandt were doubtless aware that the German problem could not be viewed, let alone solved, in isolation. Brandt's analysis is somewhat glib in that he fails to emphasize what was most crucial about the *Ostpolitik* of the SPD-FDP coalition, namely, the willingness to run more risks and to seize the initiative. The prudence of the pace of *Ostpolitik* is a matter for debate. Scheel leaves his readers with the impression that there existed a latent tendency to let the lions loose. The FRG was a political dwarf no longer and with the *Ostpolitik* it was taking infirm steps toward diplomatic assertiveness commensurate with its economic power. It behooved both the U.S. and the FRG to fathom the new realities. In the case of the latter, its policy-makers would have to recognize that merely supporting a status-quo would in the long term result in frustration as well as political ossification; in the former, its West German ally had individual interests and concerns that had to be understood, scrutinized, but above all, respected.

The two German states proceeded to carry out a series of measures improving relations prior to the Kassel summit. Bonn and East Berlin concluded a postal agreement in April 1970. They also contracted to increase the number of telephone and telex lines between them, no petty accomplishment in light of the fact that the leadership of one state still viewed contacts with the other as essentially repugnant. Another agreement changed West German tax laws in such a way as to facilitate GDR industrial import trade to the FRG, while reducing the profitability of the latter's exports.[12] These provisions were targeted at the reduction of already ballooning West

German trade surpluses with the GDR. Finally, the *Bundestag* repealed the Act of 1966 which subjected SED officials responsible for preventing *Republikflucht* (escape from the GDR) to criminal proceedings in the FRG. Upon repeal, East German officials could be guaranteed safe conduct in the FRG. Stoph's arrival was nonetheless marked by public requests for his arrest because he had headed the East German secret police for years.

Several unfortunate incidents took place during the Kassel meeting. Youths hauled down the GDR flag and destroyed it while Brandt was still greeting Stoph. Demonstrators halted the limousine in which Brandt and Stoph were riding as they were being taken to a wreath-laying ceremony. Several riots broke out as demonstrators battled in the streets. In a nation grown used to domestic tranquility, such occurrences boded ill for Brandt's pursuit of *Ostpolitik*. As if the domestic turmoil was not troublesome enough for Brandt, Stoph threatened a walkout from the meeting. Having protested the treatment in the FRG he regarded as unacceptable, Stoph telephoned Ulbricht for consultation; in light of the latter's assiduous skepticism about relations with the FRG in general, most suspected that Stoph would hurry home in a fit of disgust, jeopardizing all Bonn's efforts. To the surprise of almost everyone, Stoph stayed. Ulbricht, just returned from Moscow, had apparently once again been strongly urged to keep the inter-German dialogue going.[13] It would be safe to conclude that Ulbricht again knuckled under to Soviet pressure and reluctantly kept going a process to which he was opposed.

In private conversations, Brandt brought up a number of talking points, salient matters of contention all, the specifics of which were classified until recently.[14] Among the topics discussed were the following:

1. Stoph inquired about the possibility of both states entering the U.N., to which Brandt replied that considerable progress would have to be made in the normalization of German-German relations prior to such entry.
2. Offering to "respect the independence and autonomy of each of the two states in affairs affecting their internal sovereign authority," Brandt advocated more extensive cooperation in transportation, cultural events, science, education and trade. Stoph was somewhat skeptical.
3. Brandt reiterated the "two state" position of his

government, about which Stoph made the standard, non-committal remarks about the regulation of inter-German relations on an international-legal basis.
4. Brandt underscored the importance of a Berlin settlement to broader accord. Stoph criticized efforts to "interfere" in Berlin.
5. Both sides expressed interest in the conclusion of traffic regulation agreements.

The Kassel summit ended with little being decided. Though Stoph had not staged a walkout, East German leaders were less than anxious to reach accords with the FRG. Again the GDR was stonewalling. Brandt and Stoph agreed to disagree on several issues and to usher in a "Denkpause" (pause for thought).

During the inter-German discussions in 1970, the GDR continuously attempted to assert its demands of sovereignty in Berlin and on the transit routes. In addition to addressing quadripartite matters, the East Germans howled about FRG ties to West Berlin and Bonn's alleged schemes to annex the Western sectors. The West Germans countered that their presence in the city was governed by the Berlin Kommandatura and hence was not the business of the GDR. On a kindred point, the latter was also assertive, demanding FRG recognition of East Berlin as the capital of the GDR as a precursor to an anticipated countenancing of the GDR as a separate nation.

For all their awkward faltering, the Bonn leaders outmaneuvered their East German counterparts by engaging in a similar game. As Scheel now recounts, his government viewed significant progress on the Berlin question to be the prerequisite for German-German accords and for the *Ostpolitik* in general. Moscow's insistence that Ulbricht's regime keep talking to Bonn would not be sufficient; if the Soviet Union were genuinely interested in improved relations and attentive to a tacit acceptance of the European status-quo, it would have to pave the way for concessions on Berlin.[15] The Kremlin would thus have to lean on Ulbricht even harder to concede to a *modus vivendi* with the West. That Berlin should serve as a test case, the FRG and the U.S. were of one mind.

Meanwhile the quadrilateral negotiations on Berlin were not lending themselves to jubilee celebrations. Renowned for hard bargaining, the Soviets appeared to have been stalling. Soviet negotiator Abrasimov acquired a reputation for being an especially difficult customer. As a high-ranking party *apparachik*, he was used to giving orders and having them scrupulously followed. He understandably had little patience for Western "interests" or with requests to compromise.

With the talks showing signs of a deadlock, Bonn intensified its efforts to reach a general agreement with the Soviet Union. West German avidity was a function of notions: first, that such a treaty would catalyze the expansion of inter-German relations and, second, that the public standing of the Bonn coalition under pressure to produce would thereby be enhanced. Brandt's foreign policy adviser and confidant, Egon Bahr, laid the groundwork for the Bonn-Moscow Treaty with the so-called "Bahr text," the culmination of discussions resulting in, among other points, the "respect" for existing Eastern European boundaries.

NOTES

1. The complete text appears in: Bundesministerium für innerdeutsche Beziehungen, *Die Entwicklung der Beziehungen zwischen der Bundesrepublik Deutschland und der Deutschen Demokratischen Republik: Bericht und Dokumentation* (Melsungen: Verlagsbuchdruckerei A. Bernecker, 1973), p. 52. The translation is from Catudal, *The Diplomacy of the Quadripartite Agreement on Berlin*, p. 76.

2. *The Washington Post*, March 6, 1970; *Der Spiegel*, March 16, 1970.

3. *Der Spiegel*, March 30, 1970; for his own account: Brandt, *People and Politics The Years 1960-1975*, pp. 371-72.

4. Melvin Croan, *East Germany: The Soviet Connection* (Beverly Hills and London: Sage Publications, The Washington Papers, 1976), vol. 4, no. 36, p. 26.

5. Brandt, *People and Politics The Years 1960-1975*, p. 373.

6. See: *Der Spiegel*, March 23, 1970 and June 7, 1971.

7. Catudal, *The Diplomacy of the Quadripartite Agreement on Berlin*, p. 83; *Der Spiegel*, March 23, 1970.

8. Brandt, *People and Politics The Years 1960-1975*, p. 373.

9. Ibid.

10. Ibid.

11. Ibid., pp. 368-369.

12. Catudal, *The Diplomacy of the Quadripartite*

Agreement on Berlin, p. 110; for a recently-declassified account of FRG contingency planning just prior to the Kassel summit see: Baring, op. cit., pp. 287-88.

    13. Baring, op. cit., p. 289; *Der Spiegel*, June 1, 1970.

    14. For a more detailed account, Baring, op. cit., pp. 290-292, talking points ranged from the general logistics of a German-German *modus vivendi* to esoteric discussions of financial matters.

    15. Baring, op. cit., pp. 326-29; *Der Spiegel*, Feb. 8, 1971.

9
The Bonn-Moscow Treaty

The Bonn coalition was convinced that the "Bahr test" of May 1970 provided a near-complete framework for a treaty between the FRG and the Soviet Union. Brandt and Scheel believed the FRG to have obtained the most it could expect from the negotiations.[1] Soviet willingness to bargain seriously with the West Germans, to treat them as equals, to put aside the unfortunate events of the past, was in itself a significant breakthrough. As a crowning gesture, Moscow made no demands creating dilemmas for Bonn, such as prior recognition of the GDR or the denunciation of quadripartite rights in Berlin. Intended as the basic draft proposal for a final agreement to be negotiated by the Foreign Minister, the provisions of the text were to remain a state secret. Domestic fall-out might have untold consequences in the event the text's content became known before the signing of an actual treaty.[2]

In July the text leaked and was published in the daily, *Bild-Zeitung*, and in the weekly magazine, *Quick*. The source of the leak was never determined; some speculated it might have been East Berlin or Moscow itself, though the latter being the culprit seems most unlikely.[3] More probable is that a dismayed West German official divulged the information. Be that as it may, the Kremlin was furious and castigated Bonn for its leak-prone political system. Disclosure more or less incurred the finality of the text; Moscow refused to make additional changes.[4]

Before Scheel's trip to the Soviet Union to negotiate a draft of the Bonn-Moscow treaty, the FRG had carefully to examine the Bahr text for its compatibility with the Basic Law. Several legal questions had already been raised by potential opponents of the treaty. Might it be excluding the possibility of reunification, thus constituting a violation of the Basic Law? Would it infringe upon Allied rights in Germany? On the political level, was Bonn committing itself to concessions in Eastern Europe without adequate recompense? The Bonn working group on the text determined the provisions to be compatible with the Basic Law if in the course of the upcoming treaty negotiations the FRG postulated two conditions to the Soviets: that Bonn would continue to uphold its constitutional obligation to strive for reunification as before, and, that the FRG would ratify the treaty only after a satisfactory accord on Berlin had been achieved.

This linkage of a Berlin solution with the Bonn-Moscow Treaty became widely known as the "Junktim." Behind it was the Bonn government's judgment that the Soviet Union could not be permitted to cause tension in Berlin while renouncing the use of force in Europe. Brandt and Scheel were both at pains to underscore their position on the matter.[5] They considered the existing situation in Berlin inconsistent with the stipulations of a force renunciation agreement, and required that the Kremlin bring pressure to bear upon the GDR to end harassment and chicanery and to consent to the status-quo. Baring points out that Bonn's two preconditions or "complements" to the yet-undrafted treaty would appertain to the following crucial issues.[6]

1. Bonn could not under any circumstances tolerate a misconstruing of the renunciation-of-force agreement with a final German peace settlement. Bonn categorically rejected any notion that a Soviet-West German agreement could solve the German question, that in Bonn's view would only be possible on a multilateral basis. The FRG was prepared to accept the existing borders only insofar as it was renouncing the use of force in the latter's alteration. According to Bonn's interpretation, both parties to the agreement should regard the existing situation only as a point of departure for future developments.

2. The renunciation-of-force could not preclude an eventual German reunification, hence an accord could not be interpreted as an affirmation of the permanency of the inter-German border. The two sides agreed in May 1970 to the following annex to the Bahr text: "The agreement does not encroach upon the political goal of the FRG to participate in the creation of a peaceful new European order respecting the legitimate interests of all parties, which would allow the German people reunification in the event the latter so chose."[7]

3. Maintenance of Allied rights was of great

importance to the FRG. Bonn had to let it be understood in the Kremlin that the FRG regarded as completely unacceptable any accord interpreted as impinging upon Allied prerogative. In the general practice of international law such an eventuality would be proscribed: treaties cannot be concluded at the expense of a third not a partner to the agreement. However, the East Bloc had repeatedly threatened in the long history of Berlin crises to terminate Allied rights--ostensibly by legal means-- through the ratification of an East Berlin-Moscow agreement. There was no trusting the East Germans, for they had shown themselves willing to try any angle to undermine Allied rights.

Besides, Scheel went on to note, additional weighty political considerations faced Bonn. Many in Washington were becoming increasingly suspicious of the apparent urgency of the *Ostpolitik*. In 1970 Bonn was venturing actions regarded as unthinkable short years before. Reassurances had to be provided to concerned friends and Bonn wanted an explicit statement on the maintenance of Allied rights. Had a renunciation-of-force treaty precipitated new crises in Berlin, Brandt and Scheel would have faced major problems, foreign as well as domestic. A Berlin confrontation would likely have resulted in a governmental crisis in Bonn and the collapse of the coalition. Sanguine expectations in the FRG following the two inter-German summits would have been dashed had it appeared that the coalition was jeopardizing the protection offered by allies. Revulsion against the *Ostpolitik* would have been considerable and accusations of Bonn's having sold the West down the river wide-spread.

Before Scheel went to Moscow, the U.S. expressed overtly its skepticism in private conversations with FRG officials about Bonn's determination to anchor Four-Power rights in agreements with the Soviet Union.[8] The State Department suggested that a provision guaranteeing Allied rights be written into the treaty. Bonn did not seem to share the belief that difficulties with interpretation would be so great as to require such a specific provision; moreover, FRG leaders doubted--correctly--whether Moscow would agree to such an addendum. Among Soviet objections would be a Soviet demur about the FRG addressing Berlin matters. Bonn finally consented to dealing with quadripartite rights in clarification notes following the conclusion of a treaty.

A regular source of contention, Berlin had become even more sensitive with the convening of quadrilateral

negotiations on the divided city. Berlin was developing
into a point of friction within the Western camp in
addition to being a potential tinderbox for East-West
flare-ups. The mutual FRG-U.S. viewpoint that accords with
the East formed a sort of unified whole virtually assured
internecine quarreling if the Berlin discussions, in which
the FRG was not participating, broke down, setting off a
chain reaction. Bonn's dilemma was all too apparent: it
had vested and growing political interests in Berlin, but
had no legal competence there. Though coalition officials
were emphasizing their adherence to the position on
Berlin's interconnection with other East-West issues, they
were aware of the precarious basis for claims. A public
statement of the West German Foreign Office actually
affirmed that a "legal Junktim" on the part of the Bonn
government would not be possible because the entire matter
lay outside Bonn's jurisdiction.[9] The FDP in particular
was adamant about retaining the bond among accords in the
Ostpolitik fabric, even when such a rigid stand caused
tension with its coalition partner.[10]

In late July 1970 under pressure for success to
maintain the *Ostpolitik's* momentum, Scheel left for Moscow
in order to negotiate the treaty. The Kremlin leaders were
intransigent on Berlin, insisting that the FRG lacked
responsibility and should not be concerning itself with the
imbroglio. For a while it appeared that the negotiations
would break down and no accord would be reached, the result
of Soviet refusal to accept Scheel's preconditions. The
West German Foreign Minister made clear to the Kremlin
leaders the futility of signing an agreement devoid of a
reference to the German question, since such a compact
would be challenged by the Constitutional Court and would
have little chance of *Bundestag* ratification.[11] Gromyko
even seemed unswayed at first by Scheel's argument that the
future of the Bonn coalition might hang in the balance.
Finally Moscow did give in and agreed to the necessary
changes in the treaty. The FRG added a "separate
instrument" in the form of an exchange of notes with the
Western Powers concerning Berlin and Germany.[12] Although
not officially part of the Bonn-Moscow Treaty, both sides
have accepted the "instrument" as legally binding. In
addition, Brandt supplemented the treaty with a letter--the
so-called "German Option"--stating his government's
interpretation of the treaty as being compatible with the
provisions of the Basic Law on reunification. The Soviet
Union tacitly accepted the "German Option" as part of the
accord.[13] Several articles of the original Bahr text were

dropped from the final treaty signed on August 12, 1970, but the essence of the accord was preserved with the exception of explicit text references to the German question. Brandt and Scheel had accomplished a major breakthrough.

Despite severe criticism of the agreement in some domestic circles, the Bonn-Moscow Treaty contained successes going beyond the renunciation-of-force that was, in itself, not insignificant. One must acknowledge several important facts. First, FRG diplomacy had succeeded in separating the issue of border recognition from a mutual renunciation-of-force. The treaty precluded only the modification of the status-quo by force; it was silent on—tacitly allowing for—the peaceful, negotiated alteration of borders. As a result, the treaty was compatible with the Basic Law. Had there been prior requirements for recognition of a separate German state or FRG consent to the permanent division of Germany, the treaty would have been struck down by the Constitution Court, and would have had no chance of passing the *Bundestag* anyway. The subordination of a recognition of borders to a general renunciation-of-force represented a major concession on the part of Moscow. Moreover, the Bonn-Moscow Treaty set an important precedent in relations with the East Bloc, creating a usable, albeit only partial, frame-of-reference for additional accords, especially with Warsaw and East Berlin.

Second, the Kremlin raised no objections (in the probable absence of consultation with the GDR) to the "German Option," Brandt's letter added to the treaty package. The letter has been generally accepted as part of the treaty; at least this assumption has gone unchallenged. The letter's inclusion was additional testimonium to the treaty's concordance with the Basic Law.

Third, Moscow acceded to Bonn's insistence that the treaty contain a reference to existing Four-Power rights and responsibilities in Germany, something the Soviet Union adamantly resisted even in the early stages of negotiations. Largely because of pressure from its allies, the FRG issued a statement on Four-Power rights before signing the Bonn-Moscow Treaty.[14] Article IV of the text affirms that the accord does not affect valid agreements on Germany, only a step away from explicit Soviet recognition of Western rights.

Finally, Moscow made some allowances for the FRG on the Berlin issue. Though rejecting the "Junktim" and continuing to assert that Berlin was not the concern of the

FRG, the Kremlin did not interfere with West German assurances to the Allies, nor did it undertake actions effecting a potential crisis in the Alliance. The FRG Foreign Office, displaying what can scarcely be called modesty, later suggested that the linkage with a Berlin arrangement provided Moscow with additional incentive to reach an accord.[15] The Soviets would be loath ever to admit as much.

But the FRG's renunciation-of-force agreement with Moscow met with a measure of West German domestic resistance and raised eyebrows in Washington. Wide currency was accorded to the notion that the concessions had all been on Bonn's side. The CDU/CSU opposition in the FRG began the groundwork for challenging the *Ostpolitik* in the parliament as well as in the courts. In light of the evidence it is difficult cogently to argue that the Soviet Union had been unwilling to accommodate Bonn in various ways; what is more, there seemed to be growing support in the West German population for the *Ostpolitik*.

The FDP had made significant gains in the Hesse and Bavarian state elections held in November 1970, when West German polls were becoming plebiscites on the *Ostpolitik*. The public seemed to be showing support for the previously-underrated Foreign Minister.[16] Some coalition officials were regarding the Bonn-Moscow Treaty as a shining achievement already in the fall of 1970. The accord doubtless represented a catalyst to Bonn's Eastern initiatives. The early success, however, posed a two-fold dilemma for the Brandt-Scheel government. First, Bonn would come under pressure--internal as well as external--to maintain the momentum of its *Ostpolitik*; failure to produce jeopardized the coalition's future. Second, FRG officials--government and opposition--were fully aware that ratification of the Moscow Treaty, with the attendant prospects for the *Ostpolitik*, was contingent upon successful Berlin negotiations that were out of Bonn's hands. Thus, Bonn was completely dependent upon its allies and some FRG leaders became impatient at the slow pace of the quadrilateral talks on Berlin.

NOTES

1. Baring points out that the SPD-FDP coalition faced crucial state elections in the fall of 1970. Scheel, convinced of the diplomatic accomplishment in Moscow, would present the voters with his success: Baring, op. cit., p. 311.

2. Ibid., p. 312.

3. Indeed, it is difficult to see what Moscow stood to gain from the leak, although the possibility of the leak being another GDR effort to torpedo detente cannot be excluded. Most plausible is that the leak originated in Bonn: Baring, op. cit., pp. 312-13.

4. Whetten, op. cit., pp. 193-95; Baring, op. cit., p. 313.

5. Walter Scheel, "Die deutsche Politik des Gewaltverzichts," *Frankfurter Allgemeine Zeitung*, July 15, 1970; *Der Spiegel*, May 31, 1971 and Jan. 17, 1972.

6. These points are discussed in detail by Baring, op. cit., pp. 316-32.

7. (author's translation), Baring, op. cit., p. 318.

8. The discussion took place on July 17, 1970. See: Baring, op. cit., p. 321.

9. Ibid., p. 324; Catudal, *The Diplomacy of the Quadripartite Agreement on Berlin*, pp. 119-21.

10. Baring, op. cit., p. 325.

11. Ibid., pp. 333-34.

12. Ibid., p. 344.

13. The text is contained in: Whetten, Appendix V, pp. 224-27.

14. Baring, op. cit., p. 344.

15. Baring, op. cit., pp. 348-49.

16. Charts of state election results appear in: *German Tribune*, Dec. 10, 1970; *Der Spiegel*, June 8, 1970.

10
U.S.-FRG Differences

Notwithstanding public proclamations by the Alliance of agreement on policy, Scheel was fully aware of the complications the ambitious West German *Ostpolitik* posed for U.S. negotiating strategy.[1] Scheel is now inclined to admit--more so than at the inception of the SPD-FDP *Ostpolitik*--that the *Ostpolitik* generated the mistrust of such qualmish U.S. policy makers as Henry Kissinger and Helmut Sonnenfeldt, who feared impetuous detente policies or a precipitous conference on European security would strengthen Moscow's hand in Eastern Europe and ultimately jeopardize NATO.[2] U.S. stalling on certain East-West issues ran athwart of an FRG foreign policy under pressure to produce. A not insignificant SPD-FDP achievement would seem to have been the expeditious convening in March 1970 of quadrilateral discussions on Berlin, a result of persistent lobbying efforts on the part of the FRG.

Roger Morgan downplays the role of the FRG in encouraging its allies to seat themselves at the conference table, arguing that President Nixon had come into office with the intention of negotiating a deal on Berlin.[3] Kissinger and Nixon were supportive of the general direction of the *Ostpolitik*, insofar as Bonn was finally accepting realities U.S. analysts had long taken for granted. The Administration was nonetheless concerned about possible long-term consequences of West German policies. But if Kissinger was apprehensive about the effects of the *Ostpolitik*, Ulbricht was doubtless perturbed.

For their part, West German leaders spared no efforts to illustrate that their attempts to improve the situation in the East were predicated upon having both feet firmly planted in the West. In a speech before the European

Parliament in September 1970, Scheel emphasized that the Bonn-Moscow renunciation-of-force accord had been concluded on the basis of existing NATO military security arrangements as well as in accordance with European economic and political integration. "Without these bases, there would have been no agreement," said Scheel.[4] He went on to explain that Moscow should become accustomed to regarding the European Community as a negotiating and trading partner. The role of the EC as an international player and the importance assigned to this organization as spokesman for common trade policies by Bonn are underscored by EC chairman's signature upon the Helsinki Final Act of the Conference on Security and Cooperation in Europe. At the time the incumbent chairman was the Italian foreign minister. The EC furnishes Bonn with yet another political structure within which it is able to articulate and pursue its interests.

Moreover, Scheel asserted, the Bonn-Moscow Treaty would likely provide an impetus to European integration. Recognizing both well-timed opportunities as well as pitfalls, he suggested that his government could exploit the former while giving wide berth to the latter. In the following year, Brandt addressed himself to these issues in most explicit terms.

> Our Ostpolitik is based upon our Westpolitik. This is a fact and not a matter of doubt. Our efforts toward reconciliation and cooperation with the East are geared toward achieving greater peace and security for Europe. Thus, they also benefit Western cooperation. Here and there suspicions and fears have surfaced that there is a contradiction between the treaty with the Soviet Union and our active participation in the work of West European unification and in the Atlantic alliance. This is an assumption proceeding from false premises. I want to say this here once again with complete clarity: the Federal Republic of Germany conducts its Ostpolitik not as a wanderer between two worlds, but from a position firmly established in Western cooperation. Atlantic alliance and Western European partnership are for us the essential prerequisites for the success of conciliation with the East.[5]

That the Soviet Union expected the *Ostpolitik* to clear the way for the European security conference it desired as had the Bonn-Moscow Treaty for the Bonn-Warsaw Treaty of

December 7, 1970, was apparent. Radio Moscow proclaimed
the "historic role" of the Bonn-Moscow Treaty, and *Pravda*
noted that:

> The sides are convinced that the treaty they have
> concluded opens up favorable prospects for the
> successful development of peaceful cooperation between
> the USSR and the FRG in various spheres, in the
> interests of the peoples of both states. They
> expressed confidence that the treaty will foster the
> strengthening of security in Europe, the solution of
> the problems existing there and the establishment of
> peaceful cooperation between all European states,
> irrespective of differences in their social systems.[6]

Several months later, *Pravda* remarked with
satisfaction that the Bonn-Warsaw Treaty of 1970 opened up
new possibilities for European cooperation.

> Like the treaty that the Soviet Union and the FRG
> signed in Moscow last August, the document initialed
> in Warsaw is in the spirit of the Potsdam Agreement
> that defined European borders 25 years ago. The
> Polish-FRG Treaty is still another concrete result of
> the socialist countries' efforts to heal the situation
> in Central Europe and bolster the principle of the
> inviolability of the state borders existing there.
> Thus, the treaty's significance far surpasses the
> limits of the relations between the two countries.[7]

Moscow counted on *Ostpolitik* to help create conditions for
the convocation of a security conference recognizing the
status-quo in Europe.

Where were the real underlying dilemmas for Bonn? In
a bit of discerning analysis, Alastair Buchan identified a
contradiction in the Western European "ideal" by spelling
out some of the latter's requirements. This "ideal" he
explained,

> . . . would best be met if the pattern of the
> relationship between the countries of Western Europe,
> and the general objectives to which each subscribed,
> were such as to promote European cohesion, security,
> and prosperity, without alienating either the United
> States or the Soviet Union, or jeopardizing conditions
> of detente which could lead to a permanent settlement
> in Central Europe; in other words, to have its cake

and eat it.[8]

What is startling about Buchan's description of this
European "ideal" and its contradictions is how aptly they
apply to the nexus of the *Ostpolitik* and Bonn's policies
toward the West. The dilemma of Brandt's policies, and for
the European "ideal," was how the FRG could eat the cake
it wanted to possess. West German pieces of the puzzle,
did not fit in every respect with those of the Soviet
Union, the United States and the FRG's partners in the
European Community and this incompatibility of the puzzle's
pieces touches at many points upon the open "German
question." Such were the problems of Bonn's *Ostpolitik* in
1970 and of the Berlin situation for the Western Three.[9]

In an August 1970 interview Brandt underscored his
government's position that progress on the Berlin situation
was the *sine qua non* for the continuation of the *Ostpolitik*
as well as for the ratification of the Bonn-Moscow
Treaty.[10] "We can ratify the treaty," Brandt asserted, "if
by then progress, considerable progress, has been made
toward stabilizing the status of West Berlin." Brandt went
on to say:

> We are not thinking of security solely in the military
> sense of the word, but security also in terms of
> viability, including both a firm Western presence and
> also an acceptance by the other side of the fact that
> Berlin, for all practical purposes, belongs together
> with West Germany, and that free access to Berlin is
> necessary if Berlin is going to have a reasonable
> future.[11]

With the Berlin negotiations making very little
headway, Brandt's statement was just what Washington did
not wish to hear at the time. Fearful of the prospect of
having their hands tied, some U.S. officials began to take
umbrage with Bonn. Kissinger was uneasy about having other
would-be architects of detente erecting their own edifices.
Brandt's remark lent credence to Kissinger's suggestion
that Bonn was overestimating its political clout.

If the U.S. was disquieted, Moscow was furious. The
"Junktim" was becoming a source of contention between the
Soviet Union and the FRG; alarm bells would go off in the
Kremlin whenever Bonn addressed itself to Berlin matters.
Scheel recalls how Gromyko once screamed at him: "Berlin
is none of your business."[12] With a natural proclivity for
suspicion, Moscow resented potential restrictions upon its

freedom of maneuver, and moreover, had to endure incessant GDR complaints about West German motives.

That genuine differences in nuance as well as in substance between the FRG and the Western Allies did arise during the course of the Berlin negotiations is undeniable. Brandt's August statement alluded to the emergence of such differences; Scheel now concedes how wide the rift might have become. Reasons are not difficult to find. Brandt and Scheel spelled some of them out in a July 7, 1970 cabinet meeting, mentioning that the FRG and its allies could be setting non-coinciding goals.[13]

Far and away the most scathing U.S. criticism of Bonn's policies came from non-government circles. Such "founding fathers" of the West German state as John J. McCloy, Lucius Clay, Thomas Dewey and Dean Acheson expressed their forebodings about the *Ostpolitik* in a December 1970 encounter at the White House. Acheson even publicly labeled the *Ostpolitik* as Brandt's "mad race to Moscow," arguing that Bonn's policies were threatening to detach the FRG from the Western Alliance.[14] In a January 1971 article, George Ball, former Under Secretary of State, presented similar reprimands, demonstrating how extensive mistrust of Germany still was.[15] At the time there seemed to be a growing temptation for Bonn to follow a more independent course and to urge its allies to quicken the pace of relaxing tensions. By December 1970 the FRG had successfully negotiated the Bonn-Moscow and Bonn-Warsaw Treaties, ratification of which was contingent upon a Berlin settlement. The patience of some FRG officials would soon wear thin, for it was not only the final conclusion of the two aforementioned accords that depended upon Western diplomatic successes, but also a codified agreement with the GDR that was to be the capstone of SPD-FDP policy conceptions.

What was the salient cause for mistrust? The Brandt-Scheel government had not arrived at any new conclusions about the German question, nor had it altered the premises upon which the arguments in favor of the *Ostpolitik* had been based; such change had occurred long before 1969. In an astute observation, Alfred Grosser cited disparate FRG rallying-cries linked by policy conceptions. Under the Adenauer administration there was to be "no detente without progress on the German problem"; by the time of the Grand Coalition, this had evolved to: "detente is so fundamental to subsequent progress on the German problem that we are ready to make progress towards a detente, and we agree to the resolution of the German problem coming much later."[16]

This latter statement not only accurately described the SPD-FDP policy approach, but also corresponded closely with the course U.S. officials had been urging Bonn to follow for years and one the West had long since adopted. What put Western nerves on edge was the possibility of Bonn granting too many concessions too fast and thereby, perhaps inadvertently, launching the FRG into unilateralism damaging to Western interests.

It is ironic, however, that the FRG in certain areas actually pressed for more concessions on Moscow's part than did the U.S. Bonn was above all concerned about the existence and welfare of the some two million inhabitants of West Berlin. Few in Bonn did not hold the view that the FRG bore primary responsibility for the West Berliners and the former could ensure the well-being of the latter only by developing social, economic and administrative ties. Since few Western bargaining chips on Berlin were available, the U.S. seemed prepared to place such ties onto the negotiating table, a source of considerable concern to Bonn.

In addition it appeared that both Brandt and Scheel believed the Allies were unduly emphasizing quadripartite rights insofar as the importance of these rights would be at the expense of West German presence in Berlin. Four-Power rights and responsibilities included those maintained by the Soviet Union. The lurking trade-off between an ally's interests and an adversary's prerogative could not have been lost on Bonn. Adamant about having the Soviet Union and the GDR confirm "original" rights in Berlin, the Western Powers conveyed the impression of insensitivity to their ally's apprehensions. Kissinger, for example, still does not seem able to fathom the deep personal-emotional commitment Bonn leaders have to West Berlin, despite his vast knowledge of European problems. Perhaps such an argument gives Bonn the benefit of the doubt. Just as the FRG had somehow to come to terms with the realities of the European postwar status-quo, facts about the Berlin situation had to be faced. The West was in a weak position in Berlin, the chicanery the GDR engaged in during the quadrilateral negotiations served as adequate reminder. Thus arose the question of an alternative to bargaining on FRG presence in Berlin.[17] The West had little to offer the East Germans, rendering a deal on Berlin more feasible were the issue part and parcel of a larger matrix.

Yet another consideration about the divergence in views should be made. Though the Soviet Union did accommodate Bonn in the renunciation-of-force agreements, the concessions involved relatively manageable problems compared to the labyrinthine enigma of Berlin, aspects of which had become obscure after decades of animosity.[18] Fully aware of the perplexities, having been governing mayor of West Berlin for 9 years, Brandt should not have expected a prompt Berlin settlement favorable to the West. The Bonn coalition was coming under constituency and opposition pressure in 1971, but it nevertheless should have realized the hazards of discounting the differences on each side in the negotiations then underway. Brandt's apparent lack of patience resulted largely from the dilemma inherent in his policy approach and in the European "ideal" described by Buchan. With a minimum of friction, Bonn expected more results from detente than did its allies in a shorter period of time. The dilemma was exacerbated by the dictates of political exigencies; some in the Bonn government had allowed themselves to be persuaded that the coalition could ill afford to wait long for progress on Berlin. Scheel himself, hardly a political adventurer, was closely attentive to the need for maintaining the *Ostpolitik's* momentum upon which rested the credibility of his government.[19] The Brandt-Scheel coalition had promised its voters major benefits from the *Ostpolitik* and pledged itself to strive for "menschliche Erleichterung" in the East. The coalition leaders were expected to deliver on the goods; if their initial steps failed, they risked being turned out of office.

West German rigidity in the Adenauer years, the inability of the West to achieve any diplomatic breakthroughs in Central Europe, as well as the awkwardness with which Brandt perceived America to have handled the Wall crisis, culminated in frustration for the Chancellor and an absorbing mistrust of U.S. foreign policy.[20] Brandt was apprehensive during the quadripartite negotiations that the U.S. could have cared less about the issue of West Berliners' visiting privileges in the eastern part of their city, an important humanitarian concern for Bonn. East Berlin for all intents and purposes was lost; the most the Western Powers could accomplish there was to refuse explicitly to recognize it as capital of the GDR, while striving to maintain the last vestiges of quadripartite rights in the Eastern sector. Bonn could expect only thin gruel: additional telephone service, some postal agreements, limited accessibility to East Berlin.

On practical improvements on the Berlin situation such as traffic, supply and railroad connections, FRG views coincided quite closely with those of the Western powers throughout the course of negotiations. Such concurrence helped to smooth over rough edges. Fortunately for the Alliance, push did not come to shove and a chasm between Bonn and Washington on broader issues did not develop. The Bonn government was not placed in the unenviable position of having to choose between allegiance to its allies and its own national interests. Had the Berlin negotiations broken down, the SPD-FDP coalition might have had to make just such a choice. That such a clash of interests in the West was avoided is not attributable merely to astute Western diplomacy. Lack of imagination and sophistication in Soviet foreign policy as well as Moscow's willingness to make concessions on Berlin at least partly at GDR expense were also factors.

The sort of friction that did not materialize between Bonn and Washington, did afflict the Kremlin's relations with East Berlin during the crucial stages of the quadripartite negotiations. Not enamoured of the prospect of a Berlin accord even under the most favorable circumstances for the GDR, Ulbricht, the notorious East Bloc hardliner, attempted to checkmate Moscow's efforts once he saw the direction in which the negotiations were headed. Convinced that any East-West accommodation would become a direct threat to his regime, Ulbricht expressed his reluctance to have the Soviet Union conclude a Berlin agreement. Having realized he was not going to win full West German recognition of the GDR in the foreseeable future, Ulbricht became averse to further negotiation with the West. With the 1968 "Prague Spring" still fresh in his mind, he wanted no repetitions in his "sovereign capital." In his view a Berlin settlement would have risked just that.

NOTES

1. Baring, op. cit., p. 284; Roger Morgan, *The United States and West Germany 1945-1973* (Oxford: Oxford University Press, 1974), pp. 211-212.

2. See: Kissinger, *White House Years*, pp. 408-12 for his version, and Baring, op. cit., pp. 260-63 for Scheel's.

3. Morgan, *The United States and West Germany 1945-1973*, pp. 214-215.

4. *Agence Europe*, No. 645, September 16, 1970, p. 6;

Baring, op. cit., p. 332.

5. Address by Chancellor Brandt to the Fifth German-French Conference of Chambers of Commerce in Hamburg, September 3, 1971, *Bundeskanzler Brandt: Reden und Interviews* (Bonn: Press and Information Office of the FRG, 1971), quoted in: Helga Haftendorn, *Conflicting Priorities in German Foreign Policy* (New York: Praeger, 1985), p. 245.

6. *Pravda*, Aug. 14, 1970, *CDSP* XXII/33, p. 22.

7. *Pravda*, Nov. 23, 1970, *CDSP* XXII/47, p. 22.

8. Alastair Buchan, *Europe's Future, Europe's Choices* (New York: Columbia University Press, 1969), pp. 152-53.

9. David M. Keithly, "Whither German Social Democracy"?, *Strategic Review*, Vol. 13, No. 3 (Summer 1985), pp. 60-66.

10. Morgan, *The United States and West Germany 1945-1973*, pp. 209-11.

11. Interview with Brandt, *Time*, Aug. 24, 1970.

12. Baring, op. cit., pp. 331-32.

13. Ibid., p. 329; Nina Heathcote, "Brandt's Ostpolitik and Western Institutions," *World Today*, Vol. 26, Aug. 1970, pp. 342-43.

14. Morgan, *The United States and West Germany 1945-1973*, pp. 213-14; *New York Times*, Dec. 22, 1970.

15. This argument appeared in Ball's article, "A Reply to Arthur Goldberg", *New York Times*, Jan. 8, 1971. In an article entitled, "The Cold Warriors versus Willy Brandt," *New York Times*, Jan. 5, 1970, Goldberg defended Brandt against his leading American critics. At the time there were precious few Americans willing to rally to Brandt's cause.

16. Alfred Grosser, "France and Germany: less divergent outlooks," *Foreign Affairs*, Vol. 48, No. 2 (Spring 1970), p. 241.

17. There were several transit-route incidents during the course of negotiations, with one traffic delay lasting some 30 hours, see: Theo Sommer, "Spiegelfechtereien um Berlin," *Die Zeit*, Jan. 12, 1971; *Der Spiegel*, Feb. 8, 1971.

18. See: Gerhard Wettig, "Berlin Frage und sowjetische Westpolitik 1970/71," in *Die Sowjetunion, die DDR und die Deutschland-Frage* 1965-1976 (Stuttgart: Deutsche Verlags-Anstalt, 1977), pp. 89-91.

19. Baring, op. cit., p. 330; Wolfgang Wagner, "Das Berlin-Problem als Angelpunkt eines Ausgleichs zwischen West und Ost in Europa," *Europa-Archiv*, Vol. 26, No. 11 (1971), pp. 375-77.

20. See: Willy Brandt, *People and Politics*, pp. 20-24,

pp. 78-82; Baring, op. cit., pp. 328-330; Walter Hahn "West Germany's Ostpolitik: The Grand Design of Egon Bahr," *Orbis*, vol. 16, no. 4 (Winter 1973), p. 862.

11
Quadripartite Negotiations

Two problems stood in the foreground of quadripartite negotiations: access to West Berlin and FRG presence in the city. The access question posed a two-fold difficulty, since it involved issues of West German as well as of Allied transit. The hurdle presented by the former--West German transit--was passed with relative ease early in the negotiations, when the Four Powers decided that inter-German accords, supplementing a quadrilateral agreement, should regulate traffic and overland transit, thereby solving the "Zugangsfrage," at least for the FRG. Moscow had no objections to an FRG acquisition of more or less unrestrained accessibility to West Berlin, since this would not necessarily involve exercise of FRG authority there, and, moreover would enhance the prestige of the GDR which would negotiate the details of a transit arrangement. But the matter upon which an accord would stand or fall was the Allied demand for a Soviet guarantee of access.

The issue of Allied transit rights proved to be very sticky. Ostensibly upholding GDR interests, the Soviet Union insisted that the East Germans enjoyed full territorial sovereignty in which the authority to control all traffic between the FRG and West Berlin was inherent. In its initial position, Moscow argued that neither the occupational entrenchment of the Western Powers in Berlin nor the existing agreements--the validity of which the Soviets sometimes accepted--could legally infringe upon "established" East German sovereign rights.[1] The West's most essential precondition for a Berlin settlement was an across-the-board Soviet guarantee of unimpeded access to West Berlin. Anticipated inter-German traffic accords notwithstanding, the Soviet Union would have to underwrite all access--Allied, West German and third party--if there were to be any quadripartite treaty. Hence, opening Soviet proposals were non-starters and the negotiations deadlocked.

The Soviet side at first attempted to portray West Berlin as a sort of land-locked "independent political entity." In accordance with the time-honored principle of international law, it would follow that the surrounding state (or states) is authorized to control access to the area. According to Moscow's interpretation, landlocked states have no choice but to reach transit accords with neighboring states and, as the Soviets were quick to point out, no exception could be made for "occupation troops." In referring to customary handling of enclaves in international law, the Soviet Union lent support to the GDR position that West Berlin, as an independent political entity, would have to make separate transit arrangements with the GDR, in addition to those made between the two German states. Such a notion was completely unacceptable to both the FRG and the Allies, since to the former it would deny long-established ties, neither would there be provisions for "menschliche Erleichterung." For the latter, Moscow would be offering no explicit guarantees of access rights, nor would it confirm "original" rights of occupation.

In official statements, the Soviet Union and the GDR substantiated their positions by virtue of the 1955 Bolz-Zorin Treaty allegedly granting the GDR extensive sovereign authority. Despite some 15 years of East German noise about "illegal, anachronistic" Allied rights in Berlin as well as provisions in the Bolz-Zorin Treaty for "temporary" special arrangements for Allied traffic, it is notable that the East German regime never launched a systematic campaign against Allied military vehicles--neither rail traffic, nor convoys on the transit routes, nor the Allied military patrols that regularly make their rounds through East Berlin.

The Western Powers submitted a lengthy proposal for settlement on February 5, 1971. The proposal's very structure underscored Allied priorities in Berlin, with a preambular reference to improvements in the "Greater Berlin" area and an initial section guaranteeing free access to the city.[2] The first two annexes provided for the practical application of Soviet-guaranteed transit procedures. The third dealt with the relationship between the FRG and the Western sectors, ensuring the development of West German ties to the city, while codifying supreme Allied authority there. The FRG would be entitled to represent the interests of West Berlin abroad. As would be expected, the Allies were studiously reticent about East German authority and made no reference to the GDR.

The two concessions the Western Powers offered the Soviet Union were the only ones they were prepared to make: "demonstrative federal presence" in Berlin would be subdued and Berlin was designated as not comprising a constituent part of the FRG. There was little leeway available to the Three; theirs was nearly a maximum or "ideal situation" first proposal. It was quite evident they could not have backed down far. Moreover, the clause barring the Western sectors from constituting sovereign FRG territory had a mirror image in that it affirmed continued Four-Power jurisdiction in the city, and hence thwarted any Eastern schemes to establish any part of Berlin as an "independent political entity."[3] The only accommodation the Allies made to the East Germans was the endorsement of inter-German transit compacts following quadrilateral agreement on a far-extending framework.

Intended to be kept secret within the quadripartite negotiations, the Western proposal leaked to the West German press. Given the number of parties standing to gain from a leak, public revelation cannot have been astonishing. Though West German reaction to the Four-Power negotiations was generally restrained, many in Bonn could not have been altogether pleased with the thrust of the Allied proposal. Brandt's government found common ground with the conservative opposition in the concurrence that the Allies were disregarding West German humanitarian interests.[4] For instance, the Western Powers seemed to be skirting the issue of East Berlin. Some observers tended toward the view that inhabitants of the Eastern sector were entitled to certain rights under Four-Power authority.[5] Most Bonn officials agreed that a salient point of the "practical improvement" in the Berlin situation had to include provisos regulating but also encouraging contacts across the German-German borders. Such concerns were secondary for the Allies, at least compared with access rights.

A reduction in the FRG "presence" in West Berlin was understandably somewhat difficult to swallow for a government constitutionally committed to upholding the interests of Germans, especially one headed by a former West Berlin governing mayor in office during two severe East-West crises. With a modicum of consternation, West Germans could hardly have avoided taking cognizance of the fact that, the Berlin situation being what it was, the

Western Powers held only West German bargaining chips in negotiations to which the FRG was not party. Unable to escape their destiny, Germans had to face the bitter realities of partition during the Four-Power negotiations, as is a matter of course.

Likely informed of the Allied proposal long before the leak, the East Germans indubitably grew even more apprehensive about the outcome of a Berlin settlement. Not even mentioned in the Western draft of an accord, the East German regime concluded that a future agreement would scarcely be in its interests. Ulbricht felt he had already made sweeping concessions to the West, albeit at Moscow's insistence, by retreating from the "Ulbricht Doctrine." Ulbricht was not reassured, when, as reported in the Western press, Soviet Ambassador Abrasimov, not celebrated as a proponent of conciliatory gestures toward the West, reacted to the February proposal in a not-all-too negative manner.[6] Although Abrasimov reportedly took immediate exception with the Western Allies on the matter of East German sovereign rights, his reply fueled speculation that the Kremlin was unusually eager for a Berlin settlement.[7] One should therefore not exclude the possibility that GDR officials were leaking information to the Western press in an effort to undermine negotiations.

The East Germans tried other methods as well. On February 4, Stoph suggested publicly that West and East Berlin--the latter as "capital" of the GDR--begin negotiations on an array of issues. There could have been no question about what the GDR had in mind and it was hardly to facilitate a Berlin settlement. Offering West Berlin a separate deal on access and visitation privileges the GDR hoped to circumvent quadrilateral accords, with an aim toward eventually presenting the other powers with a *fait accompli*.[8] The tactic failed, however, when the West Berlin *Senat* rejected Stoph's proposal out of hand.

Later in the month, East Berlin was back with yet another endeavor, when Stoph proposed talks more limited in scope with the goal of promoting contacts with Berlin, i.e., across the Wall. Viewing "current efforts for a reduction of tensions in the center of Europe and for normalization of the situation of West Berlin as being of greatest importance," the GDR made a further awkward attempt to influence the quadripartite negotiations. Stoph suggested that West Berliners might be allowed to make Easter visits to East Berlin and to the GDR even in the absence of a Four-Power agreement.[9]

Failing to take the East German bait, the *Senat*

consulted the Western Powers and the FRG. East Berlin had gotten nowhere; the question whether East German diplomatic probes in West Berlin had been entirely approved in Moscow remains open. The Soviets might have found the timing inappropriate.

Prior to 1969 the West had attempted to prevent the GDR from engaging in discussions with West Berlin in order not to lend credence to the East Bloc position that the Western sectors constituted an independent political entity. The policy--not atypical in non-recognition cases--created some practical difficulties when trial balloons went up for a possible Berlin settlement. The FRG was not empowered to address Berlin matters; the East Bloc categorically rejected any West German responsibility for Berlin anyway. The U.S. had no diplomatic relations with the GDR and for years had refused to speak with it. If practical improvements in the Berlin situation were to be achieved, the GDR needed an interlocutor, and so the Allies adopted the policy of differing levels of negotiations. Major matters of the city's status would remain within the exclusive jurisdiction of the Western Powers. The West Berlin government would be entitled, contingent upon consultation with the Allies, to negotiate on some local issues with the East Germans. The rationale for the modification in policy was the following: inter-German dialogue was being carried on in any event with U.S. encouragement, and, moreover, an eventual Four-Power Berlin deal would be supplemented by German-German accords on such matters as traffic regulation, transit-route maintenance and visa requirements, all necessitating wide-ranging negotiation.

The West Berlin response to Stoph's initiative was circumspectly to welcome apparent GDR interest in humanitarian issues, while advising the East Germans of the parameters of West Berlin's negotiating authority.

Abrasimov submitted the Soviet draft proposal for a Berlin settlement on March 16, 1971. Labeled a "document of surrender" by the Berlin SPD, it certainly provided for a good deal less than the Allies were hoping for. In hindsight, however, the proposal seemed to be about par for the course and could have been worse in that it might have reflected even greater Soviet intransigence. Renowned for tough bargaining, Moscow could not have been expected to put forth a mollifying offer. The proposal's emphasis was about where a serious analyst would have expected it to be--upon the virtual exclusion of the FRG from West Berlin. Comprising two parts of general provisions and five

annexes, the draft began on a negative note: "Berlin
(West) is not part of the FRG and is not governed by it
. . . The relations between Berlin (West) and the FRG must
not contradict this."[10]

While the Western Powers described West Berlin as not
a state (Land) of the FRG, the Soviets had employed the
term, "part," possibly indicating an effort to diminish
existing ties between the Western sectors and the FRG.
Also, the proposal referred to Berlin (West) throughout, a
rather obvious attempt to give support to the East Bloc
position that only West Berlin was a subject of
negotiations. The inability of the two sides to concur on
what area was being discussed illustrated the apparent
disparity in the two positions. Moscow's proposal was
fraught with nuances, leaving many questions wide open.
Had the Kremlin backed off from the "independent political
entity" standpoint at all? Did the proposal represent
anything new, or was it a mere repetition of the Soviet
campaign throughout the 1960s to isolate West Berlin?

Worst of all, Moscow made no specific mention of what
the West had clarified as the most crucial aspect of a
deal, namely, guaranteed access. Tendering on a few vague
remarks about transit accords being "concluded between the
authorities," the Soviets kept their distance from the
issue upon which the quadrilateral negotiations would stand
or fall.

Terming the Soviet proposal a maximum bargaining
position was to go to extremes, but the Kremlin's draft for
a settlement was nonetheless very problematic, leaving many
questions unanswered. To pessimistic Western observers at
the time, it must have been adequate confirmation of the
futility of attempting to do business with Moscow in
Berlin. U.S. negotiator Rush observed: "Some on the
Western side felt the Soviet draft evidenced this
impossibility of reaching some compromise between the two
proposed agreements."[11] Soviet unwillingness to compromise
and the ensuing lack of progress in the quadripartite
negotiations would likely have meant the end of the Brandt-
Scheel coalition in Bonn.

The proposal did however contain some positive
elements, an example of which was lack of any reference to
East Berlin as the "capital of the GDR." Another was a
discernible Soviet preparedness to recognize Four-Power
"rights and responsibilities," notwithstanding the absence
of suggestions on access matters. But access and "rights"
were inexorably connected in the view of the Allies. The
acceptance of occupation prerogative and the denial of free

access were mutually exclusive. On the other hand, one could argue with some cogency that recognition of Allied rights precludes the existence of an independent political entity.[12] Moscow had come a long way from the time when it engaged in delivering ultimatums requiring complete Western withdrawal from the Western sectors of Berlin. Additionally, the Soviet proposal explicitly allowed FRG representation of some West Berlin interests abroad, including consular jurisdiction. Acceptance of such FRG authority would set a necessary precedent for further ties.

Short weeks after the submission of Moscow's proposal, the text--supposed to be kept secret within the confines of the quadrilateral negotiations--became public. The rationale for the confidentiality of the negotiating positions was to debar any party from public commitment to a particular viewpoint, although most positions could not have been difficult to surmise. The appearance of the Soviet working paper on April 15 in a major Polish daily, *Zycie Warszawy*, and on the following day in *Neues Deutschland* gave rise to the wide-spread supposition that the Soviets were behind the publication of their draft. Notwithstanding attribution of the source to certain groups in Brussels, the proposal was published only in part, in a way which seemed to demonstrate Soviet flexibility.[13] Moscow might have seen the maneuver as a possible way politically to separate Bonn from its allies. A tough stance in the negotiating sessions coupled with an ostensibly conciliatory public position--following skillful editing--had the dual effect of fostering despair in the U.S., France and Britain, while encouraging Bonn to pressure its allies into concessions. With certainty the text's publication had been intended for Western consumption. Had the Bonn coalition become too uneasy about the chances of an agreement and succeeded in convincing the Western Powers to back off from their firm stand on access, for example, then Moscow would find itself in a more favorable position. The GDR's seeming eagerness to print the text was an indication that East Berlin may have entertained a similar idea.

It is entirely possible that the Soviet leak scheme was undertaken with an eye toward the upcoming (March 30-April 9) 24th Party Congress. The draft proposal itself, offering few major concessions to the West and thus taking the hard line of Soviet officials not anxious for a Berlin deal, might have been employed to bolster the position of accord proponents as solid evidence that no one intended to give away the store. Allied rejection of the draft, the result of the absence of provisions for guaranteed access, could be cited as a manifestation of resolve, i.e., Western unwillingness to settle for anything less than the "three essentials." Furthermore, advocates of a Berlin agreement--by this time including Premier Kosygin and Party Secretary Leonid Brezhnev--could point out that sufficient efforts, the last being the leak, had been made to detach the West Germans from their allies. Attempts had been carried out; probes had met resistance. Moscow had lost a round. Kremlin leaders favoring new initiatives toward the West seemed to have covered their domestic flanks and were thus in position to strike a deal.

In late April there was again talk of U.S.-FRG disagreements. Various West German magazines, all critical of Brandt's *Ostpolitik*, published several confidential correspondences of the FRG's ambassador to Washington, Rolf Pauls, who had protested Bahr's maneuvering in the U.S. to the Chancellor. Having been dispatched to Washington in April for consultations on Berlin, Bahr it seemed had been offering U.S. officials his own suggestions, to which Pauls was not privy, on how to expedite proceedings on Berlin. Bahr, Pauls suggested, succeeded once again in raising American suspicions of Bonn, by encouraging for example U.S. consent to the establishment of a Soviet consulate general in West Berlin, something Moscow was keen upon, but Washington rejected.[14] Apparently Bahr had been asserting that a Soviet consulate general would not affect the status of the city. Accusing Bahr of exceeding his instructions, Pauls suggested also that the Chancellor's envoy was "going it alone."[15] The controversy was quickly blown out of proportion and did leave a few scars. U.S. apprehensions about Brandt's government were hardly assuaged. Britain and France became dismayed at having been excluded from discussions on an issue in which they had a good deal at stake. Above all, the opposition's campaign against the SPD-FDP coalition heated up and the *Ostpolitik* was subjected to increasing domestic criticism. The opposition press went so far on occasion as to label Bahr a tool of the Kremlin and to charge the government with perfidiousness as well as the "selling out of Berlin."[16]

Soviet willingness--established early in the quadrilateral talks--to facilitate the flow of inter-German traffic to and from West Berlin, with the attendant underwriting of a German traffic accord, represented without doubt a breakthrough in itself since Moscow implicitly acquiesced to inducing its East German ally to allow "Zugang." A quantum leap was necessary, however, between Soviet flexibility on this matter and an outright access guarantee, the absence of which would ensure the breakdown of Berlin negotiations.

Intrinsic to the issue of FRG presence in West Berlin was the representation of West Berliners abroad. Prior to 1971 the East Bloc insisted the FRG had in effect no authority to represent West Berliners. During the Berlin discussions, Bonn remained obdurate: denial of diplomatic representation was tantamount to discrimination against two million people and had to be eliminated in an agreement. Scheel affirmed FRG representation of West Berliners to be a matter of right as well as a crucial aspect of cultural, economic and social ties between West Berlin and the FRG.

In spite of vagueness, producing lingering doubts about the Soviet position, the draft proposal of March 16 appeared to go a long way in accommodating Bonn on "Zuordnung." It was the first time any such concessions had been put in writing; prior to this, Moscow had usually maintained that the FRG was under no circumstances entitled to represent West Berliners or to speak abroad in their behalf in any way. According to the Soviet argument, the Western Powers should be completely responsible for West Berliners. It did not behoove the Allies to take this task upon themselves; besides, Bonn opposed the idea. Berlin's long-term viability required a direct affiliation of its inhabitants with West Germany, of which the former was certainly a *de facto* part. West Germans of all political colorings were understandably concerned about the feasibility of a Berlin arrangement and insisted upon representing those Germans they judged themselves authorized and able to. It should not be forgotten that Bonn is still, theoretically at least, entitled constitutionally to act in behalf of all Germans. If Brandt and Scheel were committed to improving the lot of Germans in the East Bloc countries, they had yet greater cause to take responsibility for West Berliners. Scheel suggests that Bonn did not completely trust its allies on the question of representation, fearing political/diplomatic discrimination against West Berliners would continue in the event Bonn were not in charge. What is more, in light of growing domestic criticism, the coalition would be even more avid to present evidence of improvement in the West Berliners' conditions.

Had Moscow already accepted the principles of "Zutritt" and "Zuordnung" when it submitted its March draft proposal to its interlocutors? The evidence is inadequate and real movement on Berlin issues did not come until the

24th Soviet Party Congress. Nevertheless, the rejoinder Valentin Falin, who later became ambassador to Bonn, put forward publicly around the time of the proposal's submission is instructive about the question of FRG presence. If Bonn considered its ties with West Berlin to be an accepted result of the Second World War, the GDR and the Soviet Union, in the same vein, regard East German claims of sovereignty and assertions of such sovereignty, e.g., transit-route harassment, also to be post-war facts.[17] Falin then posited that the GDR would guarantee free access to West Berlin if the FRG would cease "violating" East German "sovereignty"; that is, an East Bloc guarantee would be contingent upon a decrease in the "demonstrative" FRG presence in West Berlin. Thus, Falin hinted at what the Soviet Union could accept in negotiations: a face-saving device for the GDR, allowing it to regulate non-Allied traffic across its territory as if it enjoyed complete sovereignty (that it does exercise such sovereignty should not be lost on observers). The GDR should maintain control of border checkpoints, a function it had been carrying out for years, and certain German-German traffic arrangements would be worked out following a sweeping quadripartite bargain on Berlin.

The West German weekly, *Der Spiegel*, explained some of the choices for Bonn: if there were to be guaranteed access and a modicum of Soviet-sanctioned West German ties to Berlin, then Bonn must be prepared to reduce demonstrative presence that the GDR condemned as being "dangerously provocative."[18] In assessing Falin's statement, *Die Frankfurter Rundschau* deduced that a demonstrative presence, such as parliamentary meetings and elections in West Berlin, would no longer be necessary, if the Soviet Union were prepared officially to accept the eminently more important economic, social and political ties. Moreover, what the Soviet Union was requiring of the FRG was not much apart from what the Western Powers had already effected with the suspension of Articles 23 and 144 (2) of the Basic Law, namely, a West German renunciation of claims to sovereignty in Berlin.

The SPD-FDP coalition then adopted a somewhat more conciliatory position on the question of demonstrative FRG presence, clarifying their standpoint with what was to become a leitmotif of the *Ostpolitik*: the FRG was actually giving away nothing which had not been lost decades ago. But the matter did not stop there. Parliamentary support for the coalition continued to erode. Critics of the *Ostpolitik* were becoming more voiceful and the first coalition defections to the opposition in the *Bundestag* had already taken place in June 1970.[19]

The opposition underscored the fact that East Berlin's *de facto* incorporation into the GDR had been realized with the consent, indeed the encouragement of the Soviet Union, and insisted that the West was completely justified abetting the extension of FRG authority in West Berlin.[20] Since the GDR continued to assert that East Berlin was the capital of their country, the FRG should not hesitate to engage in any sort of political activity in West Berlin it wished.

To such criticism the Bonn coalition had few answers; its political future as well as that of West Berlin were largely in Allied hands. It could only wait and encourage its allies to move forward on negotiations. Berlin realities were, however, clear to see. During the most difficult phase of the negotiations--between January and April 1971--the GDR repeatedly displayed its ability to exercise its "sovereign rights" on the transit routes, harassing travelers and causing traffic jams, doubtless with the full moral support of the Soviet Union. On access matters the Soviet Union held most of the trump cards. *Zugang* was crucial to the very existence of West Berlin, while there was precious little the Allies could do about the situation in East Berlin, the annexation of which was an accomplished fact.

By April 1971 a significant reduction in "demonstrative" FRG presence in West Berlin had ceased being a subject of controversy within the Bonn coalition. With Allied urging, the Foreign Office assented to such positive steps, but there was the practical need of selling the position to the West German public. Amidst ringing parliamentary opposition and rightist publication charges of knuckling under to Moscow pressure, an article entitled "Schwierigkeiten einer Berlinregelung" (Difficulties of a Berlin Settlement) appeared in the FDP monthly, *Liberal*.[21] Written by Wieland Deutschland--allegedly a pseudonym for high officials in the West German Foreign Office--the article examined the question of FRG ties to West Berlin and outlined the difficulties in the current quadripartite negotiations.[22] It explained why some concessions were necessary, hence preparing the FDP constituency and the general public for the possible outcome of negotiations. The author reiterated in detail the Bonn government's fundamental argument about the limitations of FRG authority in Berlin. Observing that the Soviet Union was prepared to make some far-reaching concessions, he suggested that West

Germans and their allies should be less concerned about
alleged legal positions (vermeintliche Rechtspositionen)
than about practical matters of access and ties.[23]

The Soviet Party Congress proved to be a watershed.
Sweeping decisions, whose effects already became visible
the following month, were ratified and announced in April.
A sort of diplomatic triad emerged consisting of a
preparedness to make the necessary concessions for a
breakthrough in Berlin negotiations, a new prescription for
SALT, and an initiative on the reduction of conventional
forces in Europe. On Berlin the Kremlin had drawn the
logical conclusions from recent developments: the Allies
were not going to back down under any circumstances from
their resolute position on access and original rights; the
FRG remained firmly in the Western camp and, despite some
Alliance squabbling, was not to be pried loose on Berlin.
Finally, East German intransigence was a problem that had
to be handled. If Moscow wanted a Berlin accord, it would
have to formulate policies according to these realities.
If it failed to do so, Kissinger would stall and play the
waiting game.

The Party Congress merely rubber-stamped a decision
the Kremlin had already reached on Berlin. How long before
the convening of the Party Congress the Soviet leadership
decided to accommodate the Allies can now be surmised
through Kissinger's disclosures about the channel.
According to Kissinger, Dobrynin stated in a February 10
meeting that the Soviets would in effect accept
responsibility for access.[24] A face-saving device was
provided to the GDR, whereby Moscow would issue a
unilateral declaration outlining its understanding of the
East German position on access.[25] The Soviets and the East
Germans could thereafter come forward in complete agreement
on Berlin matters; what Moscow had in mind was to lean on
East Berlin to adopt as its own whatever position its
senior ally determined to be appropriate. How Moscow was
to compel the GDR was not to be seen until after the Party
Congress. That the Kremlin made an offer on access the
second week in February representing the major breakthrough
in the Berlin negotiations meant the Soviet March 26 draft
proposal was probably a red herring. Presumably, Moscow
had already accepted large parts of the February 5 Allied
proposal one week after its submission, almost certainly
without the knowledge of the participants in the
quadrilateral discussions. Kissinger suggests the Soviet
March proposal might have been either a sop to Moscow
hardliners or evidence to the bureaucracy that more on

Berlin was not to be attained.[26] When Dobrynin requested
in the back-channel on March 15 additional concessions on
FRG presence in the Western sectors and Kissinger balked,
saying the U.S. would not go beyond the Allied position as
stated in the February draft, the Soviet ambassador
immediately backed down. Kissinger cites this retreat as a
clue to Moscow's eagerness for a treaty.[27]

On February 22, Dobrynin filed for detailed access
procedures which Moscow would examine, this almost six
weeks prior to a leaked Soviet proposal not even consenting
to the principle of access. In late March, despite the
Soviet draft proposal, Kissinger must have strongly
suspected that an auspicious accord was all but in the
bag.[28] Furthermore, Kissinger had several channels working
at once. In April he met with Bahr in Vermont to discuss
specific circumstances of the negotiations. Bahr
encouraged both sides to deemphasize legal positions as
much as possible and to concentrate on solving practical
difficulties--a notion, though hardly profound, Kissinger
somewhat surprisingly described as an "ingenious
suggestion."[29] Apparently a bit skeptical of Bahr's
trustworthiness, Kissinger made U.S. acceptance of this
approach contingent upon Brandt's personal endorsement.[30]
That Dobrynin immediately assented to Bahr's negotiating
concept without any consultation with Moscow was a sure
indication the wily Soviet ambassador was already privy to
it, increasing suspicions of Bahr's having "gone it alone"
at times, as Pauls had described. It was not impossible
that Bahr had his own "channels."[31]

Beginning on May 10, Falin (now Soviet ambassador to
Bonn), Bahr and Rush held meetings in Bonn that were to
serve as yet another channel for Kissinger and Dobrynin,
who broke up any logjams the Bonn mediators encountered.
Kissinger curbed any attempts by Bahr to withhold from
Britain and France information about the group's
proceedings. In this forum many details of access
arrangements were worked out. Conspicuously absent from
any of the presently-known channels was the GDR, and it is
almost incredible that in at least one forum the FRG was
negotiating as an apparent equal on quadripartite matters
that were, theoretically at least, not its business,
discussing provisions of a treaty to which it would not be
a party. It is somewhat of a pity that Kissinger does not
elaborate upon how he pulled off such a scheme.

Soviet ability to coordinate its bargaining efforts
with the GDR was greatly facilitated by the removal of
Ulbricht from the political scene. Citing health reasons,

Ulbricht stepped down from his major posts on May 3; that the Kremlin was keen to rid itself of Ulbricht is not a matter of much serious dispute.[32] Bark's argument as to the dubiousness of Ulbricht's fall representing a turning point in negotiations is somewhat misleading.[33] While breakthroughs came of course when all sides concurred on basic issues, such breakthroughs were probably achieved, as now can be determined, earlier than previously thought. However, there can be little doubt about Ulbricht's intransigence. He opposed an agreement of any kind. Moscow perceived the plain truth that Ulbricht would stand in its way; it would have to dispose of the East German party boss prior to reaching an accord. Although it is not possible to determine when the Kremlin decided for certain upon the untenability of Ulbricht's position, crucial to the CPSU Congress's resolution on a Berlin treaty was the elimination of the "Ulbricht problem."

The new SED chief, Erich Honecker, expressed his full support for the Soviet position on Berlin, be that what it may. Two weeks after Honecker's ascension to power, he and Stoph journeyed to Moscow for consultation with the Kremlin leaders. Following the meeting, the two East German strong men publicly confirmed "that an understanding on the question of Berlin would meet the interests of all parties to the negotiations and would remove the grounds for disputes and conflicts in this region."[34] At the 8th SED Congress in June, Honecker enthusiastically lauded the progress made in the quadripartite discussions, pledging his complete backing of the agreement coming out of them. The East Germans were on board.

According to Kissinger, the primary "working group" from May until August that forged the final, intricate technicalities of the treaty was the Falin, Rush, Bahr channel in Bonn, not the quadrilateral forum in Berlin. Few appeared aware of this arrangement until the publication of Kissinger's memoirs, even though it was Bahr who announced a consensus on the structure of an accord on May 20.[35]

Minor friction in the Bonn channel on a matter of access procedure the first week in June caused Gromyko to begin getting edgy, lest there be a breakdown in the final stages of the negotiations. Hoping to assure the expeditious conclusion of an agreement, the Soviet foreign minister devised his own version of a "mini-Junktim"--a move Kissinger considered tantamount to blackmail--by making final accord on the upcoming U.S.-Soviet summit contingent upon the completion of the Berlin agreement.

Though Gromyko's motives were not wholly apparent, his timing could not have been less propitious and the scheme backfired.[36] Kissinger had a high trump up his sleeve and he was looking for an occasion to play it. Once he realized the summit was not going to take place in the fall of 1971 in any event, Kissinger ordered Rush, who was himself becoming impatient, to stall the process until July 15. On that day Kissinger's trip to China was announced.

Reporting from Bonn, Bahr mentioned that the Russians had reacted somewhat emotionally.[37] Well they might have; the initial response in the Kremlin could not have been any less passionate. The Soviets' worst fears had been confirmed. A salient motivation on the Kremlin's part for exploring the possibilities of a Berlin settlement now proved to have been justified. Any lingering doubts of Soviet officials about the desirability of a Berlin deal must have quickly faded. Gromyko was keener than ever on the settlement and became concerned, lest Kissinger decide upon the virtues of stonewalling.[38]

Nine days after Kissinger gave Rush the green light for moving forward in the Bonn forum, the latter sent the following communiqué through the White House back-channel:

A draft of the tentative agreement is enclosed and it is still difficult for me to believe that it is as favorable as it is. It is still subject to the final approval of you, Gromyko and Brandt respectively . . . We yesterday secured from Falin practically everything that we wanted.[39]

What had been the major accomplishments? In Washington's view, first and foremost, the Soviet Union backed off from its prior refusal to regard Berlin access as quadripartite business. In accepting the access problem as international--as opposed to domestic--the Soviet Union conceded its responsibilities within the framework of quadrilateral accords and thereby implicitly recognized the continued quadripartite status of Berlin. Rush suggests Soviet consent on this point to have been the quintessential step toward agreement.

Signaling as early as February 1971 through the back-channel its willingness to offer the West an auspicious bargain, the Kremlin by May had conceded to:

1. Accept existing "ties" between West Berlin and the FRG.

2. Allow the FRG to represent West Berliners abroad, thereby ending all vestiges of discrimination.
3. Drop its demands for the elimination of all FRG institutions and officials from West Berlin in light of Bonn's flexibility on "demonstrative presence" and of its explicit respect for the GDR.
4. Guarantee free overland access to and from the city.
5. Permit West Berlin's inclusion in FRG non-military treaties.[40]

The last difficulty encountered in the negotiations concerned the Soviet demand for a consulate general in West Berlin. Although the exact Soviet motives for maintaining such a diplomatic office have never been clear, the issue was from the beginning one impinging upon the quadripartite status of the city. The U.S. speculated that the Soviet Union would proffer the consulate as evidence of quadripartite control only in West Berlin, rendering a *coup de grâce* to the concept of greater Berlin. The existence of a Soviet general-consulate in West Berlin, according to the U.S. argument, could have undermined the Western position and weakened some of the Soviet concessions on Berlin, since the Soviet Union would thereafter have two consulates--in the East and in the West--while the Allies would have but one.

But there are several other points to be made. The consulate could serve to strengthen Soviet recognition of West Berlin's ties to the FRG.[41] The Allies could henceforth argue that the Soviet Union's consulate testifies to its preparedness to accept an FRG presence as well as Allied rights in Berlin. Furthermore, if the Western Powers made clear that such a consulate could be established only with their explicit permission and operated only under their auspices, this would then be evidence of the absence of Soviet original rights in the Western sectors and thus a tacit confirmation of quadripartite status.[42]

Later developments would show the U.S. objections to be unfounded. Following the establishment of full diplomatic relations between the Western Powers and the GDR, the U.S., France and Great Britain all opened consulates in East Berlin, though they refuse to recognize East Berlin as the capital of the GDR. Reference in the 1971 Quadripartite Agreement only to the "relevant area" manifests the continuing differences in interpretation of the exact meaning of the agreement. The existence of a Soviet consulate in West Berlin hardly impinges upon the status of the city; the consulate is forbidden to address any quadripartite matters. Of course, one cannot openly discuss what is to be presumed about Soviet consulate personnel: that most are in the employment of the KGB. But such a venerated distinction does not usually disqualify Soviet officials from serving in diplomatic posts.

NOTES

1. "Allgemeiner Deutscher Nachrichtendienst," 10 and 11 January 1970; *Der Spiegel*, April 6, 1970; *Der Spiegel*, Feb. 1, 1971.
2. See: Appendix I of Catudal, *The Diplomacy of the Quadripartite Agreement on Berlin*, pp. 277-80.
3. The clause represented a rather unusual "concession" in that it also upheld the continued validity of Western prerogative in Berlin. See: Appendix I, ibid.
4. There can be little doubt that many Bonn officials felt that the Western Powers, interested in an access guarantee and a confirmation of their prerogative, cared little about other aspects of the Berlin problem. See: Baring, op. cit., pp. 328-31.
5. Indeed, East Berliners have been prosecuted in East German courts and imprisoned for demanding rights they might theoretically possess on the basis of the quadripartite status of greater Berlin. One of the most famous cases has been that of Nico Hübner, an East Berliner who refused to serve in the army of the GDR, citing the "demilitarization" of Berlin. See: *Europa-Archiv*, Vol. 33, No. 15 (July, 1978), p. 151; *Der Spiegel*, July 3, 1978, pp. 65-68, and Brandt, *People and Politics The Years 1960-1975*, pp. 101-103.
6. Catudal, *The Diplomacy of the Quadripartite Agreement on Berlin*, p. 149.
7. See: *Der Spiegel*, Feb. 15, 1971; *Frankfurter Allgemeine Zeitung*, Feb. 15, 1971.
8. *Der Spiegel*, Feb. 8 and Feb. 22, 1971.
9. See: *German Press Review* (Washington, D.C.: Press Office of the Embassy of the FRG), Feb. 10, 1971; *Frankfurter Allgemeine Zeitung*, Feb. 26, 1971.
10. See: Appendix I of Catudal, *The Diplomacy of the Quadripartite Agreement on Berlin*, pp. 277-80.

11. Kenneth Rush, "Berlin: The Four-Power Agreement" in *Current Foreign Policy* (Washington, D.C.: Department of State, GPO, 1971), p. 4.

12. In Annex IV the Soviet draft proposal did appear explicitly to accept at least some Allied rights and responsibilities in Berlin: *Der Spiegel*, April 19, 1971.

13. *Der Spiegel*, April 19, 1971.

14. By this time, neither U.S. skepticism nor expressions of concern to Bahr were new. See: Baring, pp. 320-21; *Der Spiegel*, Sept. 20, 1971. Some held the establishment of the Soviet consulate general in West Berlin to be a face-saver the West could grant without much difficulty. Bahr encouraged the U.S. to accept the consulate as a means for moving the talks along.

15. Catudal, *The Diplomacy of the Quadripartite Agreement on Berlin*, pp. 165-66.

16. For descriptions of the growing parliamentary opposition to Brandt's government, see: Baring, pp. 396-403, 405-409; *German Press Review*, Aug. 4, 1971.

17. *Frankfurter Allgemeine Zeitung*, March 19, 20 and 30, 1971; *Der Spiegel*, April 5, 1971.

18. *Der Spiegel*, April 5, 1971 and June 14, 1971.

19. Baring discusses the results of the defections, pp. 297-301, 396-403.

20. *Frankfurter Allgemeine Zeitung*, Feb. 2, 1971; *Der Spiegel*, June 14, 1971.

21. Wieland Deutsch, "Schwierigkeiten einer Berlinregelung," *Liberal*, May 1971; *Der Spiegel*, June 14, 1971.

22. *Der Spiegel*, June 14, 1971.

23. Rolf Zundel, "Wieland Deutsch oder Boris Russ?" *Die Zeit*, June 22, 1971; Erich Roper, "Zur Rechtslage Berlin," *Deutschland-Archiv*, Vol. 28, No. 8 (1971), pp. 801-804; Jens Hacker, "Der neue Rechtsstatus für West-Berlin," *Die Politische Meinung*, No. 142 (1972), pp. 78-94.

24. Kissinger, *White House Years*, pp. 825-26. Kissinger said Dobrynin's offer sounded like "a distinct possibility," describing it as precisely the Western "fallback position." Western lack of room for maneuver in the negotiations is evidenced in the minute difference between the "maximum" position as submitted in the February 5 proposal and the "fallback."

25. Ibid., p. 826.

26. Dobrynin did, however, submit the March 26 draft proposal to Kissinger in the back-channel on March 18, raising the eventuality that Moscow was reneging on most of its concessions on access. Kissinger responded with a set

of principles on Berlin, anticipating that Dobrynin would be back with what the U.S. wanted.

27. Ibid.

28. Kissinger mentions on several occasions the eagerness he detected in Soviet officials; this encouraged him to push for a deal, Kissinger, *White House Years*, pp. 414-16, 531-32, 826-28. He could not have foreseen the removal of Ulbricht in May or known what the new foreign policy initiatives emerging from the 24th Party Congress would have been.

29. Ibid., p. 828.

30. U.S. officials had their differences with Bahr. With some justification, Kissinger might have harbored suspicions of him. See: Kissinger, *White House Years*, pp. 411-12; also: Walter F. Hahn, "West Germany's Ostpolitik: The Grand Design of Egon Bahr," op. cit., pp. 859-80; "Der Mann neben Willy Brandt," *Die Frankfurter Rundschau*, Aug. 27, 1971; Catudal, *The Diplomacy of the Quadripartite Agreement on Berlin*, pp. 164-66.

31. Kissinger, *White House Years*, pp. 830-31.

32. Croan, *East Germany: The Soviet Connection*, p. 28. Ulbricht became at times pert with Soviet leaders, saying publicly for example at the 24th CPSU Congress just prior to his fall that "the Soviet comrades also had things to learn," after emphasizing his acquaintance with Lenin.

33. Bark, op. cit., p. 87; for newspaper editorials, see: Chalmers Roberts, "Soviet Move on Berlin Impasse is Expected," *Washington Post*, May 25, 1971; Ernst-Ulrich Fromm, "Moskau baut seine deutschen Gefolgsleute aus Ostberlin auf," *Die Welt*, July 12, 1971. There is some discussion of when Moscow decided to rid itself of Ulbricht. Certainly some Kremlin officials were already very impatient with him in early 1970. For discussions, see: Childs, *The GDR: Moscow's German Ally*, pp. 83-84; Gerhard Wettig, *Community and Conflict in the Socialist Camp* (London: Allen and Unwin, 1975), pp. 94-96; Bernd Weber, "Ideologiewandel von Ulbricht zu Honecker," *Aussenpolitik*, Vol. 23 (March 1972), pp. 159-67; Gregory A. Flynn, "The Fall of Ulbricht: A Lesson in Soviet Bloc Diplomacy," unpublished M.A. thesis, Fletcher School of Law and Diplomacy, 1972; *Der Spiegel*, June 28, 1971.

34. Quoted in Bark, op. cit., p. 87.

35. There was a concurrent announcement of a SALT breakthrough, Kissinger, *White House Years*, p. 829.

36. Ibid.

37. Some analysts speculated that the opening to Peking would have very adverse effects upon U.S.-Soviet

relations; Kissinger insists the opposite to have been the case, *White House Years*, p. 830.

38. Kissinger cites the example of the Berlin accord as the first major success of the linkage strategy. SALT and Berlin were kept "in tandem" and breakthroughs were made in both areas, *White House Years*, p. 833.

39. Ibid., p. 830.

40. *Der Tagesspiegel*, April 16, 1971; *Frankfurter Allgemeine Zeitung*, May 20 and 22, 1971.

41. Catudal, *The Diplomacy of the Quadripartite Agreement on Berlin*, p. 164; Schiedermair, op. cit., pp. 127-130.

42. Bark, op. cit., pp. 90-92.

12
Parliamentary Opposition to the *Ostpolitik*

By the beginning of 1972 the SPD-FDP coalition was in serious political difficulty as domestic controversy concerning the ratification of the Moscow and Warsaw treaties heated up. As sensitive inter-German negotiations for the implementation of the Berlin Agreement and on the normalization of relations between the German states were being carried on, the coalition's razor-thin majority in the *Bundestag* was eroding. The ratification debate taking shape was a part of a broader challenge to the substance of, but above all, to the speed of the *Ostpolitik*. Much was on the line, not least of which was the future of Brandt's government. If the Bonn-Moscow Treaty were not ratified, the *Ostpolitik* would stop dead in its tracks and the FRG would be viewed as being unable to deliver on an accord. Lack of parliamentary consensus on such an important issue as the ratification of the Eastern agreements would be the result of a loss of a workable *Bundestag* majority with the subsequent toppling of Brandt. In the wake of such occurrences, East Berlin would likely prove stubborn in the follow-up discussions to the Quadripartite Agreement, causing delays, and quite possibly, a prolonged breakdown. There were likely few contingencies on either side for such an eventuality, since all four negotiating partners assumed that Bonn and East Berlin would conclude an agreement on various practical matters, effecting specific provisions with a minimum of friction. Had either side backed out, the Quadripartite Agreement may not have gone into effect. A new government in Bonn would have required a good deal of time to formulate its position on issues and might have refused to ratify the Bonn-Moscow Treaty. For all the disagreements and mistrust between the U.S. and the FRG in 1970, such a

development, i.e., a different West German political
constellation, would have necessitated a reappraisal of
some aspects of U.S. policy, now partially geared to
Brandt's *Ostpolitik*.

The CDU/CSU opened its offensive against the Bonn-
Moscow Treaty at the time of the accord's initialing in
1970. In an August position paper, the opposition outlined
its difficulties with the provisions.

1. The right of the Germans to self-determination is
   jeopardized by the Moscow Treaty.
2. The determination of borders must remain reserved for
   a peace treaty.
3. The Moscow Treaty does not yield concrete improvements
   in intra-German relations; freedom of movement for
   people, ideas, and opinions has yet to be guaranteed.
4. The Moscow Treaty does not contain any constructive
   elements paving the way to a better order of peace in
   Europe.
5. The German government's policy underlying this treaty
   threatens the foundations of Western integration and
   alliance policy.
6. The Moscow Treaty has the effect of raising the
   international status of the GDR toward recognition
   under international law.
7. The treaty commitments are imbalanced, with one-sided
   consideration given to the interests of the Soviet
   Union.
8. The Moscow Treaty fails to clarify the issue of
   preserving a free Berlin.[1]

The first substantial barrier the coalition confronted
was on a procedural matter in the upper house, the
Bundesrat. Rejecting the coalition's timetable of six
weeks for the first reading of the treaty proposals, the
conservative CDU/CSU opposition, enjoying a slight majority
in the *Bundesrat*, lengthened the parliamentary agenda
considerably. The first reading would thus not take place
until late February 1972, with the second and third not
coming until May. In the interim, it was hoped, the
coalition would lose its majority in the *Bundestag*; the
opposition supposed that the longer debate went on, the
stronger its position would become.

In January 1972 the opposition formally challenged the
constitutionality of both the Eastern treaties in the
Bundesrat legal committee. Alleging the renunciation-of-
force pact and the guarantee of Poland's territorial

integrity to have constituted a recognition of an unacceptable status-quo, the opposition argued that the treaties ran counter to the reunification proviso of the Basic Law. Moreover, since the *Bundesrat* has an absolute veto over legislation affecting the boundaries and territory of German states, the opposition claimed the treaties would fall into that category of legislation subject to such a veto.

Before Scheel's trip to Moscow in 1970 for the final negotiation of the renunciation-of-force pact with the Soviet Union, the coalition had closely examined the constitutionality of the accord and thus had a ready answer to the opposition's charges in the *Bundesrat*. According to the Bonn working group, the treaty with Moscow was in accordance with the Basic Law, provided two conditions were met.[2] First, the FRG would have to confirm the German Option (stating the continued reunification mandate) in writing before the signing of the treaty. Second, the parliamentary ratification of the Bonn-Moscow Treaty would be contingent upon the success of a Berlin settlement: the "Junktim" preceding the signing. Since both stipulations had been followed, the coalition presented a well-founded argument in the *Bundesrat* legal committee. Eventually the CDU/CSU lost on both counts, when the committee ruled the Eastern treaties to be not unconstitutional and not liable to absolute *Bundesrat* veto.

In the first *Bundesrat* reading in February, however, the plenum passed a resolution specifying twelve opposition objections to the treaties.[3] Among the charges, the resolution suggested that the accords might preclude German reunification, allowed for Soviet interference in West German domestic affairs, and did not provide for an absolute Soviet renunciation of the right of intervention under U.N. Charter Articles 53 and 107. Perhaps most disconcerting for the coalition was that the Quadripartite Agreement was deemed "unsatisfactory."[4]

The judgment of the upper house represented a significant political defeat for the coalition. Although the legal committee had declared the *Bundesrat* unable to torpedo the Eastern treaties par veto, the resolution constituting the "official opinion" of the upper house clearly cast doubt upon the entire foreign political enterprise of the coalition.[5] Challenging nearly every aspect of the accords, the majority view of the upper house seemed at least to imply that the Western Powers had reached an agreement with the Kremlin not in the West German interest.

Conservative opponents fell into various categories within the rubric of two basic groups: adversaries to the *Ostpolitik* in principle and conservative critics.[6] The former consisted primarily of CSU members and of some rightist CDU elements opposing political deals with the East Bloc in general, who labeled the *Ostpolitik* a sell-out to the Soviet Union.[7] This group tended to see a dire threat to the FRG both from abroad and from evolving socialism within its borders. Unwilling to consent to accords with the East in the early 1970s under most circumstances, these irreconcilables refused support to any program for modifying the situation in the East.

Moderate CDU officials such as former Foreign Minister Gerhard Schröder and Richard von Weizsäcker made up the latter group, which, while not against the idea of the *Ostpolitik*, took exception with certain aspects of SPD-FDP policies, such as for instance, the visible urgency of the coalition, the purported dearth of advantages for the FRG, the possible difficulties for the Alliance and with allies.[8] Certainly more balanced, the "conservative critics" have since endorsed the *Ostpolitik*, at least in part; most would agree with Brandt's initial point of departure that there is no real alternative to recognizing realities. Prior to the ratification debate, von Weizsäcker began warning of the possibility of the Soviet Union opening rifts within the Atlantic community or of an impending breakdown in the West German foreign policy consensus coming in the wake of a bitter domestic debate.

As early as June 1970--before the signing of the Bonn-Moscow Treaty--the coalition faced its first defection crisis. In protest against the *Ostpolitik*, several members of the FDP, mostly from the "lost" Eastern territories of Germany, threatened to leave their party and join the CDU. This incident was a precursor of what would confront the coalition during the ratification controversy. CDU/CSU objections to the Eastern treaties were shared by many FDP parliamentarians. In regard to the Bonn-Warsaw Treaty, the CDU/CSU called for the following:

1. Creation of a *modus vivendi* based on the Oder-Neisse line and subject to a settlement by peace treaty for all of Germany.
2. Renunciation of the threat or use of force.
3. Binding and concrete arrangements for safeguarding the human rights of persons and groups, in particular the right to free movement and unimpeded contacts with relatives.

4. Creation of a German-Polish youth organization.
5. Greater exchange in the economic, cultural, and scientific fields.
6. Institution of a German-Polish chamber of commerce.
7. Establishment of full diplomatic relations with the inclusion of West Berlin.[9]

The coalition had 254 of 496 seats in the *Bundestag* at the beginning of June 1970, a thin majority of five. Were seven representatives willing to vote with the opposition, then the CDU/CSU would have been in the position to carry through on a constructive vote of no-confidence and unseat Brandt.[10] On June 17 two prominent members of the FDP, Erich Mende and Siegfried Zoglmann, established a fronde against party leader Scheel called *National-Liberale Aktion* in an effort to inveigle other party members to withdraw support from the Bonn coalition. The move was in the main unsuccessful and the FDP did not split on the issue of support for Brandt's government. In October three FDP parliamentarians, Mende, Zoglmann and Heinz Starke defected to the CDU. The coalition retained 251 seats until the occasionally bitter ratification debate of 1972.

By March 1972 it appeared that the treaty legislation was in serious trouble. One SPD representative, albeit an opponent of the pacts and one whose vote the coalition could not have counted on anyway, Herbert Hupka, joined the ranks of the CDU. Then two members of the FDP, Gerhard Kienbaum and Knut von Kühlmann-Stumm, expressed publicly their reservations with the treaties, and the coalition leaders had reason to suspect that other backbenchers in the *Bundestag* were of like mind. Assuming as most in Bonn at the time did that several FDP parliamentarians would defect, the newly-chosen opposition leader, Rainer Barzel, suggested on March 10 the possibility of a constructive vote of no-confidence against Brandt. Barzel hoped to take the reins of government with a majority fleshed out by those who had turned their backs on the coalition.

Previous to these dire auguries for the Bonn government there was little evidence of Moscow's having seriously doubted ratification of the Eastern treaties. From the viewpoint of many Kremlin officials, the FRG and the West had received such a bargain with the Bonn-Moscow Treaty, but above all with the Quadripartite Agreement, that few FRG parliamentarians would be so imprudent as to turn down the deal. Faced with the likelihood of rejection as well as a new conservative government in Bonn, Kremlin leaders began visibly to fret. True to form they opened up with bullying tactics, threatening the FRG with all sorts of redoubtable consequences such as a "return to the Cold War," should the treaties not be ratified. A Soviet official in West Berlin was even quoted as saying in regard to the eventuality of treaty legislation failure: "Then everything would be destroyed, everything we have accomplished so far. Then a Cold War would break out, and a hot one might be possible."[11] Doubtless the official was not speaking without prior approval from Moscow.

The Soviet Union was, however, forthcoming with positive gestures, designed at least in part to bolster Brandt's position domestically. First, Moscow expressed its willingness to conclude a new trade agreement with Bonn, granting the FRG the right to represent West Berlin. Second, and certainly more significant, was a GDR action at Kremlin behest to permit West Berliners to visit East Berlin and the GDR, in effect executing the procedures specified in the Quadripartite Agreement but not yet rendered official through inter-German accord. The visiting privileges, extended first during the Easter holidays at the end of March and again seven weeks later, were utilized by over 600,000 people.[12] Witnessing this tangible result of the *Ostpolitik* almost without precedent, many West Germans were naturally more favorably disposed to coalition policies. Never before had so many Westerners traveled to East Berlin and the GDR at any one time; Moscow demonstrated it could deliver.

Polls in the FRG in 1972 showed increasing popular support for the *Ostpolitik*, indicating that the parliamentary opposition was out of step with public opinion. In April 1972, for instance, 65 percent of the West Berliners viewed the Quadripartite Agreement as "satisfactory" or "very satisfactory," while 30 percent expressed disapproval.[13] 60 percent of the West Berlin population favored parliamentary ratification of the Eastern treaties.[14] Within the FRG in April, 57 percent considered the treaties to be "serving German interests" and 61 percent favored the *Ostpolitik* generally.[15]

Equally noteworthy was a visible upward trend in public endorsement of coalition policies. For instance, in October 1971, only 53 percent of the FRG's population supported the *Ostpolitik*, and in the previous summer, but 42 percent.[16] Thus public endorsement of Bonn's course seemed to be in an inverse relationship to parliamentary support. The CDU/CSU did not appear to give much heed to opinion surveys.

The parliamentary maneuver the opposition planned had

not previously been attempted at the national level, although it had twice succeeded in the state of North-Rhine Westphalia.[17] The outcome of the elections in Baden-Wurttemberg on April 23, as well as the defection of yet another FDP member of the *Bundestag*, strengthened Barzel's hand and convinced him of the potential success of the no-confidence vote. Voices in the opposition were offering the state elections in Baden-Wurttemberg--which the CDU won by its usual convincing margin--as a sort of preliminary referendum on the *Ostpolitik* that would be the primary issue in nationwide elections.

What policies the opposition would follow in the event they prevailed in the constructive no-confidence procedure were less discernible than their unconcealed objections to the treaty legislation, the Quadripartite Agreement, and the *Ostpolitik* in general. Officially the opposition demanded a renegotiation of the treaties with Moscow and Warsaw. Also desirable from the opposition's viewpoint was a more explicit Soviet statement on eventual German reunification and the compatibility of the Eastern treaties with it. There were also the "irreconcilables" in the CDU/CSU who likely would have opposed--at the time at least--any accord with the Soviet Union short of one breathtakingly favorable to Bonn. The question whether the party would be able to maintain its ranks and successfully renegotiate certain aspects of agreements, especially in chorus with allies determined to improve relations with the East Bloc, was an open one. Few then or now examined the possibilities for the CDU/CSU challenging the Quadripartite Agreement to which the FRG was not party. Might, for example, a CDU chancellor, in defiance of the Western Powers, have refused to negotiate German-German accords foreseen in the Quadripartite Agreement with East Berlin? Could such a chancellor have gone to his countrymen, labeled the Berlin accord "unacceptable," blocked a pact enabling millions of West Germans to visit East Berlin and the GDR, rejected a deal offering considerable political gains from a human standpoint, or suggested the FRG's allies had not upheld West German interests, particularly when polls showed nearly 60 percent of West Germany's population basically supported the *Ostpolitik*?

Barzel's maneuver failed; he had received only 247 of the 249 votes he needed. Brandt remained chancellor, but was governing without a majority. The vote on a budget resolution shortly after the no-confidence balloting resulted in a hung parliament, with the final tally 247 on each side. Unless the coalition could obtain the collusion of some members of the opposition, the ratification of the treaty legislation--scheduled for May--would be most dubious.

In order to win time, the second reading of the treaties in the *Bundestag* was delayed an entire week. In the interim the coalition would search for a formula allowing the opposition to assent to, or at a minimum not to reject, the treaty legislation, facilitating its passage in the lower house. Brandt emphasized that a modification of the treaties was out of the question; his government would be willing to supplement the agreements only with notes of interpretation or explanation. For its part, the CDU/CSU demanded the inclusion of mutually accepted statements--meaning of course the Soviets would have to be party--underscoring the Germans' right of self-determination and affirming the temporary nature of the existing political arrangements in Europe.[18]

The course of the discussions between government and opposition indicated disapproval of the treaties to be nowhere near as great as would have seemed to be the case in the initial stages of the ratification. Barzel's position and those of other moderate CDU officials suggested that, had the opposition formed a new government in the wake of the constructive no-confidence vote, little renegotiation would have actually taken place. Indeed, the opposition leader, long a proponent of an operative *Ostpolitik*, would presumably have continued the pursuit of limited reconciliation with the East Bloc.[19] It was the chancellorship Barzel wanted; if this he could not have, he would make efforts to achieve some degree of foreign policy bipartisanship. Clearly, the CDU/CSU was facing uphill work adjusting to its role as the opposition. As is often the case in parliamentary democracies, opposition parties are able to display an outward show of unity and even to put forth somewhat preposterous policy alternatives. Opposition reticence on the Berlin Agreement during the May discussions of the treaty legislation was an expression of general approval, albeit in some cases grudging.[20] By April Egon Bahr and his East German interlocutor, Michael Kohl, had succeeded in hammering out the inter-German traffic accords supplementing the Quadripartite Agreement.

Within opposition ranks, there was a steadily increasing tendency to support the treaty legislation at least in principle. Even such known "hard-liners" as Franz-Josef Strauss and Alfred Dregger were making positive noises about the accords with the East.[21] A generally favorable attitude facilitated the drafting of a nonpartisan declaration on the lingering German question that was approved by the Soviet ambassador and sent to Moscow. Gromyko even appeared to make a modest effort to assist the West Germans by testifying to his understanding of German problems and arranging for the Soviet media to announce for the first time the existence of Bonn's August 12, 1970 letter on German reunification, a visible acknowledgement of the direction of Soviet policy.

The final text of the nonpartisan declaration included the following points:[22]

1. The treaty pledges made in the name of the FRG do not exclude the possibility of a future peace treaty peacefully modifying Europe's geopolitical status-quo.
2. Although existing European borders have been mutually accepted, these do not have a permanent legal status.
3. The German right of self-determination remains unaffected by the treaties.
4. It will continue to be the policy and indeed the legal obligation of the FRG to strive for German reunification.
5. The rights and responsibilities of the Four Powers in Germany remain unchanged.
6. The FRG will maintain its membership in the Atlantic Alliance upon which it depends for its security and freedom.
7. The FRG will continue its efforts, together with its EG partners to realize European unification.
8. The FRG expresses its determination to maintain and develop ties with West Berlin in accordance with the Quadripartite Agreement.
9. A normalization of relations between the FRG and the GDR is desirable and a goal of West German policy.

The statement, though hardly revealing any new tenets of West German foreign policy, did allay some legitimate opposition concerns about coalition policies, while offering a face-saver to some CDU/CSU officials. Coalition leaders as well as Barzel hoped the text would enable a majority of the opposition to vote for the ratification of the treaties. But for other opposition officials the joint endeavors were still inadequate. Doubtless some CDU/CSU members were mistrustful of any *Ostpolitik* piloted by the SPD. In an important *Fraktion* meeting just before the final parliamentary balloting on the treaty legislation, Walter Hallstein, belonging to the opposition's gray eminence club, spoke out against the treaties, recommended abstention in the voting, however, to preserve unity within the ranks. Franz-Josef Strauss, unpredictable as usual, also viewed the treaties with disfavor and urged his colleagues to vote against them, but then shifted to the "fallback" position of abstaining in the vote. Such machinations caused Günter Gaus to accuse Barzel of being Strauss's puppet.[23]

The Moscow and Warsaw treaties passed the *Bundestag* on May 17 and the way was open for the coming into force of the Quadripartite Agreement. The final tally showed that of 496 representatives, 248 had voted in favor of the Bonn-Moscow Treaty, 10 against, with 238 abstentions. 248 voted for the accord with Poland, 17 against, with 231 abstentions. The CDU/CSU, all efforts notwithstanding, was unable to maintain uniformity. Two days later the *Bundesrat* approved the treaty legislation when all CDU/CSU delegates abstained.

NOTES

1. Resolution in parliamentary group and executive board of the CDU/CSU, August 1970, cited in Haftendorn, op. cit., p. 304.

2. See Baring's discussion of the working group's conclusions on the Eastern treaties, Baring, op. cit., pp. 314-316; also, *Der Spiegel*, Jan. 17, 1972.

3. See *The Washington Post*, Feb. 10, 1972 and *Der Spiegel*, Feb. 15, 1972.

4. Catudal, *The Diplomacy of the Quadripartite Agreement on Berlin*, p. 220.

5. A *Bundestag* majority of 249 would be required to ratify the treaties, *Der Spiegel*, Jan. 17, 1972.

6. Geoffrey Pridham, "The Ostpolitik and the Opposition in West Germany," Roger Tilford (ed.), *The Ostpolitik and Political Change in Germany*, pp. 50-51. Pridham actually sees three groups he calls the absolute opponents, the conservative opponents, and the conditional critics. He advances the hypothesis that opposition officials oscillated between basic opposition and flexibility. He does not, however, seem to make a clearly-drawn distinction between conservative opponents and conditional critics.

7. It should be pointed out that, given the intensity

of the political rhetoric on Eastern issues at the time, it was not always easy to distinguish between conditional critics and unbendable opponents. The CDU/CSU was in the opposition for the first time in the history of the FRG and was often quite awkward in its new role, not comfortable being the "loyal" opposition. An example of this loose rhetoric was headline appearing in the *Bayernkurier*, an arch-conservative weekly with close ties to the CSU, when Brandt assumed office in autumn 1969, referring to the new head of government as "The Sell-Out Chancellor."

8. Pridham, "The Ostpolitik and the Opposition in West Germany"; see also Richard von Weizsäcker's recent article in *Die Zeit* of October 7, 1983 entitled "Nur Zusammenarbeit schafft Frieden."

9. CDU/CSU position paper, "Beziehungen der Bundesrepublik Deutschland und der Volksrepublik Polen," DBT/VI, calendar 6/1523, Dec. 4, 1970, quoted in: Haftendorn, op. cit., pp. 304-305; *Der Spiegel*, Oct. 15, 1970.

10. The constructive vote of no-confidence is a variant of the procedure in the British Parliament for unseating the government chief, whereby the *Bundestag* must concurrently elect a new chancellor. The no-confidence vote is constructive in the sense that a government cannot be toppled unless a new government is chosen. To oust Brandt the opposition needed 249 votes in the *Bundestag*. See Article 63 of the Basic Law and, Heidenheimer and Kommers, op. cit., pp. 208-209.

11. *The Washington Post*, March 10, 1972.

12. U.S. Mission, Berlin, "Berlin 1972-An Unofficial Chronology" (Berlin: USIS, 1972), p. 2.

13. "Infas Report" (Bonn), April 17, 1972, poll of the Institut für angewandte sozialwissenschaft, quoted in: Bark, op. cit., p. 96.

14. Ibid.

15. Ibid.

16. "Infas Report", December 17, 1971 and May 3, 1972.

17. See: Baring, op. cit., pp. 403-405.

18. Ibid., pp. 437-40.

19. Ibid., pp. 440-47.

20. Though the "official opinion" of the *Bundesrat* termed the Quadripartite Agreement "unsatisfactory", there seemed to be little official discussion of Berlin issues in the *Bundestag* until the drafting of the nonpartisan statement on FRG foreign policy that mentioned the maintenance and augmentation of ties to West Berlin in apparent acceptance of the Agreement provisions, Baring,

op. cit., pp. 438-440.

21. Baring, op. cit., pp. 431-33, 435-36.

22. Author's translation of excerpts, the complete text appears in Baring, op. cit., pp. 438-40.

23. *Der Spiegel*, May 22, 1972.

13
The Quadripartite Agreement

Concluded by the U.S., France, Great Britain and the Soviet Union on September 3, 1971 and coming into force on June 3, 1972, the Quadripartite Agreement consists of two principal parts: the quadrilateral accords and the inter-German regulations. The former deal with the international legal status of Berlin, while the latter provide for the implementation of certain crucial decisions affecting Germans on either side of the border.

Status of Berlin

The agreement does not create a new status for Berlin, nor can it represent a permanent resolution to all the city's dilemmas. As is the case with the Bonn-Moscow Treaty and the Basic Treaty of 1972 between the two German states, the accord on Berlin is a *modus vivendi*; all would cease to be legally binding as a result of significantly changed circumstances in the event of a future unriddling of the German question. Though it does regulate and defuse the most contentious issues of post-war Berlin, the agreement does not pretend to solve all problems. Neither the Western Powers nor the FRG wished to have all quandaries "solved" since the absence of resolution guarantees the continued openness of the German question. From the standpoint of the U.S., Great Britain and France, the single most important aspect of the agreement is that is does not alter the existing status-quo in the city, ensuring the survival of West Berlin. Despite the disparate initial political/legal positions of the two sides, the negotiators succeeded in forging a workable arrangement that was the partial result of fostered

151

ambiguity in the accord, but also of not insignificant
Soviet concessions.

For decades the East Bloc contended that, by virtue of
the emergence of two separate German states from the
formerly-unified *Reich*, the German problem had been solved.
The division of Germany is a postbellum fact, so the
argument ran, and the possibility of GDR reunification with
a West German state is repudiated, until at some
undetermined future date, the two Germanies are united
within a communist Europe.

Bound by the Basic Law to seek eventual reunification,
the FRG could never officially accept the permanent
partition of Germany. In refusing to grant the GDR
diplomatic recognition, Bonn defines its affinity with East
Berlin as a "special relationship." Each German state
maintains a permanent representative in the capital of the
other. In conformity with European Community (EC) law,
trade between the German states is not international, but
instead is within the realm of domestic commerce. Hence,
the solution of all Berlin problems would not only be
inexpedient but also politically unimaginable if
disattached from a broader answer to the German question.
Soviet concurrence to respect the status-quo in Berlin
through a binding accord represents a sanctioning of the
continuance of this openness.

Legal scholars have raised the question whether or not
the accompanying documents actually constitute parts of the
Quadripartite Agreement.[1] Schiedermair argues that these
documents are not treaty components in the strictest
sense.[2] Given the complexity of the Berlin situation and
the uniqueness of the accord now regulating the city's
status, the question is not merely an academic one. On a
practical level it is necessary to determine what would
represent a violation and how a potential breach of the
pact should be handled. Such are persevering quandaries of
a Four-Power agreement directly affecting the two German
states.

Soviet guarantees of unimpeded access notwithstanding,
East German violation of a particular aspect of the traffic
accord with the FRG is doubtless a matter of inter-German
contention. At what point the signatories to the agreement
must exercise their rights and responsibilities remains an
open question, since the agreement calls for consultation
but does not offer any specific provisions for solving the
dilemma. A somewhat paradoxical aspect of the agreement is
that the Four Powers pledge themselves to maintaining West
Berlin's status without acceding to methods for inducing

the German states to preserve the existing situation in Berlin.

Western nations agree that the U.S., Britain and France, as outlined in the Paris Accords, provide for the continuation of Allied prerogative in Germany as well as in Berlin. As a result of Allied supremacy in the Western sectors of Berlin, there can be no question about the legal obligation of the Berlin *Senat* and other governmental organs vis-à-vis international agreements on Berlin.[3] In the 1955 Bolz-Zorin Treaty, ostensibly granting the GDR sovereignty over its territory, the Soviet Union judiciously preserved its rights in Germany, entitling Moscow in 1971 to guarantee safe passage of vehicles on the transit routes to Berlin. Implicit in the Bolz-Zorin Agreement is also the validity of multilateral accords reserving rights to the Soviet Union: the original London Protocols of 1944, the Air-Traffic Safety Agreement and the Jessup-Malik Agreement. All these treaties represent integral parts of Berlin's status and thus are unaffected by the Quadripartite Agreement.

Key Issues

Crucial to understanding what the agreement actually solves is an examination of the issues the accord deals with. The jurisdiction of the agreement can be broken down to include seven major issues.

1. The actual status of the city, the most disputed of all areas, was at the root of post-war conflict. The great "imponderable," this issue was skirted in order that a treaty on Berlin be possible. The parties to the accord can only agree to disagree upon its geopolitical authority. The Western Powers have continued to uphold the quadripartite status of greater Berlin, involving all four sectors as designated in the London Protocol. On the other hand, Moscow insisted throughout the course of the quadrilateral negotiations that only the Western sectors were a subject of discussion, as East Berlin had long since become the capital of the GDR. Agreement to disagree is manifested in the General Provisions, whereby the geographic parameters of the agreement remain undefined. Though a clever legal sleight-of-hand, this ambiguity could prove to be the long-term shortcoming of the treaty.

2. In regard to "Zuordnung" the agreement provides for the maintenance and development of "ties" between the FRG and the Western sectors, while specifying that West Berlin

does not comprise a constituent part of the FRG, and in essence affirming the suspension of the articles in the Basic Law pertaining to Berlin's status. This provision on ties allowed for such salient FRG interests in Berlin as the retention of West German officials, bureaus and courts in the Western sectors, and the diplomatic representation of West Berlin abroad. The FRG consented to reduce "demonstrative presence" and received through its allies a written confirmation of its interests in West Berlin.

The term "ties" has, however, not been without definitional problems. Moscow and East Berlin have on occasion challenged the financial, economic, cultural and legal integration of West Berlin into the FRG, but seemed to have ceased making references to the Western sectors as an "independent political entity." While the Russian word for "ties" bears no political implications, as Soviet officials emphasize in interpreting the agreement, and the General Provisions specify that West Berlin is not to be governed by the FRG, the East Bloc has avoided a confrontation on West German activities in Berlin, suggesting Moscow is generally prepared to accept the situation. The concept "independent political entity" seldom highlights official Soviet interpretations of the agreement and although Moscow's--not to mention East Berlin's--position on the issue can be said to be equivocal, the Soviets seem to have acceded to the Western view.[4]

This interpretation is spelled out in Annex II of the agreement in the form of a communication to the Soviet government. There the Allies reiterate assent to the maintenance and preservation of ties, but outline precisely which official governmental activities are not permissible. These include the performance of the duties of the Federal (FRG) President, the *Bundesrat*, the *Bundestag*, the *Bundesversammlung*, along with their committees as well as other (unspecified) state bodies of the FRG. The annex permits an amount of flexibility and the Allies are usually lenient in the practical application of their prerogative.

3. Access to Berlin was and is the overriding concern of the Western Powers because upon the exercise of this right the tenability of their position depends. Since the Western Powers maintain that access is a matter of right, both Parts I and II should be viewed as dealing with access; more specific provisions are itemized in Annex I as well as in the separate German accords. The Soviet Union guarantees the free flow of civilian surface traffic, and, in explicitly conceding to respect "individual and joint

rights and responsibilities" in Berlin, underwrites Allied military access--rights Moscow challenged in every major Berlin crisis.

While there is considerable equivocacy on broad legal questions as well as on matters of status, the various access accords are specific and in some cases quite technical. Acting on behalf of the GDR, the Soviet Union agreed in the Quadripartite Agreement to eliminate lengthy customs procedures, allowing the sealing of cargo vehicles in the FRG for passage on the transit routes. As a rule, even unsealed vehicles are not inspected. Except in the event of suspected criminal activity, private vehicles and baggage are not subject to East German control.[5] The FRG pays visa fees and transit-route charges in annual lump-sum form, eliminating any need for delay on the East German borders.

Upon FRG insistence, the accords on access procedure were made as specific as was considered feasible--though the Western Powers hardly needed persuasion on the necessity of adequate arrangements. Because the West insisted upon cramming "as many details as possible into their accord with the Soviets," East Bloc officials have had few opportunities to probe, their maneuvers before 1971 having often resulted in international incidents.[6] Thus there have been few opportunities for "gray-zone" violation of the Quadripartite Agreement by third parties, i.e., the GDR, producing a potentially irresolvable legal problem. Access procedures have functioned so well as to occasion former Berlin governing mayor Klaus Schütz to say that the Quadripartite Agreement has terminated the "dark chapter of searches and waiting times, of impediments and chicanery, of rejections and arrests, this dark chapter which started in the late forties and continued until 1971."[7]

4. Closely related to the question of West German ties to West Berlin is the issue of diplomatic representation of West Berliners. The parties to the agreement consented to permit the FRG to provide "consular services" to "permanent residents" of West Berlin. As a result West Berliners can travel in Eastern Europe on an FRG passport or with a special identity card,[8] and West Berlin companies are entitled to the usual services furnished by diplomatic missions. As a rule West Berlin businesses are not separated from West German concerns, a not insignificant mutual arrangement in light of the fact that West Berlin is the largest West German industrial city and most large German companies have offices there.

The use of the term "permanent residents" represents

another compromise, whereby the negotiators studiously avoided the quandary regarding the nationality of West Berliners. Added to the anomaly of a treaty not defining its jurisdiction is the aberration to international legal norms of not specifying the nationality of those individuals most directly affected. So long as there is a German question, the technical matter of the nationality of West Berlin's population will pose a dilemma. Because the Western Powers retain their sovereignty in the Western sectors and the latter therefore do not constitute an FRG state, West Berliners are not in the strictest sense West German citizens. West Berliners do not vote in national FRG elections, neither are the 22 West Berlin representatives authorized to cast ballots on substantive issues in the *Bundestag*; they possess only advisory powers. On top of this, the Soviet Union would be loathe ever to accept West Berlin as a constituent part of the FRG. Realizing the lack of an alternative to ambiguity on the nationality question and concerned in the main with discrimination against West Berliners as a humanitarian issue, the FRG has welcomed the political arrangement as outlined in the Quadripartite Agreement.

5. Nine articles of the inter-German accords deal with access or "Zutritt" of "permanent residents" to East Berlin and the GDR. No explicit restrictions are placed upon the right of West Berliners to travel in East Bloc states other than the GDR. West Berliners are entitled under the agreement to spend 30 days a year in East Berlin or the GDR with the possibility of an extension in hardship cases or in connection with commercial, academic, economic or cultural affairs. Despite considerable liberalization (keeping in mind before the Quadripartite Agreement, "permanent residents" had in effect no rights in Eastern Europe), the accords are discriminatory in that other Westerners have unlimited travel rights, theoretically.

Formerly, all non-official visitors to the GDR acquired a visa, while those visiting East Berlin needed have only an "entry permit" that could be obtained at the border. The distinction between such a permit and a visa was an important one involving Berlin's status. Since neither the Western Powers nor the FRG recognizes East Berlin as the *de jure* capital of the GDR, they long resisted East German issuance of visas for their territory including East Berlin. This aspect of the "Zutritt" issue was later changed unilaterally by the GDR.

6. Improved and expanded communication between West Berlin and surrounding East German areas is assured in Part

II and Annex III of the Quadripartite Agreement. German
authorities were left to flesh out this guarantee with
specifics; examples have included various postal, telephone
and telecommunications deals between the German states.
Telephone lines between East and West Germany were
increased by 30 in each direction with an agreement
concluded in December 1971.[9] By March 1972 this number
increased by 16. Between West Berlin and East German areas
60 lines in each direction were added by December 1971.[10]
In addition, more telex and telegram systems were made
operational between the GDR and the FRG as well as between
West Berlin and adjacent regions. These communications
accords were the first inter-German treaties to be reached
within the Quadripartite Agreement framework.

7. With the establishment of a Soviet general
consulate in West Berlin, Moscow gained a dignity-preserver
as well as an expanded presence in the Western sectors.
Wary of Moscow's intentions, the U.S. at first objected to
any scheme augmenting Soviet facilities in Berlin.
Preeminent among U.S. reservations about the creation of
such a consulate in West Berlin concerned the eventual
precedent it might set, appearing to lend credence to the
East Bloc position that West Berlin constituted an
independent political entity. Moreover, the Soviets might
later offer the consulate as evidence that the
quadrilateral negotiations resulted in an agreement on West
Berlin only. That a Soviet consulate general accredited to
the commandants of the Western sectors would run athwart of
Moscow's erratic claims to having had a monopoly on
original rights in Berlin was the only really cogent
Western argument in favor of the consulate's
establishment.[11]

Since the conclusion of the agreement, the consulate
has not raised any significant issues.[12] Personnel is
limited to 20 and the duties of the consulate are
restricted to performing consular functions for Soviet
citizens. Its existence has not impinged upon the status
of Berlin. Defending the Allied decision to grant Moscow
this concession, Rush stated:

> There is . . . nothing unique about one of the Allies
> having a Consulate General in Berlin or, in fact,
> having one outside of its own Sector. The French
> Consulate General is located in the British Sector
> . . . the British and French have had Consulates
> General in Berlin almost from the beginning of the
> occupation period. We now have a Consulate and are

giving consideration to raising its status to equate with the other two.[13]

Preamble and General Provisions

The "General Provisions" of the Quadripartite Agreement specify in Part I, Section 3, that the four governments "will mutually respect their individual and joint rights and responsibilities, which remain unchanged."[14] The Soviet Union therewith explicitly affirmed the original rights of the occupiers and accepted its contractual obligations vis-à-vis the Western Powers. Included in the Soviet guarantee is the accession to the maintenance of an Allied military presence in the city, respect for the "original nature" of Allied rights, safe passage in the air-corridors and on the transit-routes, and an acknowledgement of the "Air-Regime's" continuation.

The "Preamble" and the "General Provisions" in effect exclude the possibility of an overt Soviet challenge to Allied occupation rights in the Western sectors without a straightforward treaty violation. Notwithstanding disparate interpretations of some matters by the two sides and looming political problems in Central Europe, there is little controversy on the issues of fundamental importance to the Allies: Soviet-sanctioned free access to Berlin and validity of existing accords. As stated in the Preamble, the agreement affects neither wartime and post-war treaties nor attendant quadripartite rights.[15] The preambular proviso clause, furnishing a written confirmation of existing Berlin accords, is of particular significance since this represents the first such corroboration the Soviet Union has been willing to make in the post-war period. Moscow's concurrence with this treaty provision signifies a major modification of the Soviet position on Berlin. What is more, East Berlin is unable to call Allied rights into question without a Soviet transgression of the Quadripartite Agreement resulting and the risk of direct superpower confrontation developing. Thus the Preamble has a certain deterrent aspect.

Schiedermair points out a potential difficulty in the proviso clause in that specific mention of the London Protocol is lacking, there being reference only to "decisions" and "agreements." The former is a somewhat ambiguous term, implying that unilateral actions or certain political developments have altered the quadripartite status of Berlin.[16] As the unfolding of events has shown,

Soviet policies have resulted in significant deviations
from the originally-envisaged Four-Power control of Berlin
and in some cases have represented actual treaty
violations. An example is the unilateral termination of
the quadripartite administration of the city in 1948. One
is hardly at a loss to find others such as the *de facto*
incorporation of the Eastern sector into the GDR and the
deployment of regular GDR troops (NVA) in East Berlin in
violation of the demilitarized status of greater Berlin.

That "decisions" on Berlin in part conflict with
Berlin "agreements" is beyond dispute and inasmuch the
Preamble is internally contradictory. This palpable
contradiction reflects the fact that the Quadripartite
Agreement could settle only a limited number of issues. As
is often the case, international law provides precious few
answers to difficult political questions and is unable to
solve international imbroglios. A divided Europe will
invariably continue to give rise to political difficulties.
Without breaching the Berlin accord, Moscow cannot now
deliver an ultimatum to the Allies demanding the evacuation
of the city as it has done in the past. Insofar the
Quadripartite Agreement preserves a status-quo. On the
other hand it is not within the realm of possibility for
the Allies to restore quadripartite control to greater
Berlin or to modify the entrenched political-social order
in East Berlin which is the result of a "decision."

There can be no doubt that significant differences in
the interpretation of the agreement linger on both sides.
Some aspects of the accord border on legal irrelevance and
reflect inextricable political quandaries. The GDR will
persist in maintaining that the Quadripartite Agreement
applies only to West Berlin and hence has no validity
whatsoever in "democratic Berlin," i.e., East Berlin.
Expressions like "the relevant area" and "the practical
improvement of the situation" indicate, in the main,
absence of consensus in certain spheres.[17]

Moreover, Soviet concurrence with GDR actions in East
Berlin inconsistent with the city's quadripartite status
has been cause for Western concern. Portions of the
Preamble run counter to treaties between the GDR and the
Soviet Union. In the Bolz-Zorin Treaty as well as in the
GDR-Soviet Treaty of Friendship, the signatories do not
differentiate between East Berlin and the territory of the
GDR, but instead refer to East Berlin as the East German
capital. The East Bloc rejoinder to the Western argument
concerning the incompatibility of both pacts with the 1971
Quadripartite Agreement is that the emergence of East

Berlin as the GDR capital is an undeniable fact of post-war developments. It is thus inconceivable, according to the Soviet Union, that the sovereign capital of a country could be under occupation by foreign military forces. One of the oddities of East Berlin, though, is that it continues to be patrolled by U.S., British and French convoys as well as being occupied by the Soviet Army.

On a more positive note, the ambiguities of the Quadripartite Agreement represent some important compromises that were the *sine qua non* for accord. Fully aware that agreement in principle on the geographic jurisdiction of a treaty was not to be achieved, the two sides consented not to challenge one another on the prickly political/legal question of status. Agreement to disagree is best expressed in the preambular phrase: "without prejudice to their (the Four Powers') legal positions." Such a provision permits the GDR to exercise certain sovereign rights of control on the transit routes. Other prerogatives, also claimed by the GDR to constitute sovereign rights, remain officially undisputed, although not explicitly sanctioned, by the Western Allies. Furthermore, the Quadripartite Agreement provided a method whereby the FRG and the GDR could conclude traffic agreements, without the former having to recognize the latter as a separate state, something crucially important to the FRG. In short, a workable arrangement on Berlin was feasible when quadrilateral accords could be detached from the perplexing dilemmas of the German question. And in addition to the imprecise terminology and the intrinsic compromises, the accompanying documents bridge other aspects of differences in interpretation.

Whether employment of the term "relevant area" in the General Provisions would cause difficulties in actual practice was an open question in the years immediately following the conclusion of the agreement. Because of continuous GDR endeavors to assert its authority in East Berlin, there has been the risk of East German authorities challenging Allied rights. A logical consequence of the establishment of complete GDR sovereignty in East Berlin would be the elimination of Allied presence and control in East Berlin: the air control zone over the Eastern sector and Allied "flag patrols" in East Berlin. To date, no GDR action has been taken against these vestiges of quadripartite jurisdiction in greater Berlin, likely because of anticipated countermeasures. In general, the Berlin Agreement has not functioned badly.

The General Provisions define the 1971 status-quo or

the "existing situation" that has developed in the Berlin area as: the Agreement itself, the earlier accords and the post-war political development. On June 28, 1979 the GDR passed a law providing for the direct election of the 22 East Berlin representatives to the *Volkskammer*. Prior to this time, East Berlin delegates were appointed, not directly elected, in accordance with existing quadripartite election regulations. The GDR action was a manifest alteration of the "existing situation" in Berlin. Decrying this unilateral move, the Western Powers labeled it a violation of the Quadripartite Agreement. Though it admittedly set an unfortunate precedent, the direct election of East Berlin representatives was not gauged by the Allies as impinging upon the "three essentials" of Berlin and therefore did not occasion political counteraction apart from a demarche.[18]

The promulgation of the direct election law, however, points to a broader problem with the Quadripartite Agreement that may become significant in the future. The GDR could begin maneuvering into a position to undercut treaty provisions. Since the German states are not party to the Quadripartite Agreement itself, such a scheme under certain circumstances might meet with a modicum of success. The normal Soviet practice is to refer protesting parties to those allegedly authorized to handle such matters: GDR officials. The West could at some time be faced with the stark choice of pressing the issue with the Soviet Union with a consequent risk of escalation to crisis or accepting a detrimental *fait accompli*. Policies of "predictability", so desirable to Bonn, discourage sharp reactions on anyone's part to "pin-prick" chicanery. The question is at what point such maneuvers actually challenge important interests.

There have been yet other intimations of this potential difficulty with the accords. As of January 1, 1977, the GDR imposed a visa requirement for all non-Germans making day-trips to East Berlin, while stipulating that all day-visitors in East Berlin exit by midnight.[19] Although these GDR regulations do not apply to Allied diplomatic and military personnel who continue to have nearly unlimited access to the Eastern sector, through this move East Berlin did alter an aspect of the status-quo or "existing situation." Before this, non-Germans could stay in East Berlin for a 24-hour period on an entry-permit, without having to acquire a visa. After January 1977, Germans and non-official foreigners were placed into the same category.[20] In March of that year, the GDR introduced

a street toll on all non-official vehicles entering East
Berlin, while previously charges were made only on the
transit routes to West Berlin in lump-sum form.

Even more serious and provocative were the "screening-
off" measures undertaken by the GDR in October 1980.
Events in Poland caused deep unease in the party
leadership. East Germans, the majority of whom watch
western television regularly, were eagerly keeping up with
the Polish situation.

In early October the East German regime terminated no-
visa travel between Poland and the GDR, in an apparent
effort to shield the country from the Polish reform-
bacillus, and drastically raised required exchange and visa
fees to East Berlin and the GDR. Western reporters found
themselves subject to tighter restrictions and East German
police intensified the clamp-down on East Germans speaking
to the Western media, with whom unauthorized contact was
already a serious crime in the GDR. Policies of
"predictability" faced not insignificant dilemmas under
such circumstances. To what extent was Honecker's
government altering the status-quo unilaterally? Was
"business as usual" appropriate in the wake of a swift
falloff of Western visits to East Germany and a conscious
SED effort to further screen-off a population disgusted
with a daily dosage of lies? No single action since the
ratification of the Quadripartite Agreement so strangled
travel to East Germany and further isolated its people.[21]
Indeed, Honecker's actions were so prompt that he might
well have effected them without Kremlin approval.

At the same time, Honecker waxed eloquent with his
demarkation rhetoric. Breathing fire and brimstone in his
mid-October Gera speech, Honecker demanded that the FRG
recognize the GDR as a separate nation under international
law, accept East German citizenship as a different
nationality, and settle still lingering border disputes on
the Elbe.[22]

These were instances of unilateral measures undertaken
by the GDR where the predicament of holding Moscow
responsible within the Quadripartite Agreement framework is
acute; such is the dilemma in the face of "salami-tactics."
A continuing cause of some Western apprehensions is
whether, and to what extent, the Soviet Union will permit
the GDR to alter the Berlin status-quo. The upshot of any
change impinging upon the "three essentials" of the Allied
position as outlined by Kennedy would be superpower
confrontation. Still, numerous conceivable changes could
fall short of such infringement.

In contradistinction to the contractual provisions of the Preamble and Part I of the General Provisions, Part II, the treaty annexes, and the accompanying documentation apply explicitly to West Berlin and would appear to be somewhat less contentious. These provisions dealing specifically with West Berlin are directed toward practical solutions to numerous hitherto existing difficulties and augment West Berlin's vitality. Few Berlin issues are however so simple as to be in some manner unrelated to disputatious questions of status and Allied prerogative. Moscow's concession on access is crucial for two main reasons: first, because the Soviet Union was willing to assume responsibility for all access to Berlin in written form for the first time; second, by accepting such responsibility, the Kremlin reconfirmed the quadripartite status of the city. Thus there is a direct tie-in of Part II with Part I and the Preamble as well as with general issues of status. Soviet concurrence on access matters, with the ensuing acknowledgement that the GDR was not possessed of sovereign rights either on the Berlin transit routes or in the whole of Berlin, represented specific restrictions on previously-purported East German sovereignty.

Soviet guarantees of civilian access are made concrete in Part II, Section A, of the Quadripartite Agreement so:

> The Government of the Union of Soviet Socialist Republics declares that transit traffic by road, rail and waterways through the territory of the German Democratic Republic of civilian persons and goods between the Western Sectors of Berlin and the Federal Republic of Germany will be unimpeded; that such traffic will be facilitated so as to take place in the most simple and expeditious manner; and that it will receive preferential treatment.

In addition to the advantages accruing to West Berlin as a result of this certified access, the Allies gained the endorsement of their position that the transit routes do not constitute GDR territory.[23] Because of the mutually-recognized ultimate Soviet authority on the access routes, the "Zugang" guarantee is the treaty clause least burdened by ambiguities.

164

Civilian Access and Annexes

This is not to say there are not gray areas within the realm of traffic control. Regulation is almost completely in East German hands and in the exercise of such authority there is sometimes a fine line between legitimate control and chicanery. Incidents on the transit routes are often the by-product of meticulous GDR efforts to thwart alleged FRG-inspired "human-trade," one of the East Bloc euphemisms for escapes from the GDR. East German police (Volkspolizei) are as a rule more concerned about preventing refugee leakage than they are with regulating traffic flows.[24] Nonetheless, the sort of transportation chaos and traffic snarls characterizing the Berlin situation in the years preceding the Quadripartite Agreement have been nearly unknown in the past 12 years.

In Annex I the Four Powers outlined procedures for inspection and oversight of highway and rail freight traffic to West Berlin. This annex also specifies how toll and user fees are to be levied. Some details of the procedures like the sealing of freight vehicles or the inspection of personal and cargo papers were provided by the negotiators in the Quadripartite Agreement; otherwise, specifics were left to the "competent German authorities." The two German states are thus responsible for most of the technicalities and the execution of "Zugang," the parameters having been spelled out in the annex of the Quadripartite Agreement. The annex, in the form of a "communication" of the Soviet government to the Allies, is generally accepted as legally binding upon the German states, particularly because it is one of the chief bases for the inter-German accords, notwithstanding the fact that the two Germanies are not parties to the Quadripartite Agreement.[25]

Annex II, dealing for the most part with "Zuordnung," acknowledges the political, social and economic ties between West Berlin and the FRG. The accord partners affirm that these ties will be maintained and even developed in a manner consistent with the premise that "the (Western) Sectors continue not to be a constituent part of the Federal Republic of Germany and not to be governed by it."[26] The annex places tight restrictions upon the exercise of authority in West Berlin by the FRG president, FRG governmental agencies, both houses of the legislature and their respective committees. These specific references were included upon Soviet insistence as part of the agreement significantly to reduce "demonstrative" federal presence.

Soviet assent to the maintenance and development of West German ties with West Berlin was tantamount to sanctioning the continued validity of FRG civil law in Berlin--with the important exception of military law and codes. There could be no question that Berlin's viability would stand or fall on the issue of security; in a city unable to provide it, industry and business would be disinclined to invest. Inclusion of West Berlin in the FRG legal system as well as in the "D-Mark" area contributed to the bolstering of the city's political and economic stability.

This part of the Quadripartite Agreement contains a few gray areas as well; for instance, the reference to "other state bodies of the Federal Republic of Germany" exudes ambiguity. Despite Allied efforts not to push Moscow too far on this issue, there has been some friction regarding the exercise of FRG authority. Both Wettig and Catudal point out the potentially serious problems of interpretation inherent in this annex,[27] one of which was manifested in the Federal Environment Agency crisis.

In 1973 the FRG announced its intention to set up a federal environmental office in West Berlin and then FRG interior minister (later foreign minister), Hans-Dietrich Genscher made the unfortunate error of describing the establishment as "a political demonstration," drawing sharp protests and dire threats to interdict Berlin traffic and the like from the Soviet Union. The difficulty was eventually papered over by shifting the term "Federal" in the name (from *Bundesumweltamt* to *Umweltbundesamt*), which seemed to assuage Soviet nervousness.[28]

Less than enamoured of the awkward situation in which the FRG had placed them, the Western Powers have since discouraged any action that might be construed as being "demonstrative" and thus could be purported as "provocative" by the East Bloc. How the annex is to be applied remains somewhat of an unanswered question; ministries, federal offices, as well as the application of certain laws could become subjects of dispute or might be used by East Berlin as pretexts for an action.

Annex III--the "Zutritt" proviso--entitles West Berliners to travel to East Berlin and the GDR "under conditions comparable to those applying to other persons entering those areas," and provides for the improvement of communication between West Berlin and surrounding areas as already discussed. The annex does not explicitly assure free access, but instead eliminates the almost total discrimination against inhabitants of West Berlin--one of the principal goals of Brandt's *Ostpolitik*. Restoration of telegraphic and telephone communications was immensely significant to West Berliners whose interchange with East German areas had been either limited or non-existent for years.

Another prior dilemma resolved in Annex III was the "exclave issue" involving West Berlin territory detached from the city and inside the GDR. Of course the terms "exclave" and "enclave" are somewhat relative, depending upon one's perspective. The major exclave problem for West Berlin was that of Steinstücken, a small community south-west of Berlin, inhabited by 190 residents of West Berlin, and until 1971 completely encircled by East German territory.[29] During extended periods of Soviet or GDR harassment, the exclave was supplied by Allied helicopter. Within the broad framework provided by Annex III, West Berlin *Senat* and GDR authorities agreed to resolve the "problems of the small enclaves, including Steinstücken, and of other small areas" through an exchange of territory and guaranteed access.[30] In the case of Steinstücken, a sort of Berlin microcosm itself, a narrow corridor through East German territory to the U.S. sector was created.

Parts A and B of Annex IV establish the FRG right to represent West Berliners abroad and to include West Berlin in international agreements to which the West Germans are party. Both sections of the annex stress that matters of "security and status" remain unaffected by annex provisions, a reference to areas of exclusive Allied jurisdiction. FRG rights extend to the following spheres:

1. The performance of consular services for "permanent residents" of West Berlin.
2. The representation of West Berlin in international organizations and conferences.
3. The inclusion of West Berlin in non-military treaties and international agreements to which the FRG is party.
4. The participation of "permanent residents" of West Berlin "jointly with participants from the Federal Republic of Germany in international exchanges and exhibitions."[31]

Therewith Annex IV enabled West Berlin to be represented by the FRG in the United Nations, facilitating the entry in 1973 of the two German states into this forum from which they had previously been excluded. The annex also sanctioned West Berlin's participation in the European Parliament and the European Community (EC) in general, as well as validating the legal authority of EC transnational law in West Berlin.

Open questions regarding the extent of Bonn's jurisdiction in West Berlin remain. One problem is with the West German court system. As a constitutional organ, the *Bundesverfassungsgericht* has no legal authority in the Western sectors; thus the highest West German court of appeal is not empowered to settle constitutional disputes within Berlin or rule on a disputation between Berlin and the FRG.[32] The Allies must handle procedures as they are best able. The Soviet Union and the GDR protested the elevation of West Berlin courts to the same level of those of the FRG as a violation of the Quadripartite Agreement.[33] And East Bloc states have often insisted upon the separation of West Berlin from the FRG at Eastern European fairs and exhibitions even after the conclusion of the Berlin accord.[34]

These latter two individual incidents exemplify broader interpretation and administration problems: to what extent are non-parties to the Quadripartite Agreement able to protest or take countermeasures against alleged treaty violations? If they do not have such authorization, what is to be done when such attempts are made? Does attempted GDR enforcement of the Quadripartite Agreement, on the other hand, in itself constitute a violation of the accord? All of these are highly political questions to which there are few answers. Assiduously refusing to discuss any matter remotely related to Berlin's quadripartite status with East German authorities, recognizing that such a discussion would set most regrettable precedents, the Western Powers view any GDR endeavor to execute provisions of the Quadripartite Agreement as a violation. To further complicate matters, Moscow and East Berlin have on occasion rehabilitated their former position on West Berlin as an "independent political entity"--suggesting the absence of the Quadripartite Agreement--when it has behooved them to do so.[35]

That the GDR has tried to undermine parts of the Quadripartite Agreement or to address quadripartite matters completely within Moscow's realm can hardly have been unanticipated. Eager to assert its authority throughout its alleged territory, the GDR will doubtless continue to engage in demonstrative actions, causing friction in inter-German relations. Because of Moscow's restraining hand, the GDR shuns direct challenges to the Allies, risking the triggering of superpower confrontation.

In spite of GDR and Soviet hesitancy to concur with the principle, the German states, according to the Berlin arrangement, act as agents of the signatory powers. As agents, German officials are ultimately responsible to those party to the Quadripartite Agreement and are not empowered to suspend or alter the existing treaties or the status-quo these treaties sustain.[36] Thus, any termination or suspension of Quadripartite Agreement provisions by either of the German states is technically not feasible and any revision of the accord must have the full, mutual concurrence of the signatory powers.

Nearly all Berlin questions are of a highly political nature. The existence of two German states with individual and usually conflicting political interests is a Central European reality; both will attempt to strive for political advantage, given the possibilities available to them. In the nebulous field of international law, segregating the legal from the political is seldom possible; the Quadripartite Agreement, which will remain a highly politicized accord, is no exception to this axiom. Shifts in political power or faltering Allied determination in Berlin will invariably result in a significantly altered situation--to the disadvantage of the West.

German powers and responsibilities in the Berlin area depend largely upon contractual parameters defined by the Soviet Union, the U.S., Britain and France and the power relationships between them. As specified in the final protocol, the signatory powers assume authority for handling treaty violations and agree that any difficulties with implementation are wholly matters of quadripartite concern. But at the same time the Four Powers provided a framework for inter-German relations as well as the groundwork for the West German *Ostpolitik*. A direct result of the Quadripartite Agreement was the accord establishing a *modus vivendi* between the German states, concluded in the same year the Berlin treaty entered into force.

NOTES

1. Zivier, op. cit., pp. 175-76; Schiedermair, op. cit., pp. 185-86.

2. Schiedermair cites Article 1, Paragraph 2 of the

Vienna Convention on Treaties, Schiedermair, pp. 82-83.

3. Zivier, op. cit., pp. 238-240.

4. Zivier, op. cit., pp. 211-13; Gerhard Wettig, "Die Rechtslage Berlins nach dem Viermächteabkommen aus sowjetischer Sicht," *Deutschland-Archiv*, Vol. 7, No. 4 (April 1974), pp. 380-83; Catudal, *The Diplomacy of the Quadripartite Agreement on Berlin*, pp. 248-52.

5. According to the inter-German accords, the following acts constitute an illegal use of the transit routes and are thus violations of GDR law:
   a) distribution of receiving written material,
   b) the picking-up of passengers,
   c) departing from the transit routes in the absence of extenuating circumstances,
   d) committing of other crimes,
   e) not heeding designated traffic codes.
GDR officials do not have authority in other areas.

6. Catudal, *The Diplomacy of the Quadripartite Agreement on Berlin*, p. 261.

7. Klaus Schütz, "The Four-Power Agreement," *Chronique de Politique Etrangère*, Vol. 24, No. 4 (1971), pp. 549-550.

8. Zivier, op. cit., pp. 156-60, pp. 228-29. West Berliners have a special stamp indicating residence in West Berlin in their passports. The Soviets continue to require West Berliners to carry their personal identity cards as well as their specially-stamped passports for travel within the Soviet Union.

9. Zivier, op. cit., p. 253; Catudal, *The Diplomacy of the Quadripartite Agreement on Berlin*, pp. 267-68.

10. Ibid.

11. Such was apparently the argument Egon Bahr made in an April 23, 1971 meeting in Washington with high U.S. officials.

12. Certainly among the reasons that the Soviet consulate general has not raised status problems is the existence of military missions accredited to the Allied commandants. The military missions of a number of countries have been converted into consulates general while remaining accredited to the respective commandants. Thus the Soviet consulate general is only one of a number of missions accredited to the Allies. See: Walter Krumholz (ed.), *Berlin ABC* (Berlin: Press and Information Office, 1968), pp. 428-29.

13. See: Kenneth Rush, "Berlin: The Four-Power Agreement," *Current Foreign Policy* (Washington, D.C.: Department of State, GPO, 1971), p. 7.

14. For a commentary on this section of the "General

Provisions," Schiedermair, op. cit., pp. 54-59.

15. Zivier, op. cit., p. 200; Schiedermair, op. cit., pp. 5-10.

16. Schiedermair, op. cit., pp. 10-12.

17. Schiedermair, op. cit., p. 58; Gerhard Wettig, "Das Problem der Bindungen West-Berlins bei der Anwendung des Viermächteabkommens," *Deutschland-Archiv*, Vol. 12, No. 9 (1979), pp. 932-33.

18. *Frankfurter Allgemeine Zeitung*, June 29, 1979; *Die Zeit*, July 13, 1979.

19. Catudal, *A Balance Sheet of the Quadripartite Agreement on Berlin*, pp. 135-37.

20. Ibid.

21. *Der Spiegel*, Oct. 20, 1980; Peter Jochen Winters, "Kurswechsel Ost-Berlins gegenuber Bonn," *Europa-Archiv*, Vol. 36, No. 1 (Jan. 1981), pp. 31-38.

22. Haftendorn, op. cit., p. 250.

23. For additional discussion, see: Kenneth Rush, Introduction to *The Diplomacy of the Quadripartite Agreement on Berlin*, pp. 15-16.

24. Zivier, op. cit., pp. 247-48. In policing the transit routes, GDR officials are empowered to undertake the following measures:
   a) issue a warning or a fine,
   b) take into custody or confiscate certain items,
   c) refuse transit to individuals in case of access violation,
   d) arrest individuals.

25. Karlheinz Niclauss, *Controverse Deutschlandpolitik* (Frankfurt: Alfred Metzner Verlag, 1977), pp. 57-59.

26. For discussions of issues regarding Berlin "ties," see: Gunther Doeker, Klaus Melsheimer and Dieter Schroder "Berlin and the Quadripartite Agreement of 1971," *American Journal of International Law* 67 (1973), pp. 59-61; Karl Doehring and Georg Ress, *Staats- und volkerrechtliche Aspekte der Berlin-Regelung* (Frankfurt: Volkerrecht und Aussenpolitik, 1972), pp. 39-42.

27. Catudal, *A Balance Sheet of the Quadripartite Agreement on Berlin*, pp. 112-14; Wettig, "Das Problem der Bindungen West-Berlins bei der Anwendung des Viermächteabkommens," pp. 927-28; also, Karl Carstens, "Zur Interpretation der Berlin-Regelung," *Festschrift für Ulrich Scheuner zum 70. Geburtstag* (Berlin: Berlin Verlag, 1973), pp. 63-65.

28. *New York Times*, Jan. 23, 1974; *Der Spiegel*, Jan. 14, 1974.

29. The seminal work on the Steinstücken problem is:

Honore Catudal, *Steinstücken: A Study in Cold War Politics*
(New York: Vantage Press, 1971); also: Zivier, pp. 264-266;
Gerhard Wettig, "Fünf Jahre Berlin-Abkommen: Eine Bilanz,"
Aus Politik und Zeitgeschichte, vol. 42 (Oct. 1976), pp.
38-42.

30. See: Annex III, Paragraph 3 and Article 1 of the
"1971 GDR-Senat Arrangement on Exchange of Territory";
also: Schiedermair, op. cit., pp. 122-26.

31. Annex IV A, Section 1 (d); Mahncke, *Berlin im
geteilten Deutschland*, pp. 93-95; *Frankfurter Allgemeine
Zeitung*, August 15 and 20, 1973; *Frankfurter Allgemeine
Zeitung*, Sept. 18, 1973.

32. Zivier, op. cit., pp. 107-109; Niclauss, op. cit.,
pp. 110-14.

33. Zivier, op. cit., pp. 221-23; Schiedermair, op.
cit., pp. 98-101. The integration of West Berlin courts
into the FRG judicial system does raise questions about
inconsistencies with the Quadripartite Agreement. Clearly
the highest court of appeal in the FRG, as a constitutional
organ, cannot function as the foremost court in West
Berlin.

34. On several occasions the Soviet Union has insisted
upon the issuing of separate invitations to the FRG and to
the *Senat* for international gatherings ranging from
congresses to athletic events. See: Catudal, *A Balance
Sheet on the Quadripartite Agreement on Berlin*, pp. 114-16.

35. For a Soviet view, see: Viktor Boldyrew, "Das
Vierseitige Abkommen über West Berlin--ein Shritt zu
Frieden, Sicherheit und Zusammenarbeit in Europa," *Deutsche
Aussenpolitik*, Vol. 5 (September-October, 1972), pp. 873-
99; for an analysis of East Bloc positions: Gerhard Wettig,
"Die Rechtslage Berlins nach dem Viermachteabkommen aus
sowjetischer Sicht," pp. 378-88.

36. The so-called "agent theory" is no invention of
the Quadripartite Agreement and dates back to at least the
1950s. Public mention of it was made in 1958 by John
Foster Dulles. The Secretary suggested in a November 1958
telegram that the U.S. could accept "perfunctory" tasks
being carried out by GDR officials with an explicit
agreement on ultimate Soviet responsibility, Department of
State Telegram, State Department (Washington) to U.S.
Embassy Bonn, No. 1084, Nov. 24, 1958.

14
The Basic Treaty and Relations
Between the Germanies

Though the inter-German sections of the Quadripartite Agreement did not represent the first compacts made between the German states, they nonetheless set a significant precedent. For the first time the FRG and the GDR had concluded permanent agreements as equal partners without preconditions requiring inconceivable concessions on the part of one side or the other. For the FRG, "unsatisfactory" desiderata would have entailed the diplomatic recognition of the GDR, the denial of a "special relationship" between the two German states, with the attendant "closing" of the German question. These were demands the GDR unrealistically made upon the FRG; any proposals for negotiation beginning with stipulations on this order were out of the question. Such however was the intention of Ulbricht with the "all or nothing policy." Since he could not accomplish what he felt was necessary for the GDR in terms of a final elimination of the German question, he staunchly followed policies of confrontation. The quandary for the GDR was considerable: concessions to the FRG were widely viewed in the SED as acquiescence, but pursuit of the "all or nothing" policy virtually guaranteed West German refusal officially to acknowledge the *de facto* existence of the GDR.

As in the Quadripartite Agreement, mutual concession on political/legal matters is couched in the legal jargon specifying agreement to disagree: "without prejudice to the different views . . . on fundamental questions, including the national question."[1] Furthermore, the Berlin accord provided an antecedent procedure for achieving inter-German compacts, in that they would be under the aegis of Four-Power prerogative. In the traffic accords of the Quadripartite Agreement as well as in the Basic Treaty

(Grundlagenvertrag) between the two German states, the parties accept Four-Power rights and responsibilities in Germany. The Quadripartite Agreement thus offered a framework for inter-German accord, with the arrangement realized under the *plafond* of the Powers. Moreover, a notable political utility of the Traffic and Transportation Agreement was that it furnished enough confidence for the two parties to move ahead with negotiations on the Basic Treaty.[2]

Bearing major similarities to the Bonn-Moscow and Bonn-Warsaw Treaties, the Basic Treaty is nonetheless an aberrance in the international legal sphere inasmuch as it provides for a "special relationship" between two states that are not foreign (Ausland) to one another. Inherent to all these Eastern agreements is the "inviolability" of existing borders, the renunciation-of-force, and clauses upholding the validity of existing accords.[3] In follow-up "clarifications" to the agreements, the FRG stated its commitment to eventual reunification and to preserving the openness of the German question.[4] The explicit acknowledgement of Four-Power rights in the Berlin accord and in the Basic Treaty supplies the West with a guarantee of Allied participation in any European peace settlement redrawing the map of the continent.

The breakthrough on the Basic Treaty came in May 1972, though representatives of the German states had been unofficially working toward a treaty normalizing relations for some time before this.[5] East Berlin publicly declared its readiness to exchange views on an eventual accommodation that would be the precursor to the entry of the German states into the U.N. According to the East German statement, inter-German relations should be the same as those existing between "sovereign, independent" states. But setting no specific preconditions, the GDR formulation was acceptable to Bonn as a basis for serious talks.

The Brandt government was doubtless in a hurry to make progress on negotiations with East Berlin in light of the upcoming elections. Because of the hung *Bundestag*, the coalition decided in late April deliberately to lose a confidence vote and thereafter to request that the President dissolve the legislature.[6] With elections pending, Brandt could not know how long his government would remain in a position to negotiate on such a sensitive matter. Moreover, with nationwide opinion polls showing increasing support for the *Ostpolitik*, government officials hoped to have negotiations on the Basic Treaty concluded prior to the *Bundestag* elections in order that the coalition have yet another achievement in the realm of the *Ostpolitik* to present to the voters. In an election destined to be a national plebiscite on the coalition's policies vis-à-vis the East, an additional important issue would be placed before the West German electorate if a treaty normalizing inter-German relations could be drafted in time.

For its part, East Berlin was prepared to expedite negotiations in the interest of bolstering Brandt's election chances. Surmising that a Bonn coalition headed by the CDU/CSU would be more faction-ridden, more circumspect on issues of the *Ostpolitik*, and thus more difficult to do business with, the GDR looked to making a deal with Brandt while it still could. Since the conclusion of the Basic Treaty would pave the way for the admission of two German states to the U.N., East Berlin set a timetable of 1972 for this international recognition. Such a boost in the international status of the GDR would not have been in the offing with a CDU/CSU government in Bonn; considerable delay in East German U.N. entry would have been almost inevitable.

On June 15, GDR State Secretary Kohl presented Bahr with a formal proposal for a German-German accord. The draft text suggested agreement on the following:

1. A general recognition of the "principles" of peaceful coexistence between two states of different social orders.
2. The sovereign equality of all states, respect for sovereignty and independence as well as the non-interference in the internal affairs of other states in accordance with the U.N. Charter.
3. Renunciation-of-force, acceptance of existing borders and the peaceful settlement of disputes.
4. The mutual renunciation of claims by either of the German states to represent the other.
5. Encouragement of peaceful relations between European nations.
6. Endeavors to reduce armament, especially nuclear weaponry.
7. Mutual commitment to limit state authority to the geographic boundaries of the German states.
8. Cooperation in the areas of economics, finance, scholarly exchange, technology, transportation, postal and telecommunications, culture and sports.
9. The maintenance of existing agreements, bilateral as well as multilateral.[7]

The restraint of the East German proposal indicated readiness to reach accord. Conspicuously absent from the text were demands for opening diplomatic relations or recognition of East Berlin as the GDR capital. In fact, East Berlin was not mentioned at all. Silence on this issue itself represented a GDR concession. Far from being a maximum position, the proposal seemed so advantageous to the FRG that one might suppose the GDR to have placed its "fallback" position onto the table.

The response in Bonn was decisively positive. An analysis done by the inner-German affairs ministry for the cabinet hypothesized that mutually acceptable formulations could be achieved in negotiation on the nine East German "talking points."[8] Indeed, the actual Basic Treaty closely resembles the East German text, with some passages having been adopted verbatim. Only the seventh point dealing with the extension of state power was deemed by the inner-German affairs ministry study group to be unacceptable.

Even though no written demands for diplomatic recognition or other preconditions were made by the GDR immediately prior to or during the discussion of normalization of inter-German relations, East Berlin officials did engage in the usual round of redoubtable polemics. Upon delivering the text to the Bonn government, Kohl specified the immediate application of both German states for U.N. membership to be a precondition for the signing of an inter-German accord and called for complete diplomatic recognition.[9] In speeches and interviews at the time, Honecker weighed in with the same demands.[10] There are two considerations to be made with regard to this apparent contradiction. First, the exactions were largely East German blustering. Second, the emphasis placed upon U.N. membership, here in the form of a fanciful precondition, reflected an importunate desire on the part of the GDR to augment its international prestige.[11]

Whatever its motives, the latter tactic got East Berlin nowhere. Bahr abruptly rejected any conditions smacking of the former "Ulbricht Doctrine." Bonn officials would not even discuss the issue; the GDR would have either to respect the FRG obligation to eventual reunification or it could forget the entire deal. As for admission to the U.N., Bonn reminded the GDR of the necessity for Four-Power concurrence on this question and of *Bundestag* ratification of entry-legislation.[12] Essentially Bonn told the GDR to be a bit more realistic. The FRG would not fail to neglect its two chief goals in the *Ostpolitik*: human amelioration and the preservation of the openness of the German question.

Kohl announced somewhat unexpectedly on June 28 that East Berlin favored the continuation of discussions and that he would return to the preconditions "later." The remark could hardly be termed an example of logic, but it did effectively eliminate the possibility of an impasse. Kohl is then reported to have told Bahr that the GDR was interested in a prompt conclusion of an agreement.[13] Permission to show so much of the East German hand certainly came from the highest party leadership.

The August 9 inner-German affairs ministry report instructed the FRG foreign office to inform the Allies fully at every stage of the negotiations and to suggest to the Western Powers that they notify the Soviet Union that neither the coming into force of an inter-German accord on the normalization of relations nor the entry of the German states into the U.N. would in any way impinge upon Four-Power rights in Germany. A hitherto secret report prescribed the following "guidelines" to Bahr in the negotiations with East Berlin.[14]

1. The FRG government is prepared to conclude with the GDR a treaty regulating relations for that length of time in which there is the absence of a comprehensive peace agreement.
2. Official government pronouncements and the "20 Points" of the Kassel summit constitute the framework for the negotiating instructions of the West German delegation. In addition the FRG government calls attention to the *Bundestag* and *Bundesrat* resolution in connection with the ratification of the Eastern treaties.
3. In the interest of the cohesiveness of the German nation and of overcoming German division, the treaty anticipates the maximum possible amount of cooperation between the two states. There should be emphasis upon securing existing accords on trade and on postal and telegraph communications for the long term.
4. All possibilities for human amelioration both within and apart from the parameters of the treaty are to be pursued.
5. The following shall be the principles of the treaty:

   a. Both German states constitute one German nation. Cohesion of the nation is to be encouraged. *and furthermore that* 178.2
   b. The rights and responsibilities of the Four Powers in Germany remain unaffected.

      c. There is to be no modification of the FRG goal to achieve reunification through peaceful means and by the exercise of German self-determination. The treaty must not complicate reunification efforts.

      d. The basic institution of "German nationality" is not to be affected by the treaty. 13 notes

      e. The GDR is not a foreign country for the FRG; the type of relationship between the two states must be in accordance with this fact.

  6. FRG accords with third nations shall remain unaffected by the inter-German treaty.

Following the September 13-14 discussions, Bahr and Kohl issued a joint communiqué stating that negotiations had reached an "intensive" stage, an indication considerable progress had already been made. Major differences of principle, exemplified by East German talk of preconditions, were smoothed over quickly. With presumable urging from Moscow, the GDR had already begun loosening travel restrictions and improving telephone communications.

With the establishment in September of diplomatic relations first between the GDR and Finland, then between the GDR and India, East Berlin's international prestige received a dramatic lift. Recognition by other states was only a matter of time. With time now on its side, the GDR was tempted to sever any connection between U.N. admission and an accord normalizing German relations—quite an about-face from demands that mutual commitment to immediate U.N. entry be a precondition of the Basic Treaty. However, such a scheme yielded East Berlin little. The U.S. formally strengthened the linkage by announcing that it would block GDR entry into the U.N. if the latter failed to acknowledge Four-Power prerogative in Germany. No recognition of Allied rights, no U.N. admission. And Moscow's position further showed the narrow confines within which East German policies could be made. The Soviet Union was also eager to safeguard its rights in Germany and would not tolerate its junior partner calling Four-Power prerogative into question even tacitly, especially in light of the fact that Moscow had recently concluded a multilateral agreement based upon the mutually accepted existence of such rights. While no Western observer can know for sure the extent or exact nature of the Soviet pressure put upon the GDR at any particular time, one can safely assume the Kremlin wanted no problems similar to those it encountered with Ulbricht. Moscow also reminded East Berlin of the upcoming West German elections and of the advantages of doing business with the SPD/FDP coalition.

With the convening of formal Four-Power talks on October 23, 1972, pressure upon the GDR took an overt form, assuming East Berlin was not already cognizant of what it would have to do to secure U.N. membership. Requested by Moscow following the October meetings between Bahr and Gromyko, the Four-Power discussions dealt with questions pertaining to GDR and FRG membership in the U.N.[15] The Four-Power composition of the meeting was itself a mutual acknowledgement of existing rights and Moscow made clear to East Berlin that the latter would have to accept the situation.

It is likely Bahr's talks with Kremlin leaders catalyzed the inter-German negotiations, still at that time at the "intense" stage. Although Bahr hastily denied consulting Kremlin leaders in order to move the negotiations with East Berlin along, this was his primary purpose.[16] Employment of the Moscow channel had been a *modus operandi* of Bonn's *Ostpolitik* at least since 1969 and the crafty Bahr was adept at smoothing over difficulties. He appears even to have expedited the beginning of the Four-Power talks. While Bahr's meetings with Kremlin leaders were officially described as merely the routine Soviet-FRG consultations envisaged in a September 1971 agreement, Bahr and Gromyko publicly acknowledged that their discussions touched upon the issues of the inter-German negotiations, including the question of confirming Allied rights.[17]

The available details of either the inter-German negotiations or of West German pourparlers with the Allies concerning the progress made toward the Basic Treaty remain limited. Still, it can be determined that the last two matters of dispute in the German-German negotiations involved, first, the handling of the nationality question and, second, the inclusion of West Berlin in the agreement.

It is obvious that the GDR found a number of Bonn's "guidelines" for an inter-German accord to be unacceptable, in particular, any clause making reference to reunification or to a single German nationality. Without such a reference, Bonn would not have signed a treaty. Upon Bahr's return from Moscow in October, Brandt stated that his government would agree to no treaty entailing an alteration of the Basic Law, meaning of course, the constitutional requirement of active engagement for reunification.[18] The timing of Brandt's remark could hardly have been coincidental, since Bahr had doubtless brought the impasse on this issue to Gromyko's attention. As a result, Moscow might have had some advice for East Berlin. To overcome the difficulty, the preambular format of the Quadripartite Agreement acknowledging disagreements on legal principles was employed.

How West Berlin was to fit into the normalization of relations between the Germanies remained a problem until the end-phase of the negotiations. East Berlin balked at having the FRG speaking for the Western sectors in all inter-German relations. Birnbaum suggests that a weakness of the Quadripartite Agreement was the absence of any provisions relating to the effects future German-German agreements would have upon West Berlin.[19] In light of the fact that short months before, the GDR had concluded extensive traffic and communications accords with the FRG and the Berlin *Senat* regarding West Berlin, the East German position was somewhat disingenuous. Finally the two sides agreed to deal with the Berlin issue in a protocol note which allowed the FRG the authority vis-à-vis West Berlin implicitly accorded it in the Quadripartite Agreement.[20]

On November 6 the texts of the Basic Treaty were completed and two days later Bahr and Kohl initialled the documents, less than two weeks before the West German *Bundestag* elections. The impressive victory of the SPD on November 19--with 45.8 percent of the vote the best in the party's history--indicated popular support for the *Ostpolitik* and ensured the ratification of the Basic Treaty. In an election serving in the main as a referendum on the course of Bonn's policies, German voters largely approved of what the coalition was doing.

Similar in a number of ways to the Quadripartite Agreement which provided an essential framework, the Basic Treaty on relations between the FRG and the GDR is an eclectic document reflecting the interjoining of various aspects of the German problem: the absence of a peace agreement, retained Four-Power prerogative, the "existing" political situation and the interests of two German states. Any agreement disregarding these realities would be unworkable; concessions must at times take the form of provisions obscuring political dilemmas.

The Preamble and Article 2 contain explicit renunciation-of-force agreements in accordance with the principles of the United Nations Charter. Closely related is the pledge to respect the inviolability of existing borders and the sovereignty of all European states, found in the Preamble and in Article 3. Insofar the accord closely resembles the Bonn-Moscow and Bonn-Warsaw Treaties. Coupled with the repeated mention of the GDR by name, these provisions afford the East Germans considerable recognition, the realization of which had been their goal for decades. Moreover, Article 4 comprised an abandonment on the part of the FRG of the once-purported West German right of "sole representation." Thereafter, the FRG presented no challenge, explicit or otherwise, to East German sovereignty. As was the case with Poland, Bonn removed the specter of a West German "bogey," exploitable by Moscow as a pretext for political domination.

Article 6 further confirms the sovereignty and independence of both German states, asserting:

> The Federal Republic of Germany and the German Democratic Republic proceed on the principle that the sovereign jurisdiction of each of the two States is confined to its own territory. They respect each other's independence and autonomy in their internal and external affairs.

Whether this article in particular is in accordance with the Basic Law's Preamble suggesting that the FRG is entitled to speak for East Germans is dubious. Compatibility is possible only if the "representation" proviso is assumed either to be a moral obligation to other Germans or a goal for the future, as argued by the Constitutional Court in deeming the Basic Treaty to be constitutional.[21]

The treaty does address all the major FRG concerns in regard to the cohesion of the German nation. The two German states agree to disagree on the nationality issue, which is explicitly referred to in a preambular passage as a "fundamental question."[22] Some observers view this formulation as the most significant East German concession of all, since reference to a "nationality question" implies the acknowledgment of such a question's existence.[23] Bonn is therefore able without difficulty to maintain its position on the openness of the matter.

Stopping short of instituting ambassadorial representation in each other's countries, with the attendant establishment of complete diplomatic relations, the two German states exchange only "Permanent Missions" headed by a Permanent Representative. According to Article 8 of the Basic Treaty the Permanent Missions are located in the "respective government's seat," phraseology dodging any mention of capitals and circumventing the "East Berlin dilemma."

In agreeing that "the present treaty shall not affect the bilateral and multilateral international treaties and agreements already concluded by (the GDR and the FRG) or relating to them," the treaty partners assented to respect Four-Power rights and responsibilities in Germany. This prerogative will presumably be maintained until a comprehensive peace agreement renders such accords *clausula rebus sic stantibus*. Acceptance of the prerogative by the German states is tantamount to a mutual admission of certain limitations upon sovereignty, e.g., Berlin, while delineating the maintenance of the vestiges of great power control.[24]

Of equal importance to Bonn is Article 7, providing wider cooperation, increased contacts and improved communications. This article, in conjunction with the respective complementary protocols, is crucial to the objective of human amelioration that resulted in a torrent of Western visits to the GDR in the 1970s.

The adjoining treaty documentation handles various details of the inter-German accord relating to health, traffic, telecommunications, postal services and sporting events. The clauses dealing with the inclusion of West Berlin in the Basic Treaty appear also in the supplementary protocols, the result of a last-minute compromise. The protocol note, "Extension of Agreements and Arrangements to Berlin (West)," specifies: "It is agreed that the extension to Berlin (West) of agreements and arrangements envisaged in the Supplementary Protocol to Article 7 may be agreed in each individual case in conformity with the Quadripartite Agreement of 3 September 1971."

NOTES

1. For a commentary, see: Karl Birnbaum, op. cit., pp. 82-85.

2. Lawrence L. Whetten, *Germany East and West* (New York: New York University Press, 1980) pp. 83-84.

3. *The Policy of Renunciation of Force* (Bonn: FRG Press and Information Office, July 1968); Whetten, op. cit., pp. 84-85.

4. *Der Spiegel*, Oct. 9, 1972, p. 22; Birnbaum, op.

cit., p. 83.

5. Baring, op. cit., pp. 457-59.

6. In West German parliamentary procedure, the "constructive vote of no-confidence" allows the chancellor to do this, since he can be voted out of office only if his potential successor obtains a majority. See: Baring, op. cit., pp. 489-91; *Der Spiegel*, Oct. 23, 1972.

7. Complete text appears in Baring, op. cit., pp. 466-67.

8. Baring, op. cit., pp. 467-69.

9. Ibid., pp. 468-69; *Frankfurter Allgemeine Zeitung*, June 16, 1972.

10. *Der Spiegel*, June 12, 1972; Some of Honecker's remarks were published by the *Allgemeiner Deutsche Nachrichtendienst*, the East German news service, on June 9 and 12, 1972.

11. *Der Spiegel*, Oct. 23, 1972.

12. Baring, op. cit., pp. 469-71.

13. *Der Spiegel*, July 3, 1972; Baring, op. cit., p. 470.

14. Author's translation, the complete text of the guidelines appeared for the first time in Baring's book, pp. 472-73; see also: *Der Spiegel*, Oct. 9, 1972, pp. 21-22.

15. Birnbaum, op. cit., pp. 79-80; see also: Henry A. Kissinger, *Years of Upheaval* (Boston: Little, Brown and Co., 1982), pp. 131-37.

16. *Der Spiegel*, Oct. 23, 1972; Baring, op. cit., pp. 490-91; *Suddeutsche Zeitung*, Oct. 11, 1972.

17. Birnbaum, op. cit., pp. 79-80; *Der Spiegel*, Oct. 23, 1972.

18. Brandt, *People and Politics The Years 1960-1975*, pp. 332-33; Birnbaum, op. cit., p. 81.

19. Birnbaum, op. cit., p. 82.

20. *Frankfurter Allgemeine Zeitung*, Nov. 9, 1972.

21. For analyses of the Constitutional Court's decision, see: "Die Stellungnahme des Bundesverfassungsgerichts zum Grundlagenvertrag," Karlheinz Niclauss, op. cit., pp. 103-14; Eva Cieslar, et. al., *Der Streit um den Grundvertrag* (Munich: Olzog Verlag, 1973).

22. Baring, op. cit., p. 469; Brandt, *People and Politics The Years 1960-1975*, pp. 332-35, 392-94.

23. Brandt, *People and Politics The Years 1960-1975*, pp. 395-96; Barthold Witte, "Die deutsche Nation nach dem Grundvertrag," *Europa-Archiv*, Vol. 28, No. 7 (July, 1973), pp. 227-34; Baring, op. cit., pp. 492-93.

24. Discussion of Four-Power prerogative can be found in: Zivier, op. cit., pp. 195-97; Birnbaum, op. cit., pp.

77-80; Wilhelm Kewenig, "Die Bedeutung des Grundvertrags für das Verhältnis der beiden deutschen Staaten," *Europa-Archiv*, Vol. 28, No. 2 (January 1973), pp. 37-46.

15
The Framework
of European Detente

Commenting somewhat ruefully on the Basic Treaty shortly after its signing, Egon Bahr remarked that in the foreseeable future the FRG would have bad relations with the GDR in lieu of none at all and that this, in and of itself, represented considerable progress. The framework for this relationship has been provided through a more or less coordinated effort with the United States and Bonn's European allies, though the FRG has taken on a considerable amount of responsibility for relations with the East. The United States does not and cannot shoulder the political burden for the alliance that it once did, and thus the European powers no longer play a secondary role behind U.S. leadership. In relations with the GDR, Bonn is very much in the driver's seat, a role which has been in part thrust upon it, but one it is ordinarily willing to assume.

Above all, Bonn is willing because it has few alternatives to maintaining a *modus vivendi* with the other German state. The overriding goal is to make the presently insurmountable partition bearable. Because there is division, inter-German negotiations will go on. Contradictions and countervailing pressures notwithstanding, the FRG is now integrated in a Western and European framework within which the "German question" is manageable.[1] For the FRG this "manageability" entails the prerogative to maintain a special relationship with the GDR in accordance with constitutional tenets and to carry on day-to-day business with the East German state. In such relations, Bonn desires a modicum of predictability, keeping in mind that this is a relative term in light of East German duplicity and "screening-off" policies. Such policies along with fortified borders and automatic shooting devices belong to daily life in Central Europe.

Statistics on inter-German contact indicate a good deal about the managing of the German question. In 1980 over 8 million West Germans and West Berliners traveled to the GDR and East Berlin. In 1970 this number was around 2.4 million.[2] In 1970 it was not possible to telephone East Berlin from the Western sectors. By 1980 there were over 10 million such calls.[3] This, after all, the SPD/FDP coalition had promised.

The follow-on inter-German accords of the Quadripartite Agreement, the first agreement mentioning the GDR by name to which the FRG is a partner, and the series of subsequent treaties laid the groundwork for a special relationship between the German states, achieving Bonn's short-term goal of German-German coexistence (Nebeneinander). In the longer term it is Bonn's hope that a limited feeling of togetherness (Miteinander) will result from policies emphasizing human amelioration. While cognizant of the dilemmas inherent in the present *modus vivendi*, Bonn usually hesitates to respond to East German demarkation measures in a way that could thwart a coexistence fostering contacts at several levels.

Along with dilemmas, problems of priorities exist for Bonn as well. Some Germans are lacking in patience with policies placing greater emphasis upon "predictability" than on progress. Despite the blossoming of German-German detente during Helmut Schmidt's chancellorship, the former West German helmsman was criticized for what some alleged to be banal policy aims, directed toward largely practical matters of relations between the FRG and the GDR, such as opening the Teltow Canal in Berlin, construction of the Berlin-Hamburg Autobahn, and the electrification of railway lines to West Berlin (this latter project has not been undertaken to date because of costs). Too little emphasis was placed, according to this view, upon broader Central European political questions, and too little effort was being made to improve the human situation.[4]

During Schmidt's years in office, Bonn found itself increasingly in the forefront on German-German issues, and serving as a mediator between East and West at times as well. The confluence of several factors is the reason for this. Lack of leadership and the policy oscillations during the Carter Administration which so disturbed Schmidt heartened the latter to take the reins in his own hands. Profound changes in the world situation including the fall of the Shah and its aftermath, the Soviet invasion of Afghanistan, and the Soviet build-up of intermediate-range nuclear missiles, placed a number of problems at Bonn's doorstep. Thereafter, the harsh rhetoric of the Reagan Administration during its first year in office impressed upon Bonn the need to shield its relations with Eastern Europe and the GDR in light of the East-West chill. Schmidt strove to prevent aspects of the special German relationship from being held hostage to superpower rivalry.

The inter-German accords have provided a framework and forums where an East-West dialogue could continue. This framework, and above all, the advantages accruing to the two German states through it, are the why and wherefore of FRG-GDR detente during a rise in East-West tensions. The framework has also been instrumental to Bonn's venturing upon mediation.

To fathom the significance of the inter-German accords, it is necessary to realize the extent to which the relationship between the Germanies has evolved in the last fifteen years. It has indeed come far since the days of Ulbricht's resistance to the detente process and the fire-and-brimstone orations accompanying this antagonism. The GDR now has entrenched interests in the rapport with Bonn. Although the hope of some that the *Ostpolitik* would begin promoting pluralism in the GDR has proved to be illusory, a certain bifurcation of directive has characterized SED actions in the past decade.[5] The gap between East Berlin's declaratory and operative policies toward the West has widened measurably since 1971.

One of the challenges the SED now faces is the handling of the very delicately measured opening to the West. The making of policy for Honecker's regime requires the management of many contradictions; at times, the SED is torn in several directions. During the deterioration of East-West relations and the upsurge of polemics in the past several years, there has been an obvious attempt by the leadership of the German states at damage limitation, lest the benefits both derive from detente be imperiled. This has come at a time when the GDR has been especially heavy-handed with its detractors at home. East German leaders are not averse to pursuing "screening-off" policies to reduce daily contact with the West as a prophylactic against a potential infection in the GDR of the variety that afflicted its eastern neighbor in 1980-1981. But inter-German trade relations remain strong: trade volume increased from 4.6 billion marks in 1970 to well over 10 billion marks in 1980.[6] The FRG-GDR dialogue has continued, despite several cancellations of visits, at the summit as well as at other levels.[7] Transit route agreements have been concluded with almost unfailing regularity.

The inter-German relationship which appears on occasion to have approached geniality in recent years has spawned fears in the Kremlin that Marxism-Leninism in the GDR might take on the attributes of Hungarian "goulash-communism," eventually undermining the Soviet strategic position in Central Europe.[8] Such mistrust and suspicion of the East Germans have been expressed openly in the Soviet media.[9] The Kremlin has been dismayed. There can be little doubt that GDR policies have not represented part of a coordinated East Bloc strategy.

Until at least 1971, the GDR was fixed upon maintaining European tensions, in contrast to the FRG's yearning, manifested in its foreign policy, for reducing disaccord and for achieving political conciliation with eastern neighbors. Disaffection and altercation represented the well-spring of legitimacy for Ulbricht and his cohorts, alienation the raison d'être of their rule. When they deem it necessary, Ulbricht's successors do not shy away from conjuring up horrific images of imperialist plots against the socialist states, but such rhetoric falls primarily into the category of declaratory, as opposed to operative policy. It is oftentimes lip-service paid to an ideology.

On a micro level, West Berlin continues to represent a stumbling block to relations with the GDR and with the Soviet Union on some issues. Formal inclusion of West Berlin in international accords is theoretically not a problem and is made possible by the "Frank-Falin" formula specifying that treaties can be extended to Berlin "in accordance with the 1971 Quadripartite Agreement."[10] In practice the "Frank-Falin" formula is laden with frictions, the result of East Bloc adherence to a not always consistent interpretation of this agreement. An inter-German cultural accord providing for increased artistic exchange has not yet been signed, despite lengthy negotiations, because of the objections raised by the East Germans about the inclusion of West Berlin.[11] In the case of Soviet-FRG agreements, the "Frank-Falin" formula has on occasion smoothed over difficulties, but at other times has not worked.[12] In view of this, it remains somewhat of a mystery what the East Bloc states will accept in terms of the extension of treaty authority to Berlin.

In point of fact, the Quadripartite Agreement and the Basic Treaty have gone far in accommodating the GDR, and the East Berlin party bosses are appreciative of the rapproachement's value. As the first of the inter-German agreements done on a formal state-to-state basis, the Quadripartite Agreement initially received mixed reviews in the GDR. In hindsight the SED leadership doubtless recognizes how the GDR has stood to gain from the agreement and the other accords for which the latter is the cornerstone. The Quadripartite Agreement underscored the durability of the regime and enhanced its international prestige. Subsequent to East German entry into the United Nations, dozens of countries established diplomatic relations with the GDR. In a few short years, the GDR accomplished what it had been unable to do in over two decades when Ulbricht was party chief. While Ulbricht's "maximum" was not achieved by a long way, the GDR has assumed the role of an East Bloc stalwart and a major player on the world stage. An emerging irony is that the GDR as well as the FRG have some overlapping interests in European detente, at least of the kind fostering inter-governmental cooperation.

Despite SED fears of dissent and domestic criticism, the GDR has not fared badly in the past fifteen years. It has not been shaken by the domestic upheavals which have taken place in Poland or troubled by the economic difficulties of Romania. The regime has acquired the international stamp of approval it long hungered for. The GDR has retained its status as an unofficial member of the Common Market through its special relationship with the FRG. Such functional membership in the EC is of tremendous economic value to the East Germans and could have been terminated, had the former East German "maximum," with the consequent acceptance of the GDR as a foreign country by the FRG, been accomplished. As it is, the Basic Treaty accords the East German regime an official acknowledgment by Bonn amounting to recognition in all but name.

Western visits to the GDR represent a mixed blessing for the SED, bringing with them all varieties of ideas beset with dangers for regime stability, but proffering an invaluable source of hard currency.[13] Access accords are another important income source for the East Germans. In transit payments for the utilization of the Berlin highways alone, the GDR received some 230 million marks from 1972-1975.[14] This user fee was increased to 400 million in 1976 and to 507 million in 1980.[15] Added to this are the Berlin-affiliated construction projects such as the opening of a main water transport artery, the Teltow Canal, in 1978, and the Hamburg-Berlin highway completed in 1980, both of which Bonn financed. The latter yielded the GDR over a billion marks in hard currency earnings.[16]

In June 1982, the renewed "swing" arrangement between the Germanies underscored again the desire of both to expand inter-German commerce. Under this compact the GDR is entitled to an interest-free overdraft credit in its trade with the FRG.[17] In June of the following year, a CDU-led government increased the amount of available overdraft, further benefiting the GDR. That Franz-Josef Strauss, one of the leading opponents of the *Ostpolitik* in its initial phase, was primarily responsible for mediating the new credit extension is an indication of the degree of acceptance the German-German relationship has in the FRG.[18]

While the genesis of the "swing" credit and of the GDR's special affiliation with the Common Market dates back to the 1950s and neither therefore is a product of the *Ostpolitik*, these arrangements provide the GDR with considerable incentive to maintain the inter-German dialogue. In a phrase closely resembling the retention clause of the Quadripartite Agreement, a provision of the Basic Treaty states that the two German states will operate "on the basis of previously existing agreements," which refers presumably to such arrangements as the "swing" and the GDR's unofficial membership in the Common Market.[19] As if to highlight the value his country places upon the current inter-German trade structure, Honecker suggested in 1977 that the GDR would continue to avail itself of the "peculiarities" of framework of accord.[20] A drastic alteration of this framework would probably result in the elimination of these "peculiarities" so lucrative to the GDR.

Of all the actors in the East-West drama, the two German states are those most benefited, but at the same time, most directly affected by detente. What has unfolded in the current scene is an East German zeal to carry on "business as usual" on a governmental level, while persevering in crackdown campaigns at home. How else are Honecker's policies to be explained? Fortunately for the West, harsh domestic policies in the GDR have not as rule impinged upon sensitive Berlin issues, necessitating agonizing choices regarding responses and raising once again the specter of military confrontation there.

In the mid-1980s, as was the case at the time of the Quadripartite Agreement's ratification, the most glaring of the GDR's vulnerabilities lies in the deficiency of "nation-building" and in the abiding allurements of a German nationality, however vague.[21] These difficulties will confront the SED for as far into the future as anyone can see. As Christoph Bertram has pointed out, if any

proof whatsoever is needed that national allegiance cannot
be imposed by a state onto its people, the GDR serves as a
prime example.[22] Not only does the East German regime
appear unsuccessful in establishing a separate communal
identity within its borders, but now it is inclined to
celebrate the past glories of the German nation and to
invoke national traditions, including those of Prussia
formerly viewed as so abhorrent.

Of course, since the SED is most unlikely under
imaginable circumstances to have regime loyalty put to any
sort of popular test, it is difficult to gauge to what
extent, if any, passive acceptance of the GDR by its
population will make the transition to a more positive
identification with the state. Recent official emphasis
upon German history would appear to be decisive evidence
that the regime is most unsure about the emergence of an
East German sense of distinctiveness. It does not go too
far into the realm of speculation to suggest that Bonn's
notions of "Miteinander" have had an impact upon East
German attitudes about nationhood and have thus added to
SED headaches. The series of inter-German accords provide
arenas for the nurturing of such a "Miteinander" within the
relatively narrow parameters in which the German states
operate. These agreements are an integral part of that
framework in which peaceful, albeit very gradual, change is
possible. It is this framework that anchors Bonn in the
West. Barring events radically altering this structure, it
will continue to serve the FRG's national interests.

The Quadripartite Agreement symbolized a willingness
on the part of the West to come to grips with the GDR as a
sovereign state and to furnish the SED with assurances that
sovereignty will not be challenged. The rationale for this
approach involves the encouragement of East German leaders
to ease up on their isolationist measures and to begin
dismantling the barriers they erected over the years toward
the West. Since 1971, the GDR has allowed more travel to
its country, although at considerable cost in hard currency
to visitors. SED efforts to intensify "screening-off"
policies, especially those undertaken in 1980, are an
indication of the East German leadership's steadfast
uneasiness on the one hand, but of a few successes of the
Western approach on the other. It is apparent that SED
apprehension does not stem from any sort of overt threat
from the West or effront to GDR sovereignty, but instead
originates from fear of its own people and their contacts
with Western Europe.

A modicum of irony is not absent here as well. The

German states are parties only to the inter-German accords
affiliated with the Quadripartite Agreement, not with the
latter itself. Yet the Quadripartite Agreement provided
the FRG with an important means for dealing with the GDR
and for better managing the German problem. The accord
represents an integral part of a framework in which a
"Miteinander" is possible. It was one of the initial steps
toward a general Western recognition of two German states.
The Quadripartite Agreement and the Basic Treaty have
enabled the FRG to pursue the *Ostpolitik*, and to maintain
its "special" relationship with the GDR, while remaining a
member of the Western alliance and a partner of the United
States.

The accords achieved through the *Ostpolitik* are thus
compatible with the FRG's foreign political concept of
security and detente. In the case of Berlin, the
Quadripartite Agreement safeguards FRG interests in the
city, while providing a substructure which is fleshed out
through inter-German contacts at several levels. Retention
clauses provide tangible U.S. defense guarantees.

The inter-German summits of the last decade have
poignantly demonstrated that dilemmas nonetheless remain
and might become more acute on some issues. Among the most
salient is that of the European "ideal" spelled out by
Buchan. How is the FRG to promote European cohesion and
security without alienating either the Soviet Union or the
United States? Soviet anger could bring in its wake
substantial Kremlin pressure on the GDR significantly to
reduce contacts with the FRG. Can Bonn maintain and
develop the "special relationship" with the GDR when
external factors strain such a relationship and could even
jeopardize it?

Instances illustrative of the quandaries are not
difficult to find in the last few years. On the final day
of Helmut Schmidt's visit to the GDR in December 1981,
martial law was declared in Poland. Bonn, under any
circumstances most cautious about criticizing Poland for
quite obvious reasons, seemed reluctant to condemn the
Polish government, if for no other reason than for fear of
the ramifications for the German-German relationship.[23]
The very presence of the Federal Chancellor in East Germany
at the time martial law was declared in Poland gave the
appearance of tacit West German condoning of the action.
Holding the summit while the crack-down was taking place in
Poland was an indication to many that the FRG would pursue
"business as usual" policies vis-à-vis the East Bloc
regardless of what the regimes were doing to their own

people. Hence Bonn's dilemma: censure of the Polish dictatorship might bring about Honecker's wrath and a worsening of human conditions in East Germany; its absence would open Bonn to the accusation of insensitivity toward oppression in the East Bloc and would invite suggestions of German arrogance. In response to the imposition of martial law in Poland, Schmidt and Honecker issued a vague statement summoning the Poles to solve their "problems" without outside interference.[24]

The German-German relationship confronts the GDR with not altogether dissimilar quandaries. Certainly the SED did not need to agonize about its reaction to the imposition of martial law in Poland. Official propaganda instruments have periodically made all sorts of noises about the end of detente and an impending "ice-age" in East-West relations. In September 1980 as labor unrest was sweeping Poland, the GDR lashed out at Bonn, accusing it, among other things, of engaging in gross interference in the domestic affairs of Poland. "During the past few weeks the vast majority of the FRG mass media have interfered massively in affairs of the Polish People's Republic. Both in radio and television they made no secret of the fact that they are seeking a change in the socialist system of the People's Republic of Poland."[25]

Moreover, East German propaganda organs did not miss the opportunity to link events in Poland with the scheduled deployment of NATO intermediate range missiles in Europe. Commenting that the FRG was "now relying upon American missiles to realize its revanchist goals against the GDR and against Poland," *Neues Deutschland* employed strong polemics against Bonn of the sort not often heard of late.[26] The SED leaders seemed to be showing that inter-German relations would invariably sour if labor unrest in Poland continued, which suggests that their initial fear of events there was very great. "Screening-off" precautions followed the spate of SED polemics apropos West German "revanchism."

East German measures to impede travel from the East and the West to the GDR in October 1980 were the opening volleys of an intensified "screening-off" campaign. Along with the access limitations, the possibility of war was raised by Honecker in an apparent crusade to terminate the widespread "business as usual" attitude toward Bonn. In an October 7 speech, the East German party chief stated that "from the GDR . . . a war will never emanate. Unfortunately, this cannot be said of the FRG. Its agreement to the long-term armament program of NATO, the

fateful Brussels decision, has complicated the
international situation."[27]

The SED tough line against Bonn was short-lived,
however. By the end of the year the GDR was signaling its
desire to maintain the dialogue with the FRG and to avoid
sliding back into a cold war.[28] There once again were
indications of a GDR preparedness to tolerate more of the
risks intrinsic to the delicate balancing act it engages
in. The SED undertook a rather visible about-face, the
explanation for which is not hard to discern. The GDR
would not be prepared to jeopardize the relationship with
Bonn if it could help it, so SED officials began soft-
pedaling their inflamed rhetoric once they detected the
enduring docility of the East German work force, and,
indeed, its displays of resentment toward striking Poles.
Notwithstanding the narrowness of their operating radius,
the SED leaders showed they too could be vacillating.
Inter-German relations are scarcely devoid of anomalies.
SED leaders do not need often to be reminded what is at
stake for them in the special relationship with the FRG.
One cannot fail to notice that the East German leadership
was of more than one mind.

As in 1981, the GDR again made conspicuous efforts at
damage limitation following the breakdown of the Geneva
talks on intermediate range missiles at the end of 1983 and
the subsequent deployment of new NATO systems in Europe.[29]
Honecker came back with assurances that detente will
continue. Schmidt-Honecker statements about war never
again springing from German soil replaced accusations of
West German revanchism and war-planning. Once again
Honecker has spoken of the "responsibility of both German
states" to maintain the peace in Europe. After the NATO
missile deployment began, he raised concern in Moscow by
going public with an expression of hope that German
bonhomie would survive the latest rearmament rounds.

Ultimately one must view West German policies against
this background and consider the alternatives for the FRG
in the 1970s to negotiating the *Ostpolitik* accords and the
Basic Treaty. There should be little doubt that, had the
FRG not taken the initiative when it did, concluding
political arrangements with the East Bloc states and
establishing a working relationship with its eastern
neighbors, the Allies would have eventually pressured the
FRG to accept realities and to conclude a *modus vivendi* on
far less favorable terms for the West Germans than those
attainable in the early 1970s. For this reason alone, the
speed with which the SPD/FDP coalition moved on the

Ostpolitik is at least understandable. Having faced the hard realities, the FRG shifted in a little more than a decade from a partially hamstrung position to playing the role of sometime mediator.

NOTES

1. See: Robert Gerald Livingston, "East Germany Between Moscow and Bonn," *Foreign Affairs*, Vol. 50, No. 2 (January 1972), pp. 297-299; also, *Der Spiegel*, April 7, 1980.

2. Josef Joffe, "Bonns Politik nach Osten-freier, aber riskanter," *Die Zeit*, September 26, 1980, p. 10.

3. Ibid.

4. Interview with Helmut Schmidt, *Der Spiegel*, July 7, 1980; Haftendorn, op. cit., pp. 259-260.

5. Robert Gerald Livingston foresaw this possibility even prior to the signing of the Basic Treaty. See: "East Germany Between Moscow and Bonn," pp. 301-307. For a more recent analysis: "Soviets alarmed at East-West German Ties," *Christian Science Monitor*, July 31, 1984.

6. Joffe, "Bonns Politik nach Osten-Freier, aber riskanter," p. 10.

7. In 1980, for example, planned FRG-GDR summits were postponed three times due to outside events.

8. "Soviets alarmed at East-West German Ties," *Christian Science Monitor*, July 31, 1984.

9. *German Press Review*, 32, August 18, 1984; *Die Welt*, July 14, 1984.

10. The formula reads: "In accordance with the Four-Power Agreement of 3 September 1971, this agreement is extended to Berlin (West) in keeping with the procedures laid down."

11. *The German Tribune*, October 6, 1985, No. 1198, p. 10.

12. Two Bonn-Moscow agreements signed in May 1973, one on economic, industrial and technical cooperation, the other on cultural cooperation, are extended to West Berlin by the "Frank-Falin" formula. Three other agreements on cultural exchange, scientific and technological cooperation, and legal assistance have not been signed because Moscow has balked at the inclusion of West Berlin. See: *The German Tribune*, October 6, 1985, No. 1198, p. 10.

13. *Christian Science Monitor*, September 28, 1983.

14. A. James McAdams, "Surviving the Missiles: The GDR and the Future of Inter-German Relations," *Orbis*, Vol. 27, No. 2 (Summer 1983), pp. 347-348.

15. *Die Zeit*, May 16, 1980.

16. McAdams, "Surviving the Missiles," p. 347.

17. Ibid, p. 361.

18. Haftendorn, op. cit., p. 260.

19. McAdams, "Surviving the Missiles," p. 348.

20. Ibid.

21. Livingston, "East Germany Between Moscow and Bonn," pp. 304-307.

22. Christoph Bertram, "European Security and the German Problem," *International Security*, Vol. 4, No. 3 (Winter 1979/80), p. 106.

23. Interview with Helmut Kohl, *Frankfurter Allgemeine Zeitung*, December 16, 1981.

24. *Der Spiegel*, December 21, 1981.

25. *Neues Deutschland*, September 4, 1980.

26. *Neues Deutschland*, September 3, 1980.

27. Honecker speech of October 6, 1980: *Neues Deutschland*, October 8, 1980.

28. *Der Spiegel*, December 21, 1981; also, interview with Honecker in: *Neues Deutschland*, December 16, 1981.

29. Haftendorn, op. cit., p. 260.

Conclusion

The 1971 Berlin Quadripartite Agreement, in addition to suspending hostilities and significantly improving daily life in and around the city provided an important impetus for the Bonn-Moscow Treaty, FRG treaties with Poland and Czechoslovakia, as well as for the Basic Treaty between the two Germanies. Moreover, it precipitated the convening of a European security conference (Conference on Security and Cooperation in Europe or CSCE) and of negotiations on Mutual and Balanced Force Reductions (MBFR). The signing of the final protocol of the Quadripartite Agreement represented in the words of Egon Bahr, "the first joint contribution to the relaxation of tensions in Europe."[1]

Improvement of the Berlin situation made possible a *modus vivendi* between the FRG and the GDR on the basis of equality and non-discrimination. The normalization of relations between the German states promoted Brandt's goal of human amelioration by facilitating travel to East Germany and through the establishment of wider contact on an official as well as an individual level.

Immediate practical improvements in the inter-German situation were difficult to overlook. Transit route obstruction or harassment by East German officials is infrequent. From June to August 1972, overland traffic had increased 35 percent over the same period the previous year. From the time the agreement entered into force on June 3, 1972 to March 1973, West Berliners made over three million visits to East Berlin and the GDR.[2] Furthermore, the agreement permits the FRG to maintain and develop the presence in West Berlin that is crucial to the city's continued existence.

Richard Loewenthal argues that Willy Brandt conceived of the *Ostpolitik* only after having become convinced that the FRG's allies had tacitly recognized Europe's status-quo.[3] By 1969 the Bonn government attempted to afford the Soviet Union additional incentives to settle on Berlin. In exchange for progress toward "human amelioration" and a general improvement in the political atmosphere, Bonn offered to accept the Oder-Neisse line (the border with Poland) as well as to foster a special relationship between the two German states. The West, with Bonn's encouragement, held out to Moscow the possibility of a European security conference with the prospect of an international approbation of the political realities in Eastern Europe.

Viewed from this angle, it is apparent why Kissinger would refer to the Berlin deal as a *quid pro quo*.[4] While leery of granting concessions on Berlin, lest its already tenuous position there erode, the U.S. had been interested in a Berlin accord since at least 1961.[5] In Berlin the Nixon Administration, like the SPD-FDP coalition, tested the waters of detente.

There is good reason to believe that Kissinger remained suspicious of Egon Bahr and other Bonn officials involved in the pursuit of the *Ostpolitik*, and these suspicions are not without some justification.[6] Although Kissinger does not openly admit that the SPD-FDP coalition correctly gauged several diplomatic possibilities in Eastern Europe in 1969-70, he does call attention to Moscow's eagerness to deal, an eagerness that, in some areas, exceeded the FRG's. In hindsight there was little reason for the West to stall too long on Berlin negotiations.

The *quid pro quo* and test-case interpretations provide only parts--albeit critical ones--of the overall picture. Observers have at times failed to discern the implications of the Kremlin's inclination to conclude an agreement on Berlin. Kissinger describes Soviet behavior in the final stage of negotiations as characterized by an impatience it would have been a shame not to have exploited. Western recognition of the Eastern European status-quo was hardly a new goal on Moscow's wish-list. A significant relaxation of tensions in the West would free the Soviet hand for managing diplomatic business in the East. After the 1969 Ussuri River clashes, there could be no doubt about seriously deteriorating Soviet-Chinese relations and little question of the ensuing uneasiness in the Kremlin.

Less than an hour after the June 15, 1971 proclamation of Kissinger's trip to Peking, the White House reminded the Soviet Union of "the sequence of events which preceded the announcement."[7] The Soviets were faced with the specter that had concerned them for years: what if the U.S. and China should decide to become chummy at Moscow's expense? Thus, in order better to handle the political/strategic situation in Asia, Moscow saw the need to shift detente with the West into high gear. The U.S. opening to China in the wake of Soviet-Chinese hostility furnished the Kremlin with additional incentives to encourage the West German *Ostpolitik*.

Kissinger spells out the Western diplomatic accomplishments regarding a situation he aptly describes as having been "encrusted by haggling over legalisms." Prior to the Berlin accord, there had been no legal basis for "Zugang" (civilian access), above all because two German states did not exist when the quadripartite status of Berlin was established. The 1971 agreement outlined transit and access procedures in detail, "down to such technicalities as the use of sealed conveyances for manufactured goods."[8] Civilian access was contractually guaranteed by the Soviet Union, a significant reversal in light of the fact that less than a year before the Soviet Union denied all responsibility for what occurred in "sovereign" East Germany. Furthermore, the Soviet Union accepted the principle of FRG ties to West Berlin. In the words of former U.S. ambassador to the FRG, Martin Hillenbrand, West Berlin would become "even more secure as its manifold ties to the Federal Republic continue to be developed."[9]

Notwithstanding the complexity of the Berlin dilemma and the decades of acerbic chaffering over Berlin legalisms, the Quadripartite Agreement has functioned much as the West planned it would. West Berlin is accessible without friction. Traffic snarls caused by East German officials are virtually unknown. The "three essentials" (actually five essentials, according to Kissinger) are respected, albeit grudgingly. Allied military patrols continue to enter East Berlin; diplomatic and military traffic moves about quite freely in the entire city. What is somewhat ironic is that Berlin has ceased to be a seismograph of European detente. Despite the definite cooling in East-West relations, the Soviet Union has made no major attempt to "heat up" Berlin, exploiting the Western pressure point in Central Europe. Scheel's 1973 statement about Berlin being a "symbol for the degree of detente in Europe," is applicable in the 1980s only to the extent that the effects of GDR "screening-off" practices, carried out when the East Berlin party bosses perceive some danger to their regime, are felt almost immediately in the divided city in the form of travel to the eastern part becoming more expensive. The superpowers continue to grouse and complain about one another's behavior, but Berlin has not been affected to the degree that it has been in the past, notwithstanding recent GDR efforts to discourage visits to its country and to East Berlin.[10] Bark's assessment in 1974 that, "the measure of (the Quadripartite Agreement) will also very likely rise and fall according to the dilemmas of detente," has not passed muster. Few observers would dispute that the "dilemmas" of detente have increased significantly in the past decade; these have failed as yet to touch Berlin. For the forseeable future East-West tensions will not be synonymous with Berlin.

In providing a framework for the Basic Treaty between the FRG and the GDR, the Quadripartite Agreement set the stage for the most important post-war development in inter-German relations. That the Berlin accord represented a necessary precursor to the Basic Treaty now seems axiomatic for several reasons.

1. Because the FRG was permitted to maintain its ties with West Berlin, an area of serious contention had been removed. The GDR cannot now challenge the principle of FRG presence in West Berlin.
2. The FRG had accomplished one of its salient short-term goals by securing the right to extend consular protection to West Berliners, thereby ending decades of discrimination. Had the dilemma concerning West Berliners' rights abroad remained unresolved, progress on inter-German travel and transit agreements would not have been possible.
3. The inter-German accords on access regulations served as an example of how provisions on travel to the GDR could function.
4. The previous quandary for the FRG, whereby any improvement in the political atmosphere was contingent upon Bonn's diplomatic recognition of the GDR (something no FRG leader could accept), was eliminated. The GDR backed off from the preconditions it had previously laid down.
5. Not to be underestimated was the significance of Ulbricht's political demise. Ulbricht was the East Bloc leader most adamantly opposed to greater contacts between East and West, let alone any sort of accommodation. Ulbricht became a victim of the

quadripartite negotiations.
6. The agreement provided the SPD-FDP coalition with the
   tangible evidence it needed to sell its policies
   domestically and to continue the *Ostpolitik*. If on
   none other than domestic grounds, Brandt and Scheel
   could not have moved forward with the *Ostpolitik*, had
   Moscow been inflexible on Berlin or unwilling to rein
   in its East German ally. Although there was
   considerable opposition within the FRG to the
   Brandt/Scheel course--leading to constitutional court
   cases as well as necessitating premature elections--
   the Bonn government acquired the requisite support for
   a treaty with "the other Germany."
7. The agreement demonstrated that a diplomatic
   arrangement was feasible. Mutually-tolerated
   disagreement on principle enabled the FRG to detach
   its foreign policy from the German question enough to
   allow Bonn some flexibility. Following ratification
   of the Basic Treaty, both German states could become
   full members of the United Nations in 1973, and Bonn's
   allies were thereafter in a position to open full
   diplomatic relations with the GDR.

That the 1971 Quadripartite Agreement bore prominent
results is no longer a matter of serious controversy. It
represented the first real test of the Nixon/Kissinger
foreign policy. It catalyzed West German *Ostpolitik* and
was an initial, crucial step in an improvement of the
political atmosphere in divided Europe. On a more mundane
but no less important level, it provided some resolution to
the daily problems of an isolated metropolis. Millions of
Germans benefit every year. This culmination--human
amelioration--cannot be overlooked by those labeling the
Ostpolitik appeasement.
     In any analysis of the *Ostpolitik*, one cannot
underestimate Brandt and Scheel's determination to
alleviate the human suffering affiliated with Germany's
division. The quest for amelioration in the short and
longer term is an indisputable leitmotif of the *Ostpolitik*
and a theme of Bonn's management of the German problem.
While human amelioration was clearly not Brandt's only
motive--one should not disregard such considerations as for
example, national pride and increased trade and commerce--
in the first series of small, faltering steps, this
objective was clearly crucial.
     For a number of reasons, all the steps Brandt would
take, however, would have been for naught in the absence of

a far-reaching Berlin agreement. First, because Berlin had been a point of contention for years, the infeasibility of a settlement there would have resulted in considerable grounds for skepticism about any relaxation of tension across German-German borders. Second, Brandt needed a Berlin settlement in order to get his Eastern treaties ratified and to rally public support for fresh ideas about an *Ostpolitik* and for new approaches to Eastern Europe. In this sense Berlin was both a seismograph of the political atmosphere and a symbol of successful policy. Third, in Berlin many of the frictions attendant to Germany's division came to a head. If such immediate sources of contention could not be diluted, then major steps toward improvement of the German situation might not be possible.

In the pursuit of *Ostpolitik* and in Bonn's handling of the German question a number of salient themes are discernible.

1. Bonn strove finally to terminate the German bogey. An East bloc opening to the FRG, and in the longer term, it was hoped, a subsiding of Soviet predominance in East/Central Europe would ensue from a decline in mistrust of the FRG.
2. Diplomatic isolation was an ominous possibility facing Bonn in the 1960s. The FRG had to avoid being an international pariah and to formulate policies attune to those of its allies.
3. West German leaders with a modicum of vision realized that only through increased contact across the German divide could any progress be made toward reconciliation. The FRG aimed therefore to foster German intercommunication.
4. Any flexibility on Bonn's part or success in the pursuit of *Ostpolitik* was predicated on domestic support and basic consensus. The coalition had to win approval among the voters for its programs and show positive achievements of its policies.
5. A *modus vivendi* with the GDR required a "special relationship," whereby no recognition under international law would be granted and neither German state could be regarded as a foreign country by the other. A successful approach to the German question entailed Soviet and East German acceptance of Bonn's preconditions.
6. Due to the complexity even of single issues and to the immense difficulties of accord, progress was possible only through awkward probes and small steps. The

German problem could be managed, at least in the foreseeable future, only in a roundabout way, following bypaths and crooked avenues. Defusing the Berlin situation represented one of these crucial steps, improving circumstances, but leaving options open. Coalition leaders correctly perceived that a Berlin agreement would catalyze the process leading to the Basic Treaty and other accords with the GDR.

7. Through peaceful initiative and demonstrated independence, Bonn hoped to bring its political influence more into line with its economic power. By 1969, the FRG was the economic and military powerhouse of Europe, with concomitant responsibilities neither its citizens nor its leaders could shun.

The Quadripartite Agreement was the product of several factors, such as the emergence of a new political coalition in the FRG and the ability of a new U.S. administration to manage change in the post-war world. Without question the coinciding of certain political developments made the accord on Berlin possible. Moscow was intent to negotiate a relaxation of tensions on the Western borders of its empire in light of the difficulties with China. A Bonn government with a paramount commitment to human amelioration was prepared in 1970 to play the one trump it possessed: to offer to recognize the European status-quo. Moreover, Bonn was in a hurry to consummate progress toward its goals. For its part, the Soviet Union was hesitant to pass up the opportunity for the convocation of a European security conference that would bestow partial legitimacy upon its World War II conquests.

Even a renowned (and admitted) skeptic like Kissinger suggests that the Soviet Union made concessions on Berlin considered practically unthinkable in previous years. A number of Western concessions to the Soviets amounted largely to face-saving devices to the latter, a prominent example of which was the establishment of a Soviet consulate in West Berlin, a *quid pro quo* for Soviet sanctioning of an official West German presence in the city. The limitations placed upon this presence were a small price to pay as part of an agreement securing the principal Western goal in Berlin: a written Soviet commitment to guarantee civilian and military access.

Any analysis of the Quadripartite Agreement must examine the specifics of the accord as well as treat the events leading up to it. Application is of course the ultimate measure of performance. A partial answer to the

question why the arrangement has succeeded is that the
accord has something to offer all participants, even to
those not technically party to it, without requiring
conditions one or more would be incapable of fulfilling,
tempting violation or circumvention of the treaty.

The FRG maintains ties with West Berlin and tenders
protection to its inhabitants. Since the former capital of
the *Reich* remains under the post-war occupation regime, the
German question continues to be an open one and Bonn is
provided with a framework within which it can retain its
relations with the GDR while adhering to its constitutional
commitment to strive for German reunification.

The GDR gained an aura of legitimacy in the
international arena and has acquired a modicum of approval
for its *de facto* annexation of East Berlin, including the
establishment there of its seat of government. While
technically acting only as an executive agent of the Soviet
Union in controlling overland transit to West Berlin, the
GDR can point to the stationing of its officials at the
border checkpoints as well as the police patrols of the
highways as visible evidence of its sovereign rights.
East-West disagreement on the extent of this sovereignty
notwithstanding, a workable arrangement stems from the
meshing of a Western and an inter-German framework.

There is no denying the importance of the GDR as an
industrial state, nor is there any question of Soviet
determination to preserve this society. Though the West
should shun propping up communist regimes, domestic
instability within East German territory must be cause for
concern even in the West. What is important to the West
above all is that this "reality" does not impinge upon
vital interests. In defending his *Ostpolitik*, Willy Brandt
encouraged his countrymen to accept certain brutal facts,
reminding them that he was renouncing nothing not long
since lost.

International recognition of its position in Eastern
Europe has been one of Moscow's chief foreign policy goals
since the 1940s, and tranquility in East Germany assures
the Soviets of their prized forward position in Central
Europe. Certainly no one in the West should be enchanted
with this reality, but practical alternatives to its
acknowledgment are absent for the foreseeable future. The
Quadripartite Agreement facilitated official Western
dealings with the GDR and laid the foundation for a
semblance of inter-German political normalization. Moscow
was relieved of the headache of incessantly standing up for
the alleged rights of its East German ally, often

resulting, due to Soviet propensity for heavy-handedness and bullying, in confrontation.

Significant advantages accrue to the U.S., France and Great Britain, whose primary interest it was in the quadrilateral negotiations--indeed, since the 1948-49 Berlin blockade--to obtain a written guarantee of Soviet legal obligations in the city, permitting frictionless access. Because the Allies perseveringly upheld their rights of occupation and never acknowledged any "original" German authority in Berlin, while demanding that the Soviet Union concede it had responsibilities and obligations there, Moscow finally yielded.

Though it is tempting, one should avoid being too critical of the Berlin accord's ambiguities. Largely because of them the agreement was negotiable and remains operable. The term "relevant area," representing the salient compromise, involves an issue upon which no further consensus was possible. It allows differing interpretations and a degree of face-saving on both sides. Disparate interpretations of the agreement underscore its highly political nature. For example, the Soviet Union has often argued that the agreement applies only to West Berlin.[11] Moscow is able to take such a position (thereby explicitly respecting the interests of the GDR) under the conditions that it not challenge Western rights and that it accept its own obligations in Berlin. The Western Powers would not and could not concede the "Berlin problem" to be exclusively one of West Berlin. They continue to emphasize that the Quadripartite Agreement applies to greater Berlin--as opposed to only the Western sectors--even though Western rights in East Berlin are limited and in spite of GDR claims of complete sovereignty there. All parties opted for "practical improvements of the situation," and ratified the accord despite their political/legal differences. The structure of the accord enabled the parties to agree to it without haggling over esoteric legalisms. So long as both sides respect the status-quo, the accord will likely remain operable.

At a rather high level of generalization, the 1971 Quadripartite Agreement produced the following results:

First, within a broader framework, the accord represented a significant step toward a German-German *modus vivendi*, one not jeopardizing the FRG position on the German question. Providing workable regulation of the Berlin situation, it did not foreclose future unravelings of Central European dilemmas.

Second, the agreement furnished the Western Powers and

the FRG with a written Kremlin guarantee of continuing Four-Power rights in Germany and in Berlin.

Third, in concluding the Quadripartite Agreement, the Soviet Union underwrote the principle of overland access to Berlin, in an apparent *volte-face* from its previous desire to grant full sovereignty to the GDR.

Fourth, not to be underestimated is the inherent value of a treaty that has contributed to the elimination of a dangerous flash-point in East-West relations. Whether or not the agreement will endure may remain an open question, but clearly it has been instrumental in ameliorating a crisis-prone situation.

Fifth, in providing the West German public with examples of what could be achieved diplomatically, Bonn acquired a mandate for the pursuit of *Ostpolitik*. The Quadripartite Agreement and the accords following it helped nurture more coherent policies toward the East Bloc and form a basic consensus among Bonn political parties on the tenets of the *Ostpolitik*.

Sixth, a principal accomplishment of the Quadripartite Agreement lay in the mutual acceptance of Western conditions for any accord on the German question. The agreement cannot, nor does it intend to, represent a solution to the Berlin problem. Rather, this agreement was reached in an effort to alleviate practical, albeit complex, difficulties attendant to the division of Germany. To expect more from the Quadripartite Agreement or indeed from the *Ostpolitik* in the foreseeable future would run counter to the entire Western approach to the German problem. Closing remaining options would be anathema to Bonn and contrary to the commitments of the United States.

The Quadripartite Agreement is instructive about what is attainable in East-West negotiation and about what the West must anticipate in agreements with the East Bloc. Though the Soviet Union made significant concessions on the Berlin issue, the abatement of differences did not require more of Moscow than it was willing to relinquish. Worthy therefore of close examination are the nature and provisions of the Quadripartite Agreement.

One might offer the Helsinki Final Act, the contractual product of the Conference on Security and Cooperation in Europe ushered in by the Quadripartite Agreement, as an example of an infeasible multilateral treaty. The overselling of detente in the West, with the consequent unrealizable expectations about change in the East, resulted in apparent wide-spread belief that the East Bloc would actually adhere to the treaty provisions of

Basket III, committing signatory states to foster human
contacts, to improve access to information and to
facilitate cultural/educational exchange. Did the West
actually deceive itself into thinking that the Soviet Union
and its satellites would promote the free flow of
information, ideas and people because of signatures upon a
treaty? Presuming the East Bloc not to have found new
moral insight, it is unreasonable to think the Soviet Union
would observe treaty provisions whose implementation would
be tantamount to the dismantling of the Soviet empire, and
the destabilization of Soviet society. The East Bloc has
little incentive to comply with Basket III of the Helsinki
Final Act and, in practice, violates the provisions with
impunity. For all the ink spilled in the West on the
subject of Basket III implementation, the political
situation in Eastern Europe has not changed as a result of
the Helsinki Accords, nor will it.[12] Thus the Helsinki
Final Act has resolved little and has led to
disillusionment because its scope is too wide and its goals
are set too high.

NOTES

1. Quoted in: Catudal, *The Diplomacy of the
Quadripartite Agreement*, p. 214.
2. Bark, op. cit., p. 112.
3. See his reply to David Gress in *Commentary*, Vol.
76, No. 5 (Nov. 1983), p. 4.
4. Kissinger, *White House Years*, p. 824.
5. This is mentioned in a "Top Secret" (Eyes Only)
cable on "Showing Identification Papers in East Berlin."
The cable is from Gen. Lucius D. Clay to Secretary of State
Dean Rusk, Oct. 24, 1961. Clay mentions the possibility of
an agreement with the Soviet Union on Berlin--an indication
that the idea had been considered within the
Administration. However, Clay ends the cable:
We will avoid test at Friedrichstrasse today awaiting
your consideration of this recommendation. We must
probe not later than tomorrow. If unarmed probe fails
we will then proceed under our instructions to protest
and if unable to reach Soviet commandant or protest
fails, to try again with armed escort. Under these
circumstances, I doubt if armed escort will suffice.

208

> Therefore, in the event unarmed probe fails, we believe that calling in Soviet Ambassador is preferable alternative to trying armed escort.

One can speculate what the consequences of the dispatching of an armed escort might have been. Certainly the seriousness of the situation itself must have induced some far-sighted individuals to consider an agreement with the Soviets.

6. Kissinger, *White House Years*, pp. 410-12; Baring, pp. 328-332.

7. Kissinger, *White House Years*, p. 835.

8. Ibid., p. 830.

9. U.S. Ambassador Martin J. Hillenbrand, in address on September 14, 1972, *U.S. Department of State Bulletin*, No. 31, September 26, 1972.

10. In the midst of the Polish crisis in the fall of 1980, the GDR considerably raised visa fees as well as required exchange, presumably to discourage visits to East Berlin and the GDR, see: *Der Spiegel*, Oct. 20, 1980.

11. Pyotr Abrasimov, *West Berlin Yesterday and Today* (Dresden: Verlag Zeit im Bild, 1980), p. 96-127.

12. See for example: Special Report Number 89, Eleventh Semiannual Report, "Implementation of the Helsinki Final Act" (Washington, D.C.: Department of State, GPO, 1981).

Appendix A:
Quadripartite Agreement
on Berlin of September 3, 1971[1]

The Governments of the United States of America, the French Republic, the Union of Soviet Socialist Republics and the United Kingdom of Great Britain and Northern Ireland,

Represented by their Ambassadors, who held a series of meetings in the building formerly occupied by the Allied Control Council in the American Sector of Berlin,

Acting on the basis of their quadripartite rights and responsibilities, and of the corresponding wartime and postwar agreements and decisions of the Four Powers, which are not affected,

Taking into account the existing situation in the relevant area,

Guided by the desire to contribute to practical improvements of the situation,

Without prejudice to their legal positions,

Have agreed on the following:

Part I
General Provisions

1. The four Governments will strive to promote the elimination of tension and the prevention of complications in the relevant area.

2. The four Governments, taking into account their obligations under the Charter of the United Nations, agree that there shall be no use or threat of force in the area and that disputes shall be settled solely by peaceful means.

3. The four Governments will mutually respect their individual and joint rights and responsibilities, which

remain unchanged.

4. The four Governments agree that, irrespective of the differences in legal views, the situation which has developed in the area, and as it is defined in this Agreement as well as in the other agreements referred to in this Agreement, shall not be changed unilaterally.

Part II
Provisions Relating to the
Western Sectors of Berlin

A. The Government of the Union of Soviet Socialist Republics declares that transit traffic by road, rail and waterways through the territory of the German Democratic Republic of civilian persons and goods between the Western Sectors of Berlin and the Federal Republic of Germany will be unimpeded; that such traffic will be facilitated so as to take place in the most simple and expeditious manner; and that it will receive preferential treatment.

Detailed arrangements concerning this civilian traffic, as set forth in Annex I, will be agreed by the competent German authorities.

B. The Governments of the French Republic, the United Kingdom and the United States of America declare that the ties between the Western Sectors of Berlin and the Federal Republic of Germany will be maintained and developed, taking into account that these Sectors continue not to be a constituent part of the Federal Republic of Germany and not to be governed by it.

Detailed arrangements concerning the relationship between the Western Sectors of Berlin and the Federal Republic of Germany are set forth in Annex II.

C. The Government of the Union of Soviet Socialist Republics declares that communications between the Western Sectors of Berlin and areas bordering on these Sectors and those areas of the German Democratic Republic which do not border on these Sectors will be improved. Permanent residents of the Western Sectors of Berlin will be able to travel to and visit such areas for compassionate, family, religious, cultural or commercial reasons, or as tourists, under conditions comparable to those applying to other persons entering these areas.

The problems of the small enclaves, including Steinstücken, and of other small areas may be solved by exchange of territory.

Detailed arrangements concerning travel,

communications and the exchange of territory, as set forth in Annex III, will be agreed by the competent German authorities.

D. Representation abroad of the interests of the Western Sectors of Berlin and consular activities of the Union of Soviet Socialist Republics in the Western Sectors of Berlin can be exercised as set forth in Annex IV.

Part III
Final Provisions

This Quadripartite Agreement will enter into force on the date specified in a Final Quadripartite Protocol to be concluded when the measures envisaged in Part II of this Quadripartite Agreement and its Annexes have been agreed.

DONE at the building formerly occupied by the Allied Control Council in the American Sector of Berlin this 3rd day of September 1971, in four originals, each in the English, French and Russian languages, all texts being equally authentic.

Annex I
Communication from the Government of the
Union of Soviet Socialist Republics to the
Governments of the French Republic, the
United Kingdom and the United States of America

The Government of the Union of Soviet Socialist Republics, with reference to Part II (A) of the Quadripartite Agreement of this date and after consultation and agreement with the Government of the German Democratic Republic, has the honor to inform the Governments of the French Republic, the United Kingdom and the United States of America that:

1. Transit traffic by road, rail and waterways through the territory of the German Democratic Republic of civilian persons and goods between the Western Sectors of Berlin and the Federal Republic of Germany will be facilitated and unimpeded. It will receive the most simple, expeditious and preferential treatment provided by international practice.

2. Accordingly,

    a. Conveyances sealed before departure may be used for the transport of civilian goods by road, rail and waterways between the Western Sectors of Berlin and the Federal Republic of Germany. Inspection procedures will be limited to the inspection of seals and accompanying documents.

b. With regard to conveyances which cannot be sealed, such as open trucks, inspection procedures will be limited to the inspection of accompanying documents. In special cases where there is sufficient reason to suspect that unsealed conveyances contain either material intended for dissemination along the designated routes or persons or material put on board along these routes, the content of unsealed conveyances may be inspected. Procedures for dealing with such cases will be agreed by the competent German authorities.

c. Through trains and buses may be used for travel between the Western Sectors of Berlin and the Federal Republic of Germany. Inspection procedures will not include any formalities other than identification of persons.

d. Persons identified as through travellers using individual vehicles between the Western Sectors of Berlin and the Federal Republic of Germany on routes designated for through traffic will be able to proceed to their destinations without paying individual tolls and fees for the use of the transit routes. Procedures applied for such travellers should not involve delay. The travellers, their vehicles and personal baggage will not be subject to search, detention or exclusion from use of the designated routes, except in special cases, as may be agreed by the competent German authorities, where there is sufficient reason to suspect that misuse of the transit routes is intended for purposes not related to direct travel to and from the Western Sectors of Berlin and contrary to generally applicable regulations concerning public order.

e. Appropriate compensation for fees and tolls and for other costs related to traffic on the communication routes between the Western Sectors of Berlin and the Federal Republic of Germany, including the maintenance of adequate routes, facilities and installations used for such traffic, may be made in the form of an annual lump sum paid to the German Democratic Republic by the Federal Republic of Germany.

3. Arrangements implementing and supplementing the provisions of paragraphs 1 and 2 above will be agreed by the competent German authorities.

Annex II
Communication from the Governments of the
French Republic, the United Kingdom and the
United States of America to the Government
of the Union of Soviet Socialist Republics

The Governments of the French Republic, the United Kingdom and the United States of America, with reference to Part II (B) of the Quadripartite Agreement of this date and after consultation with the Government of the Federal Republic of Germany, have the honor to inform the Government of the Union of Soviet Socialist Republics that:
1. They declare, in the exercise of their rights and responsibilities, that the ties between the Western Sectors of Berlin and the Federal Republic of Germany will be maintained and developed, taking into account that these Sectors continue not to be a constituent part of the Federal Republic of Germany and not to be governed by it. The provisions of the Basic Law of the Federal Republic of Germany and of the Constitution operative in the Western Sectors of Berlin which contradict the above have been suspended and continue not to be in effect.
2. The Federal President, the Federal Government, the Bundesversammlung, the Bundesrat and the Bundestag, including their Committees and Fraktionen, as well as other state bodies of the Federal Republic of Germany will not perform in the Western Sectors of Berlin constitutional or official acts which contradict the provisions of paragraph 1.
3. The Government of the Federal Republic of Germany will be represented in the Western Sectors of Berlin to the authorities of the three Governments and to the Senat by a permanent liaison agency.

Annex III
Communication from the Government of the
Union of Soviet Socialist Republics to the
Governments of the French Republic, the
United Kingdom and the United States of America

The Government of the Union of Soviet Socialist

214

Republics, with reference to Part II (C) of the
Quadripartite Agreement of this date and after consultation
and agreement with the Government of the German Democratic
Republic, has the honor to inform the Governments of the
French Republic, the United Kingdom and the United States
of America that:

1. Communications between the Western Sectors of
Berlin and areas bordering on these Sectors and those areas
of the German Democratic Republic which do not border on
these Sectors will be improved.

2. Permanent residents of the Western Sectors of
Berlin will be able to travel to and visit such areas for
compassionate, family, religious, cultural or commercial
reasons, or as tourists, under conditions comparable to
those applying to other persons entering these areas. In
order to facilitate visits and travel, as described above,
by permanent residents of the Western Sectors of Berlin,
additional crossing points will be opened.

3. The problems of the small enclaves, including
Steinstücken, and of other small areas may be solved by
exchange of territory.

4. Telephonic, telegraphic, transport and other
external communications of the Western Sectors of Berlin
will be expanded.

5. Arrangements implementing and supplementing the
provisions of paragraphs 1 to 4 above will be agreed by the
competent German authorities.

Annex IV
A.
Communication from the Governments of the
French Republic, the United Kingdom and the
United States of America to the Government
of the Union of Soviet Socialist Republics

The Governments of the French Republic, the United
Kingdom and the United States of America, with reference to
Part II (D) of the Quadripartite Agreement of this date and
after consultation with the Government of the Federal
Republic of Germany, have the honor to inform the
Government of the Union of Soviet Socialist Republics that:

1. The Governments of the French Republic, the United
Kingdom and the United States of America maintain their
rights and responsibilities relating to the representation
abroad of the interests of the Western Sectors of Berlin
and their permanent residents, including those rights and

responsibilities concerning matters of security and status, both in international organizations and in relations with other countries.

2. Without prejudice to the above and provided that matters of security and status are not affected, they have agreed that:

    a. The Federal Republic of Germany may perform consular services for permanent residents of the Western Sectors of Berlin.

    b. In accordance with established procedures, international agreements and arrangements entered into by the Federal Republic of Germany may be extended to the Western Sectors of Berlin provided that the extension of such agreements and arrangements is specified in each case.

    c. The Federal Republic of Germany may represent the interests of the Western Sectors of Berlin in international organizations and international conferences.

    d. Permanent residents of the Western Sectors of Berlin may participate jointly with participants from the Federal Republic of Germany in international exchanges and exhibitions. Meetings of international organizations and international conferences as well as exhibitions with international participation may be held in the Western Sectors of Berlin. Invitations will be issued by the Senat or jointly by the Federal Republic of Germany and the Senat.

3. The three Governments authorize the establishment of a Consulate General of the USSR in the Western Sectors of Berlin accredited to the appropriate authorities of the three Governments in accordance with the usual procedures applied in those Sectors, for the purpose of performing consular services, subject to provisions set forth in a separate document of this date.

B.
Communication from the Government of the Union of Soviet Socialist Republics to the Governments of the French Republic, the United Kingdom and the United States of America

The Government of the Union of Soviet Socialist Republics, with reference to Part II (D) of the Quadripartite Agreement of this date and to the communication of the Governments of the French Republic, the United Kingdom and the United States of America with regard to the representation abroad of the interests of the Western Sectors of Berlin and their permanent residents, has the honor to inform the Governments of the French Republic, the United Kingdom and the United States of America that:

1. The Government of the Union of Soviet Socialist Republics takes note of the fact that the three Governments maintain their rights and responsibilities relating to the representation abroad of the interests of the Western Sectors of Berlin and their permanent residents, including those rights and responsibilities concerning matters of security and status, both in international organizations and in relations with other countries.

2. Provided that matters of security and status are not affected, for its part it will raise no objection to:

a. the performance by the Federal Republic of Germany of consular services for permanent residents of the Western Sectors of Berlin;

b. in accordance with established procedures, the extension to the Western Sectors of Berlin of international agreements and arrangements entered into by the Federal Republic of Germany provided that the extension of such agreements and arrangements is specified in each case;

c. the representation of the interests of the Western Sectors of Berlin by the Federal Republic of Germany in international organizations and international conferences;

d. the participation jointly with participants from the Federal Republic of Germany of permanent residents of the Western Sectors of Berlin in international exchanges and exhibitions, or the holding in those Sectors of meetings of international organizations and international conferences as well as exhibitions with international participation, taking into account that invitations will be issued by the Senat or jointly by the Federal Republic of Germany and the Senat.

3. The Government of the Union of Soviet Socialist Republics takes note of the fact that the three Governments have given their consent to the establishment of a Consulate General of the USSR in the Western Sectors of Berlin. It will be accredited to the appropriate authorities of the three Governments, for purposes and

subject to provisions described in their communication and as set forth in a separate document of this date.

Agreed Minute I[2]

It is understood that permanent residents of the Western Sectors of Berlin shall, in order to receive at appropriate Soviet offices visas for entry into the Union of Soviet Socialist Republics, present:
  a. a passport stamped "Issued in accordance with the Quadripartite Agreement of September, 1971";
  an identity card or other appropriately drawn up
  b. document confirming that the person requesting the visa is a permanent resident of the Western Sectors of Berlin and containing the bearer's full address and a personal photograph.

During his stay in the Union of Soviet Socialist Republics, a permanent resident of the Western Sectors of Berlin who has received a visa in this way may carry both documents or either of them, as he chooses. The visa issued by a Soviet office will serve as the basis for entry into the Union of Soviet Socialist Republics, and the passport or identity card will serve as the basis for consular services in accordance with the Quadripartite Agreement during the stay of that person in the territory of the Union of Soviet Socialist Republics.

The above-mentioned stamp will appear in all passports used by permanent residents of the Western Sectors of Berlin for journeys to such countries as may require it.

September 3, 1971

Protocole n I

Il est entendue que les résidents permanents des secteurs occidentaux de Berlin, pour obtenir dans les services soviétiques compétents des visas d'entrée en Union des Républiques Socialistes Soviétiques, présenteront:
  a. un passeport muni du cachet: "Délivré en conformité de l'Accord Quadripartite due 3 September 1971".
  b. une carte d'identité ou un autre document dûment établi, confirmant que la personne sollicitant le

218

visa est un résident permanent des secteurs
occidentaux de Berlin et contenant l'adresse
complète du porteur et sa photographie personnelle.
     Pendant leur séjour en Union des Républiques
Socialistes Soviétiques les résidents permanents des
secteurs occidentaux de Berlin qui ont obtenu un visa selon
ces procédures peuvent disposer a leur convenance des deux
documents ou de l'un d'entre eux. Le visa délivré par un
service soviétique servira de titre pour l'entrée en Union
des Républiques Socialistes Soviétiques, tandis que le
passeport ou la carte d'identité servira de titre pour les
services consulaires, conformément à l'Accord
Quadripartite, pendant le séjour de ces personnes sur le
territoire de l'Union des Républiques Socialistes
Soviétiques.
     Le cachet ci-dessus mentionné figurera sur tous les
passeports utilisés par les résidents permanents des
secteurs occidentaux de Berlin pour voyager dans les pays
qui l'exigeraient.

le 3 september 1971

Agreed Minute II[3]

     Provision is hereby made for the establishment of a
Consulate General of the USSR in the Western Sectors of
Berlin. It is understood that the details concerning this
Consulate General will include the following. The
Consulate General will be accredited to the appropriate
authorities of the three Governments in accordance with the
usual procedures applying in those Sectors. Applicable
Allied and German legislation and regulations will apply to
the Consulate General. The activities of the Consulate
General will be of a consular character and will not
include political functions or any matters related to
quadripartite rights or responsibilities.
     The three Governments are willing to authorize an
increase in Soviet commercial activities in the Western
Sectors of Berlin as described below. It is understood
that pertinent Allied and German legislation and
regulations will apply to these activities. This
authorization will be extended indefinitely, subject to
compliance with the provisions outlined herein. Adequate
provision for consultation will be made. This increase
will include establishment of an "Office of Soviet Foreign
Trade Associations in the Western Sectors of Berlin", with

commercial status, authorized to buy and sell on behalf of
foreign trade associations of the Union of Soviet Socialist
Republics. Soyuzpushnina, Prodintorg and Novoexport may
each establish a bonded warehouse in the Western Sectors of
Berlin to provide storage and display for their goods. The
activities of the Intourist office in the British Sector of
Berlin may be expanded to include the sale of tickets and
vouchers for travel and tours in the Union of Soviet
Socialist Republics and other countries. An office of
Aeroflot may be established for the sale of passenger
tickets and air freight services.

The assignment of personnel to the Consulute General
and to permitted Soviet commercial organizations will be
subject to agreement with the appropriate authorities of
the three Governments. The number of such personnel will
not exceed twenty Soviet nationals in the Consulate
General; twenty in the office of the Soviet Foreign Trade
Associations; one each in the bonded warehouses; six in the
Intourist office; and five in the Aeroflot office. The
personnel of the Consulate General and of permitted Soviet
commercial organizations and their dependents may reside in
the Western Sectors of Berlin upon individual
authorization.

The property of the Union of Soviet Socialist
Republics at Lietzenburgerstrasse 11 and at Am Sandwerder 1
may be used for purposes to be agreed between appropriate
representatives of the three Governments and of the
Government of the Union of Soviet Socialist Republics.

Details of implementation of the measures above and a
time schedule for carrying them out will be agreed between
the four Ambassadors in the period between the signature of
the Quadripartite Agreement and the signature of the Final
Quadripartite Protocol envisaged in that Agreement.

September 3, 1971

Final Quadripartite Protocol

The Governments of the United States of America, the
French Republic, the Union of Soviet Socialist Republics
and the United Kingdom of Great Britain and Northern
Ireland,

Having in mind Part III of the Quadripartite Agreement
of September 3, 1971, and taking note with satisfaction of
the fact the agreements and arrangements mentioned below
have been concluded,

220

Have agreed on the following:

1. The four Governments, by virtue of this Protocol, bring into force the Quadripartite Agreement, which, like this Protocol, does not affect quadripartite agreements or decisions previously concluded or reached.

2. The four Governments proceed on the basis that the agreements and arrangements concluded between the competent German authorities (list of agreements and arrangements) shall enter into force simultaneously with the Quadripartite Agreement.

3. The Quadripartite Agreement and the consequent agreements and arrangements of the competent German authorities referred to in this Protocol settle important issues examined in the course of the negotiations and shall remain in force together.

4. In the event of a difficulty in the application of the Quadripartite Agreement or any of the above-mentioned agreements or arrangements which any of the four Governments considers serious, or in the event of non-implementation of any part thereof, that Government will have the right to draw the attention of the other three Governments to the provisions of the Quadripartite Agreement and this Protocol and to conduct the requisite quadripartite consultations in order to ensure the observance of the commitments undertaken and to bring the situation into conformity with the Quadripartite Agreement and this Protocol.

5. This Protocol enters into force on the date of signature.

DONE at the building formerly occupied by the Allied Control Council in the American Sector of Berlin this day of   1971, in four originals, each in the English, French and Russian languages, all texts being equally authentic.

For the Government of the United States of America: (K.R.)

For the Government of the French Republic: (J.S.)

For the Government of the Union of Soviet Socialist Republics: (P.A.)

For the Government of the United Kingdom of Great Britain and Northern Ireland (R.J.)

September 3, 1971

NOTES

1. *Europa-Archiv*, Vol. 26, No. 19 (Oct. 1971), pp. D.441-D.462; U.S. Department of State, "Berlin: The Four-Power Agreement," Current Foreign Policy (Washington, D.C.: U.S. Government Printing Office, 1971), pp. 13-14.

2. Initialed by the four Ambassadors on September 3, 1971.

3. Initialed by the four Ambassadors on September 3, 1971.

Appendix B[1]

Treaty on the basis of relations between the Federal Republic of Germany and the German Democratic Republic

The High Contracting Parties,

Conscious of their responsibility for the preservation of peace,

Anxious to render a contribution to detente and security in Europe,

Aware that the inviolability of frontiers and respect for the territorial integrity and sovereignty of all States in Europe within their present frontiers are a basic condition for peace,

Recognizing that therefore the two German states have to refrain from the threat or use of force in their relations,

Proceeding from the historical facts and without prejudice to the different views of the Federal Republic of Germany and the German Democratic Republic on fundamental questions, including the national question,

Desirous to create the conditions for co-operation between the Federal Republic of Germany and the German Democratic Republic for the benefit of the people in the two German States,

Have agreed as follows:

Article 1

The Federal Republic of Germany and the German Democratic Republic shall develop normal, good-neighbourly relations with each other on the basis of equal rights.

Article 2

The Federal Republic of Germany and the German Democratic Republic will be guided by the aims and principles laid down in the United Nations Charter, especially those of the sovereign equality of all States, respect for their independence, autonomy and territorial integrity, the right of self-determination, the protection of human rights, and non-discrimination.

Article 3

In conformity with the United Nations Charter the Federal Republic of Germany and the German Democratic Republic shall settle any disputes between them exclusively by peaceful means and refrain from the threat or use of force.
They reaffirm the inviolability now and in the future of the frontier existing between them and undertake fully to respect each other's territorial integrity.

Article 4

The Federal Republic of Germany and the German Democratic Republic proceed on the assumption that neither of the two States can represent the other in the international sphere or act on its behalf.

Article 5

The Federal Republic of Germany and the German Democratic Republic shall promote peaceful relations between the European States and contribute to security and co-operation in Europe.
They shall support efforts to reduce forces and arms in Europe without allowing disadvantages to arise for the security of those concerned.
The Federal Republic of Germany and the German Democratic Republic shall support, with the aim of general and complete disarmament under effective international control, efforts serving international security to achieve armaments limitation and disarmament, especially with regard to nuclear weapons and other weapons of mass destruction.

Article 6

The Federal Republic of Germany and the German Democratic Republic proceed on the principle that the sovereign jurisdiction of each of the two States is confined to its own territory. They respect each other's independence and autonomy in their internal and external affairs.

Article 7

The Federal Republic of Germany and the German Democratic Republic declare their readiness to regulate practical and humanitarian questions in the process of normalization of their relations. They shall conclude agreements with a view to developing and promoting on the basis of the present Treaty and for their mutual benefit co-operation in the fields of economics, science and technology, transport, judicial relations, posts and telecommunications, health, culture, sport, environmental protection, and in other fields. The details have been agreed in the Supplementary Protocol.

Article 8

The Federal Republic of Germany and the German Democratic Republic shall exchange Permanent Missions. They shall be established at the respective Government's seat.
Practical questions relating to the establishment of the Missions shall be dealt with separately.

Article 9

The Federal Republic of Germany and the German Democratic Republic agree that the present Treaty shall not affect the bilateral and multilateral international treaties and agreements already concluded by them or relating to them.

Article 10

The present Treaty shall be subject to ratification and shall enter into force on the day after the exchange of notes to that effect.

IN WITNESS WHEREOF the plenipotentiaries of the High Contracting Parties have signed this Treaty.

DONE at.....................on...............1972, in duplicate in the German language.

For the Federal Republic   For the German
of Germany   Democratic Republic

Supplementary Protocol to the Treaty on the Basis of Relations between the Federal Republic of Germany and the German Democratic Republic

I

Re Article 3

The Federal Republic of Germany and the German Democratic Republic have agreed to form a Commission composed of agents of the Governments of the two States. They will review and, where necessary, renew or supplement the marking of the frontier existing between the two States and draw up the necessary documentation on the course of the fontier. In the same way the Commission will contribute to regulating other problems connected with the course of the frontier, e.g. water management, energy supply and the prevention of damage.

The Commission shall commence its work after the signing of the Treaty.

II

Re Article 7

1. Trade between the Federal Republic of Germany and the German Democratic Republic shall be developed on the basis of the existing agreements.

The Federal Republic of Germany and the German Democratic Republic shall conclude long-term agreements with a view to promoting the continued development of their economic relations, adapting outdated arrangements, and improving the structure of trade.

2. The Federal Republic of Germany and the German Democratic Republic proclaim their intention to develop co-operation in the fields of science and technology for their mutual benefit and to conclude the necessary treaties for this purpose.

3. The co-operation in the field of traffic which began with the Treaty of 26 May 1972 shall be widened and intensified.

4. The Federal Republic of Germany and the German Democratic Republic declare their readiness to regulate their judicial relations as simply and expediently as possible by treaty in the interests of those seeking justice, especially in the fields of civil and criminal law.

5. The Federal Republic of Germany and the German Democratic Republic agree to conclude an agreement on posts and telecommunications on the basis of the Constitution of the Universal Postal Union and the International Telecommunication Convention. They will notify the Universal Postal Union (UPU) and the International Telecommunication Union (ITU) of the conclusion of that agreement.

The existing agreements and the procedures beneficial to both sides will be incorporated in that agreement.

6. The Federal Republic of Germany and the German Democratic Republic declare their interest in co-operation in the field of health. They agree that the appropriate treaty shall also regulate the exchange of medicaments as well as the treatment of patients in special clinics and sanatoria as far as practicable.

7. The Federal Republic of Germany and the German Democratic Republic intend to develop their cultural co-operation. To this end they shall enter into negotiations on the conclusion of intergovernmental agreements.

8. The Federal Republic of Germany and the German Democratic Republic reaffirm their preparedness to assist the appropriate sports organizations, after the Treaty has been signed, in bringing about arrangements for the promotion of relations in the field of sport.

9. Agreements are to be concluded between the Federal Republic of Germany and the German Democratic Republic in the field of environmental protection in order to help prevent hazards and harm to each other.

10. The Federal Republic of Germany and the German Democratic Republic will conduct negotiations with a view to enhancing the acquisition of each other's books, periodicals, radio and television productions.

11. The Federal Republic of Germany and the German Democratic Republic shall, in the interest of the people concerned, enter into negotiations to regulate non-commercial payment and clearing procedures. In this connexion they shall, in their mutual interest, give priority to the early conclusion of agreements on social grounds.

Protocol Note

Owing to the different legal positions with regard to questions of property and assets these matters could not be regulated by the Treaty.

Extension of agreements and arrangements to Berlin (West); representation of interests of Berlin (West)

Identical Statement by both Parties on signing the Treaty:
"It is agreed that the extension to Berlin (West) of agreements and arrangements envisaged in the Supplementary Protocol to Article 7 may be agreed in each individual case in conformity with the Quadripartite Agreement of 3 September 1971.
The Permanent Mission of the Federal Republic of Germany in the German Democratic Republic shall, in conformity with the Quadripartite Agreement of 3 September 1971, represent the interests of Berlin (West).
Arrangements between the German Democratic Republic and the Senate shall remain unaffected."

Political consultation

Identical Statement by both Parties on signing the Treaty:
"The two Governments have agreed to consult each other in the process of the normalization of relations between the Federal Republic of Germany and the German Democratic Republic on questions of mutual interest, in particular on those important for the safeguarding of peace in Europe."

NOTES

1. *The Bulletin*, Press and Information Office of the Government of the Federal Republic of Germany (unofficial translation). No. 38/Vol. 20, Bonn, November, 14, 1972; *Europa-Archiv*, Vol. 28, No. 1 (October 1973), pp. D.1-D.24.

Bibliography

Archival Materials

Dwight D. Eisenhower Library, Abilene, Kansas
      Eisenhower, Dwight D.: Records as President, White
      House central files, 1953-1961
      Herter, Christian A.: Papers, 1957-1961
      Oral History Transcripts:
            Anderson, Dillon
            Bissell, Richard M., Jr.
            Bohlen, Charles
            Clay, Lucius D.
            McCloy, John J.
            McCone, John A.
            Murphy, Robert D.
            Twining, Nathan F.
John F. Kennedy Library, Waltham, Massachusetts
      Kennedy, John F.: Presidential Papers, 1961-1963
      National Security Files 1961-1963
            Countries: Germany/Berlin
            CIA, Defense, State
            National Security Council
            Subjects: Berlin
      Oral History Interviews
            Acheson, Dean
            Amory, Robert
            Barnes, Donald
            Bohlen, Charles
            Chayes, Abram
            Clay, Lucius D.
            Couve de Murville, Maurice
            Fulbright, J. W.
            Harriman, Averell

            Mansfield, Mike
            Nitze, Paul
            Sorenson, Theodore C.
            Thompson, Llewellyn
            Tyler, William
U.S. Mission Library, Berlin
     Document Collection: 1945-1958
U.S. National Archives, Washington, D.C.
     Document Collection on Germany/Berlin: 1945-1959
     JCS File: 1945-1961
     Departments and Agencies Files
     NSC Files
     Senate Hearings

Books and Memoirs

Abrasimov, Pyotr. *West Berlin*. Dresden: Verlag Zeit im
     Bild, 1981.
Adenauer, Konrad. *Erinnerungen, 1959-1963*. Stuttgart:
     Deutsche Verlags-Anstalt, 1968.
Baring, Arnulf. *Machtwechsel*. Stuttgart: Deutsche Verlags-
     Anstalt, 1982.
Bark, Dennis L. *Agreement on Berlin*. Washington, D.C.:
     American Enterprise Institute, 1974.
Binder, David. *The Other German: Willy Brandt's Life and
     Times*. Washington, D.C.: The New Republic Co., 1975.
Birnbaum, Karl E. *East and West Germany: a modus vivendi*.
     Lexington, Mass.: Lexington Books, 1973.
Brandt, Willy. *People and Politics The Years 1960-1975*.
     Boston: Little, Brown and Company, 1976.
_____. *Über den Tag Hinaus-Eine Zwischenbilanz*.
     Hamburg: Hoffmann and Campe, 1974.
British Information Services. *Berlin and the Problem of
     German Reunification*. London: 1961.
Buchan, Alastair. *Europe's Future, Europe's Choices*. New
     York: Columbia University Press, 1969.
Bundesministerium für gesamtdeutsche Fragen. *Dokumente
     Deutschland-Frage*, Series I and II. Bonn, 1961.
Bundesministerium für gesamtdeutsche Fragen. *Dokumente zur
     Deutschlandpolitik*, Series III and IV. Bonn/Berlin:
     Alfred Metzner Verlag, 1963-1970.
Bundesministerium für innerdeutsche Beziehungen. *Die
     Entwicklung der Beziehungen zwischen der
     Bundesrepublik Deutschland und der Deutschen
     Demokratischen Republik*. Melsungen:
     Verlagsbuchdruckerei Bernecker, 1973.

Bundesregierung. „Die Berlin-Regelung. Das Viermächte-Abkommen über Berlin und die ergänzenden Vereinbarungen. Bonn: Presse-und Informationsamt, 1972.

Calleo, David. The Atlantic Fantasy: The U.S., Nato, and Europe. Baltimore: The Johns Hopkins University Press, 1970.

Cate, Curtis. The Ides of August. New York: M. Evans and Co. Inc., 1978.

Catudal, Honoré M., Jr. A Balance Sheet of the Quadripartite Agreement on Berlin. Berlin: Berlin Verlag, 1978.

_____. The Diplomacy of the Quadripartite Agreement on Berlin. Berlin: Berlin Verlag, 1978.

_____. Kennedy and the Berlin Wall Crisis. Berlin: Berlin Verlag, 1980.

Childs, David. The GDR: Moscow's German Ally. London: Allen and Unwin, 1983.

Cieslar, Eva et al. Der Streit um den Grundvertrag. Munich: Olzog Verlag, 1973.

Croan, Melvin. 1976. East Germany: The Soviet Connection. The Washington Papers, Vol. 4, No. 36. Beverly Hills: Sage Publications.

Dahm, Georg. Völkerrecht, Vol. 3. Stuttgart: Deutsche Verlags-Anstalt, 1961.

Doehring, Karl and Ress, Georg. Staats-und völkerrechtliche Aspekte der Berlin-Regelung. Frankfurt: Athenäum Verlag, 1972.

Drath, Viola Herms (ed.). Germany in World Politics. New York: Cyro Press, 1979.

End, Heinrich. Zweimal deutsche Aussenpolitik: Internationale Dimensionen des innerdeutschen Konflikts 1949 und 1972. Cologne: Wissenschaft und Politik, 1973.

Flynn, Gregory A. The Fall of Ulbricht: A Lesson in Soviet Bloc Diplomacy. Unpublished M.A. thesis, Fletcher School of Law and Diplomacy, 1972.

Foreign Office (U.K.). Selected Documents on Germany and the Question of Berlin 1944-1961. London: H.M.S.O., 1961.

Gasteyger, Curt. Die beiden deutschen Staaten in der Weltpolitik. Munich: Verlag Piper and Co., 1976.

Görgey, Laszlo. Bonn's Eastern Policy 1964-1971. Hamden, Conn.: Archon Books, 1972.

Gusseck, Lutz. Die internationale Praxis der Transitgewährung und der Berlin-Verkehr. Frankfurt: Athenäum-Verlag, 1973.

234

Haftendorn, Helga. *Security and Detente Conflicting Priorities in German Foreign Policy.* New York: Praeger, 1985.

Hanhardt, Arthur M., Jr. *The German Democratic Republic.* Baltimore: The Johns Hopkins University Press, 1968.

Hanrieder, W.F. *The Stable Crisis: Two Decades of German Foreign Policy.* New York: Harper and Row, 1970.

Heidelmeyer, Wolfgang et al. (eds.). *Documents on Berlin,* 1943-1963, Munich: Oldenbourg Verlag, 1963.

_____. (ed.). *Dokumente zur Berlin-Frage 1944-1962.* Munich: Oldenbourg Verlag, 1962.

Heidenheimer, Arnold and Kommers, Donald. *The Governments of Germany.* New York: Harper and Row, 1975.

Hennig, Ottfried. *Die Bundesprasenz in West-Berlin.* Cologne: Verlag Wissenschaft und Politik, 1976.

Hofmeister, Burkhard. *Bundesrepublik Deutschland und Berlin.* Darmstadt: Wissenschaftliche Buchgesellschaft, 1975.

Hubatsch, Walther, et al. (eds.). *The German Question.* New York: Herder Book Center, 1967.

Kaiser, Karl. *German Foreign Policy in Transition: Bonn Between East and West.* London: Oxford University Press, 1968.

Keesing's Research Report. *Germany and Eastern Europe Since 1970.* New York: Charles Schribner's Sons, 1973.

Kissinger, Henry. *White House Years.* Boston: Little, Brown and Company, 1979.

Kissinger Henry A. *Years of Upheaval.* Boston: Little, Brown and Company, 1982.

Krumholz, Walter (ed.). *Berlin-ABC.* 2nd ed. Berlin: Press and Information Office, 1968.

Ludz, Peter. *Deutschlands Doppelte Zukunft: Bundesrepublik und die DDR in der Welt von Morgen.* Munich: Oldenbourg Verlag, 1974.

Mahncke, Dieter. *Berlin im geteilten Deutschland.* Munich: R. Oldenbourg Verlag, 1973.

Mampel, Siegfried. *Der Sowjetsektor von Berlin.* Berlin: Alfred Metzner Verlag, 1963.

Morgan, Roger. *The United States and West Germany 1945-1973.* London: Oxford University Press, 1974.

_____. 1978. *West Germany's Foreign Policy Agenda.* The Washington Papers, Vol. 6, No. 54. Beverly Hills: Sage Publications.

von Munch, Ingo (ed.). *Dokumente des geteilten Deutschland.* Stuttgart: Kroner Verlag, 1968.

235

Nelson, Daniel J. *Wartime Origins of the Berlin Dilemma*. University, Alabama: University of Alabama Press, 1978.

Niclauss, Karlheinz. *Controverse Deutschlandpolitik*. Frankfurt: Alfred Metzner Verlag, 1977.

Nolte, Ernst. *Deutschland und der Kalte Krieg*. Munich: Piper Verlag, 1974.

Office of the Registrar. *John F. Kennedy. Containing the Public Messages, Speeches, and Statements of the President*. Washington, D.C.: Government Printing Office, 1962.

Riklin, Alois. *Das Berlin-Problem*. Cologne: Verlag Wissenschaft und Politik, 1964.

Royal Institute of International Affairs. *Documents on International Affairs*, 1951. London: Oxford University Press, 1954.

Schick, Jack M. *The Berlin Crisis 1958-1962*. Philadelphia: University of Pennsylvania Press, 1971.

Schiedermair, Hartmut. *Der völkerrechtliche Status Berlins nach dem Viermächte-Abkommen vom 3. September 1971*. Berlin: Springer Verlag, 1975.

Schlesinger, Arthur M., Jr. *A Thousand Days: John F. Kennedy in the White House*. Boston: Houghton Mifflin, 1965.

Schutz, Wilhelm Wolfgang. *Deutschland-Memorandum*. Frankfurt: Fischer Bücherei, 1968.

Slusser, Robert M. *The Berlin Crisis of 1961*. Baltimore: The Johns Hopkins University Press, 1973.

Tilford, Roger (ed.). *The Ostpolitik and Political Change in Germany*. Lexington, Mass.: Lexington Books, 1975.

U.S. Congress. *Documents on Germany, 1944-1970*. Committee on Foreign Relations. Washington, D.C.: Government Printing Office, 1970.

U.S. Department of State. *Documents on Germany 1944-1959*. Washington, D.C.: Government Printing Office, 1959.

_____. *U.S. Reply to Soviet Note on Berlin*. Washington, D.C.: Government Printing Office, Department of State Publication 6757, 1959.

U.S. Mission (Berlin). *Berlin Accessways, Transportation, Communications and Utilities, 1949-1976*. 3rd ed. Berlin: Economic/Commercial Sections, 1976.

_____. *Post-War Berlin-An Unofficial Chronology*. Berlin: USIA, 1961-1977.

Wettig, G. *Community and Conflict in the Socialist Camp: The Soviet Union, East Germany and the German Problem 1965-1972*. London: Oxford University Press, 1975.

Whetten, Lawrence L. *Germany East and West*. New York: New
York University Press, 1980.
_____. *Germany's Ostpolitik*. New York: Oxford
University Press, 1971.
Zivier, Ernst. *Der Rechtsstatus des Landes Berlin*. Berlin:
Berlin Verlag, 1977.

Articles

Anthon, Carl G. "Germany's Westpolitik," *Current History*,
Vol. 62, No. 396 (May 1972), pp. 234-38.
Barker, Elisabeth. "The Berlin Crisis 1958-1962,"
International Affairs, London, Vol. 39 (January 1963),
pp. 59-73.
Bechtholdt, Heinrich. "Der Bilateralismus deutscher
Ostpolitik," *Aussenpolitik*, Vol. 21, No. 1 (January
1970), pp. 5-8.
_____. "Ulbricht's Niederlage in Osteuropa,"
Aussenpolitik, Vol. 18, No. 3 (March 1967), pp. 125-
138.
_____. "Die zweite Etappe der deutschen Ostpolitik,"
Aussenpolitik, Vol. 21, No. 12 (December 1970), pp.
209-12.
Beer, K.W. "Acht Verhandlungspunkte," *Deutsche
Korrespondenz*, Vol. 20, No. 4 (January 1970), pp. 2-8.
Bender, Peter. "The Special Relationship of the Two German
States," *The World Today*, Vol. 29, No. 9 (September,
1973), pp. 389-97.
Bertram, Christoph. "European Security and the German
Problem," *International Security*, Vol. 4, No. 3
(Winter 1979/80), pp. 105-116.
Birnbaum, Karl. "Gesamteuropäische Perspektiven nach dem
Berlin-Abkommen," *Europa-Archiv*, Vol. 27, No. 1
(January 1972), pp. 1-10.
Black, Hilary. "The East-West German Treaty," *The World
Today*, Vol. 28, No. 12 (December 1972), pp. 512-15.
Blumenwitz, Dieter. "Der Grundvertrag zwischen der
Bundesrepublik Deutschland und der DDR," *Politische
Studien*, Vol. 24 (January-February, 1973), pp. 3-10.
Boldyrew, Viktor. "Das Vierseitige Abkommen über West
Berlin--ein Schritt zu Frieden, Sicherheit und
Zusammenarbeit in Europa," *Deutsche Aussenpolitik*,
Vol. 5 (September-October, 1972), pp. 873-99.
Carstens, Karl. "Zur Interpretation der Berlin-Regelung,"
Festschrift für Ulrich Scheuner zum 70. Geburtstag.
Berlin: Berlin Verlag, 1973.

Cramer, Dettmar. "Bonn und Ost-Berlin: Kleine Schritte auf dem Weg zur Normalisierung," *Deutschland-Archiv*, Vol. 8, No. 3 (March, 1975), pp. 225-26.

Doeker, Gunther et al. "Berlin and the Quadripartite Agreement of 1971," *American Journal of International Law*, Vol. 67 (January, 1973), pp. 44-62.

Duckwitz, Georg Ferdinand. "Die Wende im Osten," *Aussenpolitik*, Vol. 21, No. 4 (April, 1970), pp. 649-57.

Franklin, William M. "Zonal Boundaries and Access to Berlin," *World Politics*, Vol. 16 (October 1963), pp. 1-31.

Grosser, Alfred. "France and Germany: less divergent outlooks," *Foreign Affairs*, Vol. 48, No. 2 (Spring 1970) pp. 235-44.

Hacker, Jens. "Die Bindungen Berlins (West) zum Bund als Problem der Ostvertragspolitik der Bundesrepublik Deutschland," *Osteuropa-Recht*, No. 3-4 (1974), pp. 205-34.

_____. "Der neue Rechtsstatus für West-Berlin: Die Ostverträge und das Berlin-Abkommen," *Die politische Meinung*, Vol. 142 (May-June, 1972), pp. 78-94.

Hahn, Walter F. "West Germany's Ostpolitik: The Grand Design of Egon Bahr," *Orbis*, Vol. 16, No. 4 (Winter, 1973), pp. 859-80.

_____. "Whither Germany?" *Orbis*, Vol. 16, No. 1 (Spring, 1972), pp. 289-93.

Heathcote, Nina. "Brandt's Ostpolitik and Western Institutions," *The World Today*, Vol. 26, No. 12 (August 1970), pp. 334-343.

Joffe, Joseph. "Westverträge, Ostverträge und die Kontinuität der deutschen Aussenpolitik," *Europa-Archiv*, Vol. 27, No. 3 (February, 1972), pp. 111-24.

Kaiser, Karl. "Prospects for West Germany after the Berlin Agreement," *The World Today*, Vol. 28, No. 1 (January, 1972), pp. 30-35.

Keithly, David M. "Whither German Social Democracy?", *Strategic Review*, Vol. 13, No. 3 (Summer 1985), pp. 60-66.

Kewenig, Wilhelm. "Die Bedeutung des Grundvertrags für das Verhältnis der beiden deutschen Staaten," *Europa-Archiv*, Vol. 28, No. 2 (January, 1973), pp. 37-46.

Kreutzer, H. "Berlin im Bund," *Zeitscrift für Politik*, No. 1 (1960), pp. 116-143.

Leicht, Robert. "Von den zwanzig Kasseler Punkten zum Grundvertraf," *Frankfurter Hefte*, Vol. 28, No. 4 (1973), pp. 241-48.

238

Livingston, Robert Gerald. "East Germany Between Moscow and Bonn," *Foreign Affairs*, Vol. 5, No. 2 (January 1972), pp. 297-309.

Lush, Richard. "The Relationship between Berlin and the Federal Republic of Germany," *The International Comparative Law Quarterly* 3, (1965), pp. 742-87.

McAdams, A. James. "Surviving the Missiles: The GDR and the Future of Inter-German Relations," *Orbis*, Vol. 27, No. 2 (Summer 1983), pp. 343-370.

Mahncke, Dieter. "The Berlin Agreement: Balance and Prospects," *The World Today*, Vol. 27, No. 12 (December, 1971), pp. 511-21.

_____. "In Search of a modus vivendi for Berlin: Prospects for Four-Power Talks," *The World Today*, Vol. 26, No. 4 (April, 1970), pp. 137-46.

_____. "Das Viermächte-Abkommen über Berlin," *Europa-Archiv*, Vol. 26, No. 20 (1971), pp. 703-714.

Mahnke, Hans H. "Die Konferenz über Sicherheit und Zusammenarbeit in Europa (KSZE) und die deutsche Frage," *Deutschland-Archiv*, Vol. 8, No. 9 (September, 1975), pp. 922-33.

_____. "Zur Rechtslage Berlins: Einige Korrigierende Bemerkungen," *Deutschland-Archiv*, Vol. 4, No. 9 (September 1971), pp. 901-909.

_____. "Rechtsprobleme des Grundlagenvertrages," *Deutschland-Archiv*, Vol. 7, No. 2 (February, 1974), pp. 130-49.

_____. "Zum Status von Berlin," *Deutschland-Archiv*, Vol. 8, No. 8 (August, 1975), pp. 835-42.

Meesen, Karl. "Das Problem der Staatsangehörigkeit nach dem Grundvertrag," *Europa-Archiv*, Vol. 28, No. 15 (1973), pp. 515-24.

Merkl, Peter H. "The German Janus: From Westpolitik to Ostpolitik," *Political Science Quarterly*, Vol. 89, No. 4 (Winter, 1974-75), pp. 803-24.

Morgan, Roger. "The Ostpolitik and West Germany's External Relations," in Roger Tilford, (ed.), *The Ostpolitik and Political Change in Germany*. Lexington, Mass: Lexington Books, 1975, pp. 95-108.

Nawrocki, Joachim. "Schwierigkeiten mit den 'drei Z': Die DDR und das Viermächte-Abkommen über Berlin," *Deutschland-Archiv*, Vol. 7, No. 6 (June, 1974), pp. 582-95.

Nelson, D.N. "The Early Success of Ostpolitik: an Eastern European Perspective," *World Affairs*, Vol. 138, No. 1 (Summer, 1975), pp. 32-50.

Pridham, Geoffrey. "The Ostpolitik and the Opposition in West Germany," in Roger Tilford (ed.) *The Ostpolitik and Political Change in Germany*. Lexington, Mass.: Lexington Books, 1975, pp. 45-58.

Rexin, Manfred. "DDR-Politik nach dem Grundvertrag," *Liberal*, Vol. 15, No. 3 (March, 1973), pp. 170-79.

Riklin, Alois. "Berlin als völkerrechtliches Problem," *Schweizer Monatshefte*, No. 4 (1966), pp. 703-718.

Roper, Erich. "Zur Rechtslage Berlin," *Deutschland-Archiv*, Vol. 28, No. 8 (August 1971), pp. 801-805.

Rush, Kenneth. "The Berlin Agreement: An Assessment," *The Atlantic Community Quarterly*, Vol. 10, No. 1 (1972), pp. 52-65.

_____. "Berlin: The Four-Power Agreement" in *Current Foreign Policy*. Washington, D.C.: Government Printing Office, 1971.

Schmitt, Matthias. "Ökonomische Perspektiven in der Ostpolitik," *Aussenpolitik*, Vol. 22 (April 1971), pp. 193-208.

Schröder, Gerhard. "Germany Looks at Eastern Europe," *Foreign Affairs*, Vol. 44, No. 1 (October 1965), pp. 15-25.

Schulz, Eberhard. "Die DDR als Gegenspieler der Bonner Ostpolitik," *Europa-Archiv*, Vol. 26, No. 8 (1971), pp. 283-92.

Spittmann, Ilse. "Von Kassel nach Moskau: Die SED und der deutsch-sowjetische Vertrag," *Deutschland-Archiv*, Vol. 3, No. 10 (October, 1970), pp. 1103-15.

Wagner, Wolfgang. "Aussichten der Ostpolitik nach dem Abschluss der Berlin-Verhandlungen," *Europa-Archiv*, Vol. 27, No. 3 (February, 1972), pp. 79-86.

_____. "Das Berlin-Problem als Angelpunkt eines Ausgleichs zwischen West und Ost in Europa," *Europa-Archiv*, Vol. 26, No. 11 (1971), pp. 375-82.

Weber, Bernd. "Ideologiewandel von Ulbricht zu Honecker," *Aussenpolitik*, Vol. 23, No. 3 (March, 1972), pp. 159-67.

Wettig, Gerhard. "Aktionsmuster der sowjetischen Berlin-Politik," *Aussenpolitik*, Vol. 19, No. 6 (June, 1968), pp. 325-39.

_____. "Berlin Frage und sowjetische Westpolitik 1970/71," in *Die Sowjetunion, die DDR und die Deutschland-Frage 1965-1976*. Stuttgart: Deutsche Verlags-Anstalt, 1977.

_____. "Das Berlin-Problem Rückblick und Gegenwart," *Aus Politik und Zeitgeschichte* (March 1, 1969), pp. 3-26.

_____. "Fünf Jahre Berlin-Abkommen: Eine Bilanz," *Aus Politik und Zeitgeschichte* (October 8, 1976), pp. 3-46.

_____. "Das Problem der Bindungen West-Berlins bei der Anwendung des Viermächteabkommens," *Deutschland-Archiv*, Vol. 12, No. 9 (September, 1979), pp. 926-37.

_____. "Die Rechtslage Berlins nach dem Viermächteabkommen aus sowjetischer Sicht," *Deutschland-Archiv*, Vol. 7, No. 4 (April, 1974), pp. 378-88.

Whetten, Lawrence L. "Appraising the Ostpolitik," *Orbis*, Vol. 15, No. 3 (Fall, 1971), pp. 856-78.

_____. "The Role of East Germany in West German-Soviet Relations," *The World Today*, Vol. 25, No. 12 (December 1969), pp. 507-20.

Winters, Peter Jochen. "Kurswechsel Ost-Berlins gegenüber Bonn," *Europa-Archiv*, Vol. 36, No. 1 (January 1981), pp. 31-38.

Witte, Barthold. "Die deutsche Nation nach dem Grundvertrag," *Europa-Archiv*, Vol. 28, No. 7 (July, 1973), pp. 227-34.

Newspapers and Periodicals

Aussenpolitik
Christ und Welt
Der Monat
Der Spiegel
Deutsche Aussenpolitik
Die Welt
Die Zeit
The Washington Post
The New York Times
Frankfurter Allgemeine Zeitung
Neues Deutschland
Frankfurter Rundschau
Süddeutsche Zeitung
Tagesspiegel
The German Tribune
Current Digest of the Soviet Press
German Press Review
Agence Europe
Foreign Broadcast Information Service (FBIS)
Le Monde
Pravda

Index

Dewey, Thomas, 113
Diplomatic representation,
127–128, 134, 154,
155–156, 166–167, 181
Direct election law, 161
Dobrynin, Anatoly, 84,
130–131, 136(n24),
136–137(n26)
Dregger, Alfred, 146
Dulles, John Foster,
171(n36)

East Berlin. *See* Berlin
EC. *See* European Community
EDC. *See* European Defense
Community
Election law, 161
Erfurt summit, 91–93
Escapees. *See* Refugees
European Advisory
Commission, 6
European Community (EC),
110, 112, 152, 167, 189
European Defense Community
(EDC), 12
European Parliament, 167
Exclave issue, 166

Falin, Valentin, 128, 131,
132
FDP. *See* Free Democrat Party
Federal Republic of
Germany (FRG)
policy changes, 53–63
political parties, 69–70,
72–73, 146. *See also*
entries for individual
parties
public opinion in, 144,
201, 206
trade credits, 54–55, 71,
77, 96–97, 144, 187, 190
See also Demonstrative
federal presence
Finland, 178
France, 53–54, 69–70, 78,
88, 126, 131, 134, 151,

153, 157, 168, 205. *See also*
Occupation rights;
Quadripartite Agreement
Frank-Falin formula, 188,
195(n10), 195(n12)
Free Democrat Party (FDP),
68, 72–73, 74–75, 81(n20),
94, 104, 142–143
FRG. *See* Federal Republic of
Germany
Friendship Treaty, 33, 87
Fulbright, J. William,
37(n54)

Gaus, Günter, 148
Genscher, Hans-Dietrich, 165
German Democratic Republic
constitution, 60
negotiating position, 86–87
penal code, 59, 60. *See*
also Honecker, Erich;
Ulbricht, Walter
"German Option," 104–105, 141
Goldberg, Arthur, 117(n15)
Görgey, Laszlo, 58
Grand Coalition, 54, 113
Great Britain, 78, 88, 126,
131, 134, 151, 153, 157,
168, 205. *See also*
Occupation rights;
Quadripartite Agreement
Gromyko, Andrei, 68, 71, 104,
112, 132–133, 147, 179, 180
Grosser, Alfred, 113
Grundgesetz. *See* Basic Law

Haftlingsfreikauf, 68
Hallstein, Walter, 147–148
"Hallstein Doctrine,"
12–13(n7), 54, 55, 69, 74,
84
Helsinki Accords, 207
Helsinki Final Act, 206–207
Hillenbrand, Martin, 199
Honecker, Erich, 132, 162,
176, 187, 190, 193, 194
Hübner, Nico, 135(n5)

246